DANIEL
DEFOE

by

FRANCIS WATSON

KENNIKAT PRESS
Port Washington, N. Y./London

DANIEL DEFOE

First published in 1952
Reissued in 1969 by Kennikat Press
Library of Congress Catalog Card No: 70-86578
SBN 8046-0642-0

Manufactured by Taylor Publishing Company   Dallas, Texas

DANIEL DEFOE

CONTENTS

I. WHO WROTE *Robinson Crusoe?*   *page* 1

II. THE CHILD OF DISSENT   38

III. THE SHORTEST WAY TO THE PILLORY   72

IV. THE GREAT POLYGRAPHER   116

V. MATERIALS OF A MASTERPIECE   166

VI. AUTUMN HARVEST   191

READING NOTE   228

CHRONOLOGY   231

INDEX   235

ILLUSTRATIONS

ROBINSON CRUSOE, 1719   *facing page*
                                                              80

The first and most illustrious of many repre-
sentations, from the copperplate frontispiece
by Clark and Pine to the first edition of 1719.
Crusoe's appearance in the familiar costume,
devised during his third year on the Island, is a
little inconsistent with the sinking of his ship
in the background—unless that be intended
for the other vessel which foundered with all
hands before his eyes in his twenty-fourth year
of solitude

Collection Sir Louis Sterling, Kt.

DEFOE PILLORIED AND AT LARGE   81
The Whigs' Medley. A satirical print of 1711 by
G[eorge] B[ickham], exhibiting Defoe in his
pillory appearance of 1703 and also, fully
wigged, in his study, a Dissenting mischief-
maker well matched with the Pope, the Devil,
Oliver Cromwell, the Knave of Hearts and the
Knave of Clubs. Attention was drawn to these
impressive portraits, outstanding among the
few remaining engraved likenesses of Defoe,
by Mr. E. W. H. Meyerstein in *The Times
Literary Supplement*, 15 February 1936

British Museum Print Room

Illustrations

facing page

LONDON MARKET SCENE C. 1720   96
    The Borough Market, c. 1720, from a print.
Lively engravings of daily activity such as this
are rare before Hogarth, and Defoe's narratives lacked a contemporary illustrator
Collection Kenneth Monkman, Esq.

DEFOE'S HANDWRITING   97
    The first page of copy for the printer of the
Review of the State of the British Nation, 31
December 1709. The bulk of each number of
the *Review* consisted of an essay on a current
political or economic topic, and for nine years
Defoe was writing a dozen pages or so of copy
each week in addition to his other activities
British Museum Dept. of MSS.

Chapter One

WHO WROTE *ROBINSON CRUSOE*?

THE whitest thing in Bunhill Fields, the old Dissenters'
Burial-Ground off the City Road, London, is the
granite obelisk erected in 1870 over the bones of Daniel
Defoe, and newly cleaned in 1949. Nearby in that small
and crowded plot opposite Wesley's Chapel lie John
Bunyan the tinker and William Blake the hosier's son,
and the parents of Oliver Cromwell, and Isaac Watts who
wrote hymns, and Thomas Stothard who illustrated
Robinson Crusoe. It is also, this monument to Defoe, very
nearly the tallest thing standing, in 1952, between Bunhill Fields and the gaunt and scaffolded tower of St.
Giles-in-Cripplegate, nearly half a mile to the south.
Were it not for a projecting wing of the artillery
barracks, one could stand beside Defoe's grave today and
look almost to Guildhall over the flat wilderness left by
the German bombers in the parish of St. Giles, where
nearly three centuries earlier the Plague began and the
Fire stopped. Spared by that famous conflagration that
Defoe perhaps remembered and certainly recorded, all
that area he knew so well lies now like a map, with the
ragwort and the fireweed growing over it and low walls
and fences to mark the streets: Bunhill Row where
Milton came to live in his old age, Ropemaker Street
where Defoe himself died almost secretly, Milton
Street that was once Grub Street of the hacks and booksellers, and so down to Fore Street where Defoe's father

B   I

plied his trade as a butcher. It lies bare to the sky now, but the open places that Defoe knew in his crowded parish are all but lost under buildings: only Finsbury Square and Finsbury Circus remind us that here was once the great grassy tract of Moorfields, where fugitives from the Great Fire encamped, where the apprentices gathered at intervals to break up the brothels, and where Defoe's Colonel Jack ran in boyhood with his thievish companion. West of this, where the warehouses and offices that had obliterated Defoe's London have been swept clean away again, little is left among the bracken and the rusted pipes except what was there long before him—a fragment of the old London Wall near the church in which his family worshipped.

No classical epitaph could touch the memory more sharply than the simple notice of the death of Daniel Defoe, 'of a lethargy,' on April 26, 1731. He was over seventy when this merciful extinction advanced upon him, an old man who had achieved a popular master-piece with his 292nd work (at a cautious estimate) and now, after extraordinary vicissitudes of fortune, hunted and haunted by his last pursuer, had crept back to die in the parish of St. Giles-in-Cripplegate where he was born. Who was he? 'Mr. Dubow, Cripplegate,' was entered in the record of burial. The parish register amended this to 'Daniel de Foe, Gentleman'; the Victorian obelisk commemorates simply the Author of *Robinson Crusoe*. But we still ask the question.

It is an unusual literary celebrity that can survive the centuries without a familiar portrait and even without an adequate collected edition. Some men can live in a subtitle. *William Dampier, Pirate and Hydrographer*, is the engaging inscription under Thomas Murray's painting, in the National Portrait Gallery, of a remarkable Englishman who will be mentioned more than once in these pages. How could one thus succinctly catalogue the other remarkable Englishman who is their subject? Daniel Defoe, Tradesman and Novelist? Turncoat and Topographer? Hosier and Journalist? Pamphleteer and Spy? Dissenter and Public Relations Officer? He was, or has been called, all these things by turn or together. He has also been described (by Professor W. B. Trent) as 'the greatest of plebeian geniuses,' and as the man who established English realistic fiction (says Professor Ernest Baker) 'on granite foundations.'

But there is no portrait of Daniel Defoe in the National Portrait Gallery. There is no original portrait of him known to exist, and it is hard to know how far to trust the few engravings. It has become natural to speak of Defoe's England as we speak of Shakespeare's England or Chaucer's England. But England's Defoe must be conjured up, in his physical aspect, from a verbal description:

'He is a middle-sized, spare man, about fifty years old, of a brown complexion, and dark-brown coloured hair, but wears a wig; a hooked nose, a sharp chin, grey eyes, and a large mole near his mouth: was born in London, and for many years was a hose-factor in Freeman's Yard in Cornhill, and now is the owner of the brick and pantile works near Tilbury Fort in Essex.'

Among pen-pictures of the great writers this is certainly of the oddest. It reads like a criminal *dossier*, which is what it is. Defoe was wanted for seditious libel when that description was issued, in 1703, with the offer of a reward for his discovery. And his subsequent appearance in the pillory is probably, next to his authorship of *Robinson Crusoe*, the most readily remembered fact of his existence on this earth. By Dr. Jonathan

Swift, indeed, the creator of *Robinson Crusoe*—a resounding success when *Gulliver* was taking shape as an idea—could be pointedly ignored: 'The fellow that was pilloried, I have forgot his name.'

It is still *Robinson Crusoe* that sends us in search of Daniel Defoe, and then in his elusive company in search of his times; a voyage of discovery in reverse, from the Island at the mouth of the Orinoco to the England of James II, William and Mary, Anne and the first two Georges. The *Life and Strange Surprizing Adventures of Robinson Crusoe* was written 'by himself,' the *Journal of the Plague Year* by 'A Citizen.' The name on a title-page may be 'Andrew Moreton' or 'A Gentleman,' 'The Author of *The True-Born Englishman*' or 'An Officer.' It may be D.D. or D.F. or nothing at all. To Defoe's contemporaries the concealment must often have been no thicker than that of calling a rogue a 'r—e' or the victor of Blenheim 'the D— of M—gh.' But if he had advertised his own name—Daniel Foe, later altered to Daniel De Foe—more freely among the three hundred and seventy-five separate works he is authoritatively presumed to have published[1], there would not have been so open a field for the 'probable ascription' of upwards of three hundred more to the hand whose versatile industry relaxed at length in a lethargy abundantly earned.

From this prodigious journalism sprang *Robinson Crusoe*. When Macaulay in an echoing phrase declared that every schoolboy knew who imprisoned Montezuma and who strangled Atahualpa he may have been flattering his young contemporaries. But he intended the contrary. He was contrasting outlandish and unnecessary knowledge with the general ignorance of more relevant historical matters. With a similar asperity those who

[1] See the bibliography in the *Cambridge Bibliography of English Literature*.

would speak at length of Daniel Defoe commonly begin by assuming that every schoolboy knows who found a footprint in the sand and who saw the goat's eyes shining in the inky darkness of the cave. They may be right. Despite the rivals for juvenile attention which magistrates now and then deplore, *Robinson Crusoe* still finds new editions year by year. Pantomime has remained incongruously faithful since David Garrick played Crusoe, with Pantaloon, Columbine, and Harlequin Friday thrown in, in Sheridan's three-part version of 1781. Even the American 'Funnies' have adopted, beside the extravagancies of Superman, this pioneer of courageous commonsense.

That is one aspect of this extraordinary creation. For some of us a juvenile version of *Robinson Crusoe* was the very first book in which we learned to read our own language, half aloud, a finger following the line and pausing in memorable perplexity at the name Xury or the word pallisade. In its other aspect *Robinson Crusoe* is what the Germans call a *Weltbuch*. Its literary ancestry is still debated. Its literary progeny still populates the world's libraries. Its hero is part of our human sign-language, one of a handful of universally recognised figures that can as easily turn up in a Russian political cartoon or a South American advertisement as in an English pantomime. And it contains a central incident which Robert Louis Stevenson rightly placed in the best company:

'Crusoe recoiling from the footprint; Achilles shouting over against the Trojans; Ulysses bending the great bow; Christian running with his fingers in his ears . . . each has been printed on the mind's eye for ever.'

It is almost unnecessary to add that neither of these aspects—the juvenile and the classical—can have lain within Defoe's conception, when in about his sixtieth year, after so many shifts of fortune, he found himself, in Paul Dottin's words, 'peacefully settled at Stoke Newington with but one problem, the necessity of furnishing the booksellers with enough copy to supply himself with an adequate income.' Where he collected the bones of his story will be considered in the proper place, but what he made out of them is something to be clear about at the outset. For *The Life and Strange Surprizing Adventures of Robinson Crusoe, of York, Mariner*, is still the first and best reason—despite the later fiction, despite the remarkable one-man paper *The Review*, despite the *Tour* and the *Plague Year* and the excellent best of the pamphlets—for tracing at this day the life and strange surprising adventures of Daniel Defoe.

*   *   *

The right place to begin is not therefore in the Northamptonshire village of Grandfather Foe, but on the first page of *Robinson Crusoe*: which first page, in any edition, does not carry us very far into the narrative so sensationally promised in the title of a mariner of York '*Who Lived Eight and Twenty Years, all alone in an un-inhabited Island on the Coast of America, near the Mouth of the great River of Oroonoque; Having been cast on Shore by Shipwreck, wherein all the Men perished but himself. With an Account how he was at last strangely deliver'd by Pyrates.*' We are presented, briefly and convincingly, with the necessary details of birth, parentage and name. We are apprised of the rambling thoughts that early filled young Crusoe's head. After a thousand words or so the boy born in the first sentence has got upon a London-bound vessel at Hull and is running into the terror and sickness of a storm. But it is not the storm that will cast him on the Island for twenty-eight years. We need fifty odd pages of circumstantial narrative before we are ready for the heart of the matter.

Compare this method with another, that of Swift, whose *Voyage to Lilliput* appeared seven years later, in 1726. Lemuel Gulliver reaches maturity and his first ship on page one, starts the voyage that makes the story on page two, is wrecked on three and already tied down by the Lilliputians on page four. This beautifully athletic approach is one of the delights of Swift's style, and for two reasons appropriate to his purpose. The first reason is that Lemuel Gulliver, unlike Robinson Crusoe, is to be less a character than a literary contrivance for provoking the opportunities of satire. The sooner he is in Lilliput the better. The second reason is that Gulliver's adventures are to be frankly impossible while those of Crusoe, however unlikely, are to be made not only credible but vividly real.

So we are given the warming-up pages, establishing our belief in Crusoe's identity, leading us to a natural and effortless acquaintance with him, introducing us to the reasonable business that took men abroad in his days and gently persuading us—what with storms, Moorish slavers and the beasts and men of the West African coast—that strange things can happen to those who go voyaging. Those first fifty pages are often mutilated in abbreviations of the book, but they are not tedious. Perhaps we come to them now with a respect exaggerated by the consciousness that we are reading the first fifty pages of English realistic fiction. It is what Defoe himself called, with assumed modesty, 'homely plain writing', and critics have exhausted themselves in the attempt to determine where artlessness ends and art begins. It is an easy, enjoyable, picturesque flow of prose that is

neither Elizabethan nor Augustan, avoiding exuberance
and pretending to no refinement. The homely plain
writing in the event found a homely plain audience: a
new audience, many think, and surely a wider one than
either Defoe or his bookseller expected. A public of
porters and oyster-wenches and old women, said the
town Wits, who were as fearful as a modern highbrow
might be to be caught reading a best-seller. If we call it,
less contemptuously, a middle-class public, we shall at
once enter upon one of the peculiar fascinations of the
life and writings of Daniel Defoe. We seem to be in at
the birth of a style and a literary form. Are we also
witnessing the emergence of a social class?

   Robinson Crusoe's father encourages us to think so.
His brief appearance at the beginning of the book fulfils
a stock purpose. The wiseacre vainly attempting to
restrain the roving ambitions of youth is not uncommon
in the picaresque tradition. But what is it that Crusoe
senior recommends, and that Crusoe junior keeps
remembering though he disobeys the advice? Not
merely prudence and *terra firma*, but a precise and
positive place in society: the Middle Station of Life,
defined as a mean between 'the mechanick part of mankind' and the great and wealthy with their warring
passions and anxieties. The middle classes of our own day
would hardly recognise themselves in the old man's
picture of an existence 'not embarras'd with the labours
of the hands or the head, not sold to the life of slavery
for daily bread, or harrast with perplex'd circumstances,
which rob the soul of peace, and the body of rest.' Even
for Defoe's day the delineation is doubtless brightened
for the occasion. Crusoe the younger, at any rate, does
not altogether forget this sober advice. The restless
adventurer in him is at war with the resourceful citizen,

and those who have acclaimed him as a typical Englishman have the nation of shopkeepers in mind as well as
the voyagers to the world's ends. Finally it is the citizen
who survives the conflict, even on an uninhabited island.
Is it Defoe's own conflict, his own repentance of the
ventures that went wrong in his career, of the bold
voyages in political society that came to wreck through
a change in the weather or an error in navigation?
Nearing sixty, after hazards and calamities and humilia-
tions, does he long above all things for the anonymous
security of 'the middle state, or upper station of low
life?' The author himself gave colour, in his Third Part
of *Robinson Crusoe*, to an interpretation of the tale as
personal allegory; and the gaps and doubts in our
information about him have stimulated the search for
such internal evidence. Some of the surmises that have
been made are indeed extravagant; but it is not altogether
fanciful to feel, as one reads the book, that by the time
that Defoe had cast his hero on the Island he was
beginning to identify himself with him. The skill of the
circumstantial manner beguiles us up to that point. But
when once Crusoe is alone, so utterly alone that the
narrative *must* either be autobiography or invention, it is
Defoe for whom we look in that costume of goat-skins.
With the imaginative act of identification which the
author was bound to make, if he had not made it before,
when Crusoe's companions perished in the sea, the
temperature of the work rises to that at which a masterpiece can be precipitated (a masterpiece to some so unaccountable that they have even found a Bacon for Defoe
and attributed *Robinson Crusoe*, without evidence or ado,
to his political patron Robert Harley, Earl of Oxford).
'An employment quite remote to my genius,' Crusoe
has remarked of his tobacco-planting business in Brazil,

which seemed to be tempting him to settle down to middle-class felicity. The Island at the mouth of the Orinoco awaits his genius.

It is a testing-ground in which the specimen is to be isolated. In the experiment that has become immortal, the ingredients of Defoe's best-seller combine perfectly. Sermons and narratives of exploration were already, to judge by the lists, the safest money-spinners for the book-sellers. On Crusoe's Island we have both. We have also the opportunity to enjoy the inquisitive intelligence that produced one of the earlier of Defoe's works, the enterprising and still very readable *Essay Upon Projects*. The grass-roots of political economy may be revealed under the tropical sunlight of an island virgin to the colonist, where the tools must be contrived before the work can be done; where salvage from the wreck, beloved of every boy, is also the capital for a one-man company; where a device as ancient as the wheel will have to be produced afresh, and where the cultivation of food-grains will be reached, as doubtless it was reached in human beginnings, by observation out of accident. Whatever is sincere in the tremendous verbosity of Defoe's Protestantism will have to express itself in the thoughts of a man alone with God, a man hitherto content, as Crusoe confesses, with 'a certain stupidity of soul, without desire of good or conscience of evil.' And his relations with his fellow-beings must leave some trace, surely, upon Crusoe's solitude, as well as upon the deliverance from solitude through Friday, then through Friday's father and the Spaniard, and finally in the return to civilisation. If Defoe, tossed and battered by the world, had had a touch of Swift's misanthropy, we should know it after reading *Robinson Crusoe*. The fellow that was pillo-ried could make enemies, but he was no foe of mankind.

Whatever detail or idea was gleamed from Alexander Selkirk's narrative or Dampier's voyages or Knox's *Historical Relation of Ceylon*, or any other Crusoe source-book, Friday was Defoe's delightful invention. It may be that Friday was created partly for the literary purpose of introducing dialogue into an account that had to cover twenty-eight years. The need of this device of dialogue strikes one in the debates, occasionally aloud, which the solitary Crusoe holds with himself, considering first one view and then another; and in the voices which speak to him in dreams; even in the squawking of that 'honest, sociable creature,' his parrot. Yet Friday, so inseparable from Crusoe in our own mental picture, is almost an afterthought. He is ignored in the title-page presenting the castaway 'who lived all alone in an uninhabited Island.' Nor does Defoe seem in any sort of hurry to produce this second character. The time-scale of the narrative, so often telescoped by abridgments or in the reader's memory, is noteworthy. Crusoe is fifteen years on the Island before he sees the terrifying foot-print on the shore and goes tearing back to what he ever after refers to as his 'castle'—a most veracious touch. He spends two years more in 'the constant snare of the fear of man,' securing himself and his belongings, before he first sees the gruesome remains of a cannibal feast at the south-west point. It is in his twenty-third year of residence, being now well prepared, that he observes the savages themselves, on his own side of the Island; and in his twenty-fifth year, that is ten years after the footprint incident, Friday is discovered and rescued. Only three years afterwards Crusoe finds the means of leaving the Island, having been upon it twenty-eight years, two months and nineteen days. The exact reckoning is characteristic, and so is the coincidence of

Crusoe's deliverance 'from this second captivity, the same day of the month that I first made my escape in the *barco-longo* from among the Moors of Sallee.' To match those early adventures there is a kind of epilogue to the First Part of *Robinson Crusoe* in the journey with Friday from England to Spain and back across the Pyrennees in winter, with wolves and bears for good measure of excitement. And already, in the concluding paragraphs, a further volume is foreshadowed.

The Second Part of *Robinson Crusoe* is little read now, and the Third not at all. But we learn something of Defoe's market, as of his literary fertility, by noticing that Part II was issued in August 1719, only four months after Part I, of which four editions were already in print (as a mere operation of publishing this could not be approached today). Early in October of the same year the first serial edition began its run in the tri-weekly *Heathcote's Intelligence*, and Part III was on sale by August of the following year. The comparative failure of this Third Part, the *Serious Reflections of Robinson Crusoe*, can only be called deserved. But the Second Part, containing Crusoe's return visit to his Island, now colonized by Spaniards and Indians, his travels to the Orient and back overland through Siberia and Russia, seems on its first printing to have sold even better than Part I. Even if we attribute some of this popularity to the interest already created by the first appearance of Crusoe, we must still conclude that it was the lively reporting of travel and adventure that made the strongest appeal to Defoe's public.

That element remains, even though the earth be shrunken to a pattern of tarmac runways. And there is the sea, which we are in danger of forgetting in the fascination of Crusoe's island-life. 'I had read *Robinson*

Crusoe many times over and longed to be at sea,' is the simple testimony of a seaman (John Nicol) of Nelson's day; and the sailor is bracketed by Charles Lamb with the serving-maid in his relegation of Defoe's fiction to 'kitchen-reading.' Before *Crusoe* and the tales and histories of Defoe's last decade there is not much evidence of his intense interest in geography and travels, which must have been based on wide and thorough study: but in *Captain Singleton*, which followed close upon *Crusoe*, he not only made surmises of the route across Africa which were confirmed long afterwards, but also 'discovered' the strait called Bass's Strait, between Southern Australia and Van Diemen's Land (Tasmania), seventy-eight years before Bass went there. In his earlier writings the masts and rigging are to be descried, if at all, over his shoulder. He was not much of a sailor himself. There is a probability of one or more mercantile voyages to Spain and Portugal in his young days, but when he was urged to make a venture to Cadiz to recover from his bankruptcy in 1692 he found 'a secret aversion to quitting England.'

A Londoner and a tradesman need not quit England to write of ships and the sea, at all events not if he is a Daniel Defoe. Pondering one of his 'projects' he examined the guns on the *Royal Charles* with an interest worthy of Pepys. The forest of shipping in the Port of London fascinated him: he knew the cargoes and the prices and dues upon them, whither and whence they were bound, and all the language of weather and manoeuvre. One of his enterprises, the Tilbury tile-factory, kept him in sight of the Thames traffic, and he stored up much to say of these matters in the later *Tour Through Great Britain*. Indeed a special feature of the *Tour* is the attention paid to coastal matters of every kind, from the trading-fleets of Hull to a fight between French men-of-war and an English convoy which he watched from the Lizard. Like his own Colonel Jack, Defoe was 'always upon the inquiry, asking questions of things done in publick, as well as in private,' and happy especially in talking with 'old soldiers and tars.' Crusoe's voyages, the storms, the changes of wind and current, are given us with convincing detail. The impressionism of a later literary fashion is not to be looked for, but there are unforgettable touches—in the *Tour* it is the fury of the sea on the Cornish coast: 'How high the waves come rowling forward, storming on the neck of one another;' in *Robinson Crusoe* a few words, from a pen so prolific of them, give suddenly to the imagination a Van de Velde seascape: 'Our ship making her course towards the Canary Islands, or rather between those Islands and the African shore, was surprised in the grey of the morning by a Turkish rover of Sallee, who gave chase to us with all the sail she could make.'

It seems to have been to some extent due to Rousseau that Defoe's masterpiece, or the First Part of it, came to find that place in juvenile literature which it has ever since retained—not entirely to its just advantage. The book had been known and talked about, translated and imitated across the Channel during the forty years before Rousseau's *Emile* appeared in print. *Emile* is a text-book of educational and philosophical theory under the thin disguise of fiction, and the author's own text-book, he tells us, was *Robinson Crusoe*. Henceforward, among the translations and *Robinsonades* in many literatures, more or less pedagogic versions abound. For here was instruction in natural piety and natural science, in self-help as well as submission to Providence, uniquely combined with every innocent excitement. To judge of the pleasure with which a late eighteenth-century father could put such a book into the hands of his son, or a schoolmaster prepare a series of lessons upon it, one has only to conceive of a time when *Robinson Crusoe* did not exist, indeed when there were no 'children's books' at all: for on that shelf *Crusoe* is the first as well as the greatest.

If Rousseau helped to give *Robinson Crusoe* to the young, he certainly recommended it to the European Romantics. From Werther and the Byronic hero and the 'Man of Feeling' Crusoe appears unsentimentally remote. By his very solidity he survives them. Yet the idea of Defoe's book, the central situation and its philosophical consequences, were such as Rousseau could fasten upon with his almost lunatic passion for primitive virtue, strangely and powerfully combined with rational enquiry into the social contract. Through his great influence, as well as through its own, the story of a man preserving himself alone upon an island was to provide morals for misfits. Crusoe's own serious reflections, as a commercial sequel, might remain unread; but a later generation of young men escaped in imagination to his Island and there nourished their spleen against society. With no machinery of government to control him and no church to admonish him, Crusoe was recognizably good. He exalted the stature of man, and by implication placed upon the social system the onus of its justification. Political revolution and literary romanticism both called him brother, while Friday, not to be overlooked, was cast for the rôle of The Noble Savage.

It would be possible to show, with copious and sometimes diverting illustrations, that all this was very proper. With his Island (not, as is so often said, a *desert* island), Defoe does broadly infer a criticism of a society which had not continuously treated him well; and in Part Two,

in Siberia, he gives Crusoe a memorable interview with
an exiled Russian aristocrat who philosophically declines
the chance to return to court. Crusoe, save for his
monumental indifference to sex, is a very human individual (too human, some critics have complained, in
the face of dehumanizing circumstances). He does not,
like his distant literary progeny, weep aloud in a wild
ecstasy on the smallest provocation, but he lets us know
for a fact that in an emotional crisis his teeth 'would
strike together, and set one against the other, so strong,
that for some time I could not part them again.' He
knows fear and anger and compassion, remorse and
magnanimity, much doubt and searching of himself and
going about with God. Before his eyes, after long years
alone, an approaching vessel goes to pieces with all
hands lost, and he can touch the heart and nerves with a
cry: 'That but one man had been sav'd! O that it had
been but one!' The sequence of emotions upon the
disturbing discovery of the footprint can still attach
readers weaned on the psychological novel, though the
conflict be played out over months and years instead of in
the clouded crystal of a moment of time which has engrossed some of Defoe's successors.

As for Friday, he owes his claim to the title of Noble
Savage, as he owes everything else, to his master. If
Robinson Crusoe were not a popular hero, a practical
Protestant hero to replace the discredited mediaeval
hagiology, his servant would no more live in the mind's
eye than Ariel without Prospero or Hanuman without
Rama. He *is*, after all, a servant, utterly at Crusoe's
command. The project of obtaining such a servant had
begun to grow in Crusoe's mind as soon as he realized
that Caribs from another island occasionally visited his
own. In the event Friday responds completely to kindness,

as Defoe suggested in more than one of his books that slaves would respond—an idea of some novelty, no doubt, but springing from the desire of getting better service as much as from humanity or religion. In religious as well as in practical matters Friday proves instructible; posing in the process, with a childish and heathen logic, some difficult questions of theology such as suited Defoe's enquiring and somewhat paradoxical temper. He shows courage, and devotion, and filial piety. But he is also a comic—in his daring game with the bear in the Pyrennees, and on the Island in the drolleries of his conduct and his speech (Defoe was seriously interested in variants of English pronunciation). It is plain that Defoe's Friday cannot be acquitted of complicity in the pantomime and music-hall tradition of a far from noble savage. If we seek the literary roots of the Noble Savage theme we must probably go back before *Robinson Crusoe*, at least to Aphra Behn's *Oroonoko, or the Royal Slave*, of 1688, with its superior African hero and heroine, victims of the slave-trade. And for any practical mobilization of opinion against slavery as such we have to wait for the Quaker petition to Parliament of 1783, more than fifty years after Defoe's death—although some lines in Defoe's *Reformation of Manners* (1702) have been picked out as a denunciation of the Trade.

Backwards and forwards the bookworms have burrowed, until *Robinson Crusoe* itself is perforated almost to illegibility: back to find a negro hero in Aphra Behn, goats and cats in Selkirk's narrative, the Island itself in *Krinke Kesmes*; forward not only to the *Swiss Family Robinson* and the like, but towards Rousseau, towards the French Revolution, towards the Emancipation of Slaves. Some comment on Crusoe's ancestry and influence is not to be avoided in a book on Daniel Defoe. But there is a question that is more

c

important than his share of responsibility for social up-
heaval in Europe. As a text-book for Rousseau, as the hero
in our own day of a Soviet film, it must be admitted that
the endearing figure in the goatskin cap, with his parrot
and his Carib servant and his ingenious umbrella, looks
more than a little out of place. But as an Englishman of
the early eighteenth century, as the Englishman, the true-
born Englishman, as Defoe himself translated from Stoke
Newington, and moreover as the sort of Englishman who
was in fact translated with momentous consequences to
North America, Crusoe is as large as life. The historical
perspective persuades us to look back from 1789 to see
by what tides in the mind of European man the pyramidal
form of society was washed away. Instead we should be
looking forward from 1689 to see why England *avoided*
the French Revolution.

*   *   *

To Defoe, twenty-eight at the time and of respectable
Dissenting stock, 1689 (or the previous year of William's
landing) was an *annus mirabilis*. He became the defender
and perhaps even the confidant of William III, trouncing
his detractors and keeping his memory green through
the hurly-burly politics of the reign of Anne. That he
became 'Queen Anne's man' also, after pamphleteering
himself into Newgate prison and the pillory, is chiefly
the story of the mild Whig Daniel Defoe in alliance with
the mild Tory Robert Harley (and then with Godolphin)
—a notable story of moderation served by keen intelligence at a time when the country needed both. That
story covers among other things the first formative
development of British journalism, and here at least
there can be no disputing Defoe's impressive share of
parenthood. It covers many of Defoe's journeys through

the whole kingdom which produced, besides material for the well-known *Tour*, the confidential reports on public and private opinion which have only been appreciated with the partial publication of the Harley MSS. It covers in history the peaceful Union with Scotland, which Defoe laboured to promote and then to consolidate. And it ends with the death of Queen Anne in 1714 and the accession of the first Hanoverian. With George I the extreme Whigs came into their own; and Defoe, who had served, and well served, ministries of moderate Whigs and even of High Tories under the check of Harley, extricated himself from danger by a manoeuvre which may have debased and constricted his journalism, but turned his best powers into a new and wonderful field. His Georgian age was the age of *Robinson Crusoe* and *Captain Singleton*, of *Moll Flanders* and *Roxana* and *Colonel Jack*, of the *Journal of the Plague Year* and the *Tour*, in fact of nearly everything for which he is now widely known. 'It is hard,' his friend John Dunton had said of him, 'to leave off when not only the itch and inclination, but the necessity of writing, lies so heavy upon a man.'

When that itch and that necessity pounced upon the idea of *Robinson Crusoe*, Defoe had a vast amount of work and experience behind him. He had been 'shipwrecked more often by land than by sea.' His voyaging in strange waters had been done (at any rate for the most part) in his library and his counting-house, in dockside conversations, in the reporter's calling which may or may not have brought him into contact with the ex-castaway Alexander Selkirk in Bristol. Defoe sat like Henry the Navigator on his cliff, looking out upon oceans where others adventured. But there was one island that he knew like the back of his hand, and that was Britain.

He saw Britain as it could not be seen from a villa at Twickenham or a vast new country seat, or even from Wills' Coffee-House and the Kit-Cat Club. He knew it, in the first place, as a business-man, a liveryman of a City Company, engaged successively in a variety of trading and manufacturing enterprises; a commercial traveller, also, over the atrocious roads that had for so long hindered economic progress and yielded only slowly, after the Act of 1706, to the turnpike-system. It was failure in business, it has sometimes been said, that made Defoe a writer, but this is a little misleading. It is true that the full flood of his publications can be dated from 1697, after his first bankruptcy and the closure of his hose-factor's business. But he had written before that, and he went into business again afterwards. It was writing that made him a writer, the itch first and then the necessity. But neither his political activities nor the later success of his popular tales could extinguish his absorbing interest in the subject of trade. Crusoe's cargoes and enterprises are enumerated; Roxana and Moll Flanders, quite apart from the mercantile character of their amours, know all about shipments and bills of exchange and capital stock. The *Tour* is rich in information of the internal trade of Britain, and in the *Compleat English Tradesman* Defoe gives us the costume of a countrywoman, garment by garment, and tells us where each was made. Writing about trade, he once affectionately confessed, was 'the whore I really doated upon and designed to have taken up with.' If nothing else had set him apart from the smart literary coteries to which as a young man he had seemed to aspire, this passion for the market-place would have done so.

Yet in the market-place England was becoming a world power. Learning from the Dutch, fighting them

at sea, and then in alliance with them against the
ambitions of Louis XIV, the English were building up
their mercantile empire with the City of London as
headquarters. The sixteen-nineties, following the 'Revolution Settlement' of William III, saw the establishment
of the Bank of England, the first Fire Insurance Companies, the new East India Company, the proliferation
of joint-stock undertakings. The 'middle part of mankind' that was pushing forward in England as in the
Netherlands had the character of an evolutionary force,
intellectually adventurous but with a material stake in
constitutionalism and stability. Of that middle class,
and of the Dissenting community that formed so important a part of it, came Defoe, acutely conscious of
the wealth and standing of the new business-gentry. In
his writings can be studied, not only the play of economic
and political forces which were slowly preparing
Britain to become the greatest trading and industrial
nation on earth; but also the curious growth of the
'double ethic' which we have since taken so much for
granted that it is only now being examined historically
—the development, that is, of a separate business code,
a compendium of rules for economic behaviour quite
independent of any philosophic or theological concept
of man. Charles Lamb was so shocked by the conduct
recommended by Defoe in *The Compleat English Tradesman* that he could only imagine the intention was satirical.
But Defoe the Dissenter and Defoe the merchant are
there in the middle of it all.

Defoe the writer has been called an excluded genius,
and it is commonly assumed that it was his middle-class
origin alone that kept him out of the charmed circle of
Wits and Beaux. He was not even, as was Samuel
Johnson a generation later, a down-at-heel University

scholar. He was educated at a Dissenters' Academy, and it was Dissent more than birth which set a gulf between him and the intellectual aristocracy. This has been well pointed out by James Sutherland, who observes that Alexander Pope was the son of a London merchant and Matthew Prior's uncle kept a tavern. Even the last great poems of Milton had to await their reputation until his attitude to the Church by law established could be forgiven, or forgotten, along with his republicanism. Dryden went over to the Church of Rome yet kept his great place among men of letters, but there was a needle's eye for the Puritan camels who had made such a trampling among the theatres and the bookshops and the poets' taverns. The eclipse of the greatest Puritan is referred to by Defoe in his poetic lampoon of 1702, *The Reformation of Manners*:

> Let this describe the Nation's character,
> One man reads Milton, forty Rochester.

And it was not alone, as Defoe pretended, the superior attractions of the lewd over the sublime that dictated the fashion.

Nor was it entirely a party matter, for the party system was only developing into an instrument of parliamentary government during the eighteenth century. Tories and Whigs, succeeding to Cavaliers and Roundheads, can be seen in an over-simplified view as supporters of the Church and the squirearchy on the one hand, and on the other the commercial and Dissenting interests. Yet whether Whigs or Tories formed the Ministry, the landed classes and the Church were in fact in the dominant position, pre-eminent in society and setting the standards and fashions in literature and the arts. A Dissenter—even one with Defoe's capacity for teasing his fellow-Dissenters—could not be an Augustan. Where-ever one might look for Daniel Defoe in his fifties (and like Colonel Jack's mother, he kept very good company), it would not be with Lord Burlington on the Grand Tour. The whole history of Puritanism and the reaction from it stood in his way.

That the social pattern found equilibrium under an agreed settlement of Crown, Parliament and Church was due, Carlyle thought, to the fact that the centre of gravity was sufficiently low for stability. The gulf between the aristocrat and the mob was not unbridge-able. The bourgeois who prepared revolution in France had other ways to satisfaction in England. Defoe, if he could not decorate the elegant summit of the structure, had some advantage in being near that centre of gravity. He never questioned class distinctions and he spent a deal of ink on the shortcomings of servants and work-men. But he certainly appreciated the phenomenon of fluidity in the social pattern. He delighted to watch the merchant-princes displaying their opulence and putting capital into the land (where it was needed) while the younger sons of the landed aristocracy turned their hands to trade. And the gibes about oyster-women had some substance. Defoe was *interested* in the lower orders. Aubrey had commented upon the widening literacy of the times, and if Defoe succeeded in giving common folk something to read besides the Bible and Foxe's *Book of Martyrs* it was partly because he at least recognized their existence. In the years just before the accession of William and Mary he travelled much through the country, investigating, as he said, 'the common people, how they live, and what their employment.' In giving them their kitchen-reading—not only in tales of pirates and highwaymen, thieves and whores, but also in such improving works as the *Family Instructor*—he anticipated the sort of success achieved a little later by Hogarth with his popular engravings. If anyone should have painted Defoe's portrait it was Hogarth, who could conceivably have done so when he was young and Defoe was old. Hogarth in fact is Fielding's artist, not Defoe's; but Gin Lane was produced by the new cheap poison that Defoe condemned, and one cannot look at the Shrimp-Girl without feeling that Defoe knew her kind.

The England whose degree of freedom, toleration, and scientific progress drew such admiration from Voltaire and Montesquieu, visiting us in the 1720's, is still something of a marvel to the historian. It was not only the realm of Newton and Locke, developing that 'natural' approach to philosophy and politics which a terrible French logic was to carry to a bloody end. It was also a tight little island, proud of military and commercial success, conscious (from time to time) of being a leading European State. In the age that produced Arbuthnot's *John Bull*, Arne's *Rule, Britannia* and *The Roast Beef of Old England*, Defoe was using new and ringing terms: 'Great Britain,' 'Empire,' 'British Sovereignty at sea.' But with his *True-Born Englishman* he dealt racial snobbery so honest and resounding a thwack that two centuries later educated Indians were quoting it against us; and what is no less significant, it was received with popular delight in the England of his own day. In that England there were disease and dirt and yahoos and whipping at the cart's tail. But the general condition of the people, no less than their progressive institutions, astonished foreign visitors. The seal of the period, to a modern historian, is set by the Glorious Revolution of 1688—glorious because almost bloodless, observes G. M. Trevelyan, in distinction from 'the short,

fierce, destructive blaze of *la gloire*.' And for forty-odd
years thereafter, seeking Defoe in the crowd of better-
known Englishmen, we nearly always find him on the
side of just those developments the history-books under-
line as contributing at the same time to our political
liberties and to the enduring character of that constitutional settlement: parliamentary control of finance,
for instance; electoral reform and measures against
corruption; the subservience of the executive to the
judiciary; the safeguarding of the Succession, the Union
with Scotland; above all (and despite Defoe's occasional
violence in argument) the broadest measure of tolerance
consistent with security. Crusoe, when man came at last
to his Island, did not contemplate a Utopia, a Soviet, or a
Republic of the Saints. He thought of himself 'merrily'
as a monarch by right of ownership of the territory:

'It was remarkable, too, we had but three subjects,
and they were of three different religions. My man
Friday was a Protestant, his father was a Pagan and a
Cannibal, and the Spaniard was a Papist: however, I
allow'd Liberty of Conscience throughout my Dominions.'

Liberty of conscience was a live idea, and the Settlement of Church and State in 1689 produced a climate in
which religious toleration had a chance to develop. But
the Settlement itself and all its fruits could be destroyed
if Catholics could conspire with foreign foes or Non-
conformists dispute the authority of the Established
Church. Toleration, we know today in a political
context, has always this problem and this limitation, and
it was one which Defoe the Dissenter saw clearly. The
Settlement, in which Whigs and Tories contrived to
adjust their differences of outlook in a joint recognition
of national necessities, has since been seen as the firm

foundation of the constitution which has served us so well. But its permanence cannot have been so apparent to the men who made it and built upon it. It was an English (and Welsh) compromise. Scotland accepted William and Mary, but in a partisan spirit which postponed a peaceful settlement until 1707, or rather until the defeat of Jacobitism forty years later. Ireland, conquered for the new régime by the sword and exploited by Whig and Tory alike, is sundered to this day. The English people who disappointed the watchful Louis XIV by accepting William of Orange without another disastrous conflict, presumably did so because they were tired of civil war. But to be tired of conflict is not necessarily to be sure of freedom from disaster. From the excitements of Defoe's early boyhood—the Plague, the Fire, the Dutch in the Medway—he passed to manhood in a society nervous of fifth columns and aware that it had not yet balanced monarchical with parliamentary power. In the Glorious Revolution itself, swift as it was to accomplish mighty things, there were more chances and dangers than the winds that carried William's fleet to Devon instead of to the agreed assignment on the Yorkshire coast. And in the years that followed, the titles of many of Defoe's pamphlets offer a calendar of public concern: *An Argument Shewing that a Standing Army, With Consent of Parliament Is not Inconsistent with a Free Government (1698); The Danger of the Protestant Religion Consider'd, from the Present Prospect of a Religious War in Europe (1701); The Shortest Way with the Dissenters (1702); Advice to the Electors of Great Britain, occasion'd by the intended Invasion from France (1708); An Essay on the South Sea Trade (1711); Hannibal at the Gates (1712); And What if the Pretender Should Come? (1713); What if the Queen Should Die? (1713).*

That all these and many other writings from the hand of Defoe were directed in some measure against extremist agitation and panic remedies, only illustrates the fact that public passions had been aroused and required to be moderated. Defoe's method, very often, was to carry to absurd conclusions an argument which he aimed to demolish. The most celebrated example of this is *The Shortest Way with the Dissenters*, which suavely proposed measures so violent that the Dissenters were as disturbed at the possibility as the High-Church Party was wounded by the hoax. It is true that when the London mob at length grasped the nature of Defoe's rash jest they gave him a friendly reception in the pillory. But his tricks, and he played plenty of them, made him as many enemies as direct attack. For Swift, settled respectably in the bosom of the Church, the irony of which he was such a master was a safer weapon, worn as of privilege by gentlemen and wits. For the Dissenting tradesman it was always dangerous, yet always attractive; and the propensity to use it is not unconnected with an aspect of his reputation which demands some thought. William Minto called Defoe 'a great, a truly great liar, perhaps the greatest liar in English literature,' and the phrase has been echoed again and again. What exactly does it mean?

In its way, of course, it is a tribute. To call Defoe, as a novelist, an accomplished liar is rather like calling David Garrick an accomplished hypocrite. But the theatre has long been accepted as the ground of make-believe. Literature, in Defoe's day, had nothing to correspond with our idea of fiction. There was respectable reading-matter—history, politics, the Classics, sermons and religious treatises and the Bible, voyages and travels, the new scientific essays stimulated by Charles II's patronage of the Royal Society. Beyond these there were the tediously artificial 'romances' notably by the feminine followers of Mrs. Behn, which Defoe despised as a sensible citizen. Fiction, in this latter dress, found serious approval neither with the intellectual aristocracy nor with the sober reading public. Fact was the recognized medium both of entertainment and instruction, and it was fact which Defoe's readers demanded. When it began to be rumoured of *Robinson Crusoe* that the whole thing was a work of imagination (not, be it noted, that it had been transcribed from Selkirk), the author's defence was to suggest that it was by way of being a personal allegory. Allegory might be accepted from Defoe as it had been from Bunyan: but not fiction.

There is thus no sharp dividing line between Defoe's accounts of the wars in Germany or the court of Sweden or a voyage round the globe (as accurate as his sources would allow and as vivid as the method of personal narrative could make them), and a book like *Moll Flanders* or *Robinson Crusoe*. Almost all that one can say is that in the latter the main interest is in the exploits and fortunes of a single individual, while in the former it lies in the events in which the narrator shares a part. To go further than that is to apply subsequent library-labels that will not fit. Yet we cannot help trying to fit labels. We are content, no doubt, with the superb verisimilitude of the books we call his novels. But we want to know, when we take up the *Journal of the Plague Year* or the *Memoirs of a Cavalier*, whether we can rely on them as history. Objective research proves that we cannot altogether do so, and the notion of the 'great liar' begins to be extended from a judgment of craftsmanship to a judgment of character. A volume on English literature, published in 1950 in a 'Teach Yourself'

series, coolly declares that Defoe was 'constitutionally incapable of telling the truth.' Macaulay, who had
his own turn of persuasive prose, was both tendentious
and inaccurate; but nobody ever said that of him.

Defoe's reputation as a writer and a man (and the
two are hard to separate) has had a curious and fluctuating
history; but the extreme estimate of his unreliability is
now much out of date. If the literary convention that
demanded the appearance of truth is recognized, the
skill and energy with which Defoe satisfied it can be
praised. His art as a novelist, it is often said, was to make
fiction as real as fact. Looked at another way, it was to
translate fact into fiction. Investigation tends more and
more to uncover the solid material, in something
experienced or something read, with which he built and
ornamented his narratives. In a busy and varied career
he can have wasted little. A detail recaptured is as
bright as new, and it sparkles still for us. For that very
reason, perhaps, we judge his occasional lapses from
historical or autobiographical truth more severely. The
inaccuracies and inventions in the *Journal of the Plague
Year* may affront our ideas of historical method. But
consider that remarkable work—one of several in which
Defoe treated of the supernatural—the *True Relation of
the Apparition of Mrs. Veal*. This was celebrated by Sir
Walter Scott and other as a work of fiction put out as
fact, a brilliant device to serve as a puff for a fellow-
writer. It has since been proved to have been indeed a true relation of evidence, a straightforward
piece of reporting on a matter of topical and popular
interest.

What, then, of those works of Defoe which are often
indexed under the general head of 'hoaxes'? *The
Shortest Way With the Dissenters* sometimes figures as one.

Another, credibly attributed to Defoe although he dis-
avowed it, is the *Minutes of the Negotiations of M. Mesnager*,
which purported to reveal the preliminaries to the Peace
of Utrecht, and did so in a light favourable to Defoe's
former patron, Robert Harley, Earl of Oxford. They
were published—this is the point that nobody missed—
at the very moment in 1714 when the fallen Minister
was about to stand his trial on a charge of high treason.

Literary or political forgery clearly comes under a
different head from the conventional disguise of fiction
as fact. If Defoe sinned in this respect, he did so in good
company. To take only one example, Swift faked an
account of Prior's mission to Paris, purporting to come
from a French valet. Subterfuges, hoaxes, deceptions
litter the annals of the time. It was said that Pope could
not take tea without a stratagem. Perhaps Titus Oates's
enormous exploitation of popular prejudices in the reign
of Charles II (and of fears that were not unjustified) was
too dire in its effects to be classed with the practical
jokes for which the Wits and the Beaux held something
like a licence. Defoe may have witnessed the dreadful
punishment of the author of the Popish Plot, a sight to
frighten any political journalist whose manoeuvres might
fall foul of authority. He also knew of the elaborate
tricks and mystifications—'bites' as they were called[1]—
which later kept the clubs and coffee-houses happy: the
hounding of the fortune-teller Partridge with reports of
his own death was one of the more notorious of these.
It was in the seventeen-fifties, after Defoe's day, that
wholesale hoodwinking became fashionable, as in the
carefully fostered rumours of an earthquake that sent
seven hundred coaches rolling out of London to the

---

[1] Cf. Defoe's *Fortunate Mistress* (*Roxana*): 'Thus his project of coming to
bed with me was a bite upon himself, while he intended it for a bite upon me.'

West. But Defoe may be allowed a 'bite' to challenge the inner circle of the men-about-town in his account of the disappearance of the Island of St. Vincent in a volcanic eruption, contributed to *Mist's Journal* in 1718. The original report, received in a letter from Barbados, proved to have been greatly exaggerated, but Defoe's sensational description had sold out the paper. Assailed by rival journalists he replied pleasantly in the same sheet that St. Vincent was now reported to have been found again: 'but we must acknowledge, we do not believe one word of it.'

That example, as it happens, is from the latter and darker days of Defoe's periodical journalism. His own famous *Review* was by then dead. He was anonymously increasing the popular circulation of *Mist's* and *Applebee's* and other papers, and at the same time carrying out the service to George I's government which has been found so equivocal—secretly directing Tory journals in such a way as to remove their sting. There is a sentence which well suggests the character of journalism in Defoe's time and his own contributions to it. It is on the first page of the *Journal of the Plague Year*, where he makes his saddler-chronicler remark: 'We had no such thing as printed newspapers in those days to spread rumours and reports of things, and to improve them by the invention of men, as I have lived to see practised since.' That might not have satisfied C. P. Scott as a definition of the function of newspapers, but it was not said in irony. The demand for readable matter grew quickly greater in Defoe's day than the ready supply of news; improvements by the invention of men were demanded and provided in the quest for what Fleet Street now calls 'readership' and pursues with at least equal zeal. *The Review*, of which for nine years the entire

contents came almost certainly from Defoe's own hand,
stands out from all its rivals: not only for the technique
of presentation, enlivened by anecdote, reminiscence,
snatches of character and conversation, fictitious correspondence; but because his policy and attitude were those
of moderation rather than prejudice. 'The first that
deservedly leads the way is Daniel De Foe,' wrote John
Dunton in 1706 in his *Secret History of the Weekly Writers*.
Dunton had been his friend and schoolfellow; but he
felt himself to have been injured by Defoe in the writing
business and he need not have been generous in tribute
to a man with many enemies.

The testimony of those enemies for long held considerable weight. Needy, greedy Dan, the viper, the toady,
the man with a pen for sale, confronts us in the broad-
sheets of his time. The hooked nose and the large mole
itemized in the order for his apprehension were as fair game
as Pope's dwarfish body for the hostile pamphleteer.

> With a long nose and mouth as wide;
> With blobber lips and lockram jaws,
> Warts, wrinkles, wens and other flaws,
> With nitty beard, and neck that's scabby
> And in a dress that's very shabby.
> Who this should be I do not know
> Unless a Whig? I guess he's so—
> If I am right, pray take a throw!

That, of course, was a High Tory invitation to those
who gathered at the pillory at Temple Bar. But it was
not long before Whigs also were throwing curses instead
of flowers, when they began to suspect that Defoe's pen
was sold to their political opponents. The hunt seems
often to have run the other way, and the impression grows
that Defoe himself was feared, the more so as his
journalism became more clandestine. Never quite sure

behind which bush he was lurking, his enemies struck out whenever he appeared in the open, and when he did not they prodded the undergrowth with a nervous ferocity.

Not all the attacks on Defoe were undeserved. But in an age when mud was flung so indiscriminately it is right to ask why more should have stuck upon him than upon others. The commonest aspersion, that of political turncoat, has been taken a great deal too seriously. In an age of trimmers and Vicars of Bray it is clear that Defoe was on the whole truer to his political and religious principles than most public men. He spoke of Dryden (in the *Consolidator*) as 'having his extraordinary genius flung and pitched upon a swivel . . . every day to change his principle, change his religion, change his coat, change his master, and yet never change his nature.' Had Defoe been content to quote the temper of his times in defence of such shifts as he made he could have justified himself as fully as he tried to do in his *Appeal to Honour and Justice* of 1715. But he loved to cover his tracks. The money that he took from Ministers was earned honestly and for the most part without sacrifice of principle. His mistake, for the sake of his subsequent reputation, was to deny that he took money at all. Few preachers are entirely consistent in their practice. Defoe preached a great deal, and often movingly. Lapses about which a different character might hardly have troubled disturbed his conscience and were argued out of it in public. The labyrinth in which he thus found himself assorted ill, when opened by later research, with the candour of his prose. The Victorians lost something of an idol, a martyr to freedom of speech and worship, when William Lee (himself an ardent admirer) uncovered among other things the correspondence with Lord Stanhope, Secretary of State in the

D

fourth year of George I's reign. The fallen idol, exasperating biographers by the necessity of checking his own statements, became for some the man 'constitutionally incapable of telling the truth.' More recent studies have rescued him from this absurd charge and have come to rest somewhere between the extremes. There are no sure grounds for concluding, as has been done in some cases, that Defoe's own story is that of a constant and painful conflict between his fundamentalist upbringing and his worldly commonsense. The further one reads in and about him (even with a consciousness of his shifts of mood and circumstance) the more of a piece does he seem: neither scoundrel nor saint, but with a fair human measure of vanity, honesty, charity, folly, foresight, greed, altruism, magnanimity and pettiness; and with a more than human measure of industry and vitality.

The results of that industry, too formidable in bulk for any editor who has so far ventured his hand, have been whittled down by rough agreement to a dozen or so volumes. The whole world knows *Robinson Crusoe*, if only partially; but it is a creation that exists very nearly in its own right—so that the 'literary critic' of a daily paper, who recently confessed that he had forgotten that Defoe wrote the book, joins hands with thousands to whom it scarcely occurs that the book had an author at all. The fame of *Moll Flanders*, persistent but for a period somewhat furtive, now stands deservedly and unashamedly high, followed at a little distance by *The Fortunate Mistress* and *Colonel Jack*. *Captain Singleton* has not been republished since Aitken's excellent edition at the end of the last century; but the *Memoirs of a Cavalier*, the *Journal of the Plague Year* and (since Prof. G. D. H. Cole rescued the original text) the main part of the *Tour Through the Whole Island of Great Britain*, are easily obtained in standard editions. Of the works that require to be hunted out in second-hand bookshops, the most sought after are probably the *Apparition of Mrs. Veal*, *The Shortest Way with the Dissenters*, the *Essay upon Projects*, *The Compleat English Tradesman* and *A Plan of the English Commerce*, possibly also the curious *History of the Devil*. With few exceptions the tracts and pamphlets are left to the specialist, or tasted in selections and anthologies such as those of Henry Morley, John Masefield, and Professor W. P. Trent of Columbia University, to whose influence is due much of the great interest now shown by American scholars in the inexhaustible subject of Defoe and his writings. Among American contributions the publication of a fascimile edition of the complete *Review* is of particular value, since the best of Defoe's journalism was previously unknown except by the occasional quotations of scholars. As for Defoe's verse, on which at one stage in his life he would have wished his fame to be based, we are content with the quantitative estimate that he wrote more lines than Milton. Only *The True-Born Englishman* stands out memorably with the rough vigour of its early attack on racial snobbery. The success of this defence of William of Orange gave great and natural satisfaction to its author, who put out his own collected (or selected) editions in 1703 and 1705 as the *Writings of the Author of the True-Born Englishman*. And it is with a reading of this satire that the B.B.C. has elevated Daniel Defoe among the Wits and Beaux of its Third Programme.

Defoe is indeed the one writer of his time who might prompt a passing reference to so modern a development as broadcasting. Of none of the great Augustans does one feel, as one feels instinctively with Defoe, that he might have adapted himself without too much effort to the age in which we live. He would no doubt have abandoned his versification by now, finding no fashion to which he cared to aspire; and pamphlet-literature no longer holds the field. But there are other fields which he would surely have had the energy to invade; and he would have found a Press, daily and weekly and monthly, avid for fact and for sensation or for a twilit association of the two. In economic, political, military, and scientific affairs Defoe's eager curiosity would not, perhaps, find the climate of today less congenial than his own. If theological controversy has lost its vogue we are not less beset than his generation by problems of belief and action, by encroachments upon liberty of thought, by conflicts of loyalty involving State and Church and individual. Above all he would have found, after the long picnic on Parnassus, that writing is a trade again. The ivory tower, like other stately homes of England, is too expensive and too troublesome to maintain. We are back with Defoe, forced to find a market beyond that of the literary cliques, or with his successor Fielding who declared that he had to choose between being a hackney-writer or a hackney-coachman. We can imagine that Defoe would not be altogether surprised that the domestic servants whom he found so unsatisfactory have now disappeared, so that 'kitchen-reading' gains a new significance and the practical lessons of Crusoe a new value.

In the corner of this freshly colonized kitchen stands the loudspeaker-extension, for we too live in a 'projecting age.' The commerce of words, with broadcasting, advertising, the cinema, and the daily newspapers, is not fertile in masterpieces; nor would Defoe's contemporaries have thought it at all likely that his works would be read two centuries after his death. The aristocracy of letters showed neither indignation nor sympathy when he stood unjustly in the pillory. Only Alexander Pope (and that in a private conversation very different from the tone of the *Dunciad*) came near a shrewd judgment:

'The First Part of *Robinson Crusoe* is very good. De Foe wrote a vast many things; and none bad, though none excellent, except this. There is something good in all he has written.'

The technical qualities of Defoe's writing have long been acknowledged. If we turn to him today with a new interest, it is to one who all his life lived on his precarious luck, who sought with admirable persistence an outlet for his words and a living for his family, and found an unexpected immortality. There is nobody quite like Defoe in the literatures of other lands. Even in the abundant variety of English he is unique; outside the main stream, perhaps, but a tributary of capital importance.

Chapter Two

THE CHILD OF DISSENT

CRUSOE is an uncommon name, derived (Defoe tells us) from the German *Kreuznaer*. In the London Telephone Directory you will find but one Crusoe (happily enough, Crusoe's Fish-Buffets) and upwards of sixteen hundred Robinsons. The combination of the quotidian with the exotic seems exactly right for its subject.

It happened also that there was one Crusoe among the pupils at Charles Morton's Academy at Newington Green (Stoke Newington) north of London, in the sixteen-seventies. This was Timothy Crusoe, later described by John Dunton as 'the Golden Preacher . . . that could pray two hours together in Scripture language,' although 'not yet arriv'd at *perfection*, as appeared from his sloth in tying the conjugal knot.' One of Tim Crusoe's schoolfellows was Samuel Wesley, who was to become the father of a more renowned golden preacher, with the world for his parish. Another was Daniel Foe, son of James Foe, of the parish of St. Giles-in-Cripplegate. A third was the amiable John Dunton himself. In the hunt that still goes on for the historical Daniel Foe or Defoe there are broken trails and false directions in plenty, and no firm attachment that we can trace save perhaps his loyalty to King William III, alive and dead. And so it is curious to find paths that began at the Dissenting Academy in Newington crossing again: Tim Crusoe remembered when a character needed a name;

Dunton exchanging comparatively friendly knocks with Defoe in the new world of journalism; Sam Wesley also flitting in and out of contemporary controversies.

It was in many cases a charitable education that boys received (his 'fund-companions', Defoe called them) in the Dissenting Academies of which London and its neighbourhood had several. Most of them were established during the last thirty years of the seventeenth century, when times were as bad for the dissenting Protestant sects as for Roman Catholics. The Act of Uniformity of 1662, and the other restrictive measures which followed it, would have made it as difficult for a Dissenter to teach as to preach if they had been strictly enforced. For these measures applied not only to University professors and readers, and to the masters, fellows, and tutors of Colleges, but to all schoolmasters and even private instructors. From them, as from ministers of religion, the law required after the Restoration unfeigned assent to the Book of Common Prayer and rejection of the Solemn League and Covenant of the Presbyterians that had been associated with the Great Rebellion. In other words it enjoined on all teachers, on pain of loss of employment, conformity with the Church of England. The purge was strictly carried out in the Universities and endowed schools, but clearly less strictly, or less regularly, in the private institutions thereupon set up by dispossessed Dissenters. To these private Academies even conforming parents sometimes sent their children. The character of many of the Academies, and the very number of Dissenters, counselled a degree of toleration. Yet none of them could think themselves or their institutions safe from persecution.

The test was a religious test, but it would be wrong to think of it as a heresy-hunt. Doctrinal questions were bound up with considerations of political security, which counselled the reservation of office and the influential professions to the dominant interests after the return of the monarchy—to the landed gentry and their allies in the Church. As Defoe himself was to put it in a memorandum written (probably) in 1794, 'the Papist, the Church of England, and the Dissenter have all had their turns in administration.' And he added sagely: 'Whenever any of them endeavoured their own settlement by the ruin of the parties dissenting, the consequence was supplanting themselves.'[1] The turn of the Dissenters had come with the Commonwealth and the Protectorate, with Presbyterianism in the lead and a comparative toleration for all the Protestant sectarians. For the social and political appreciation of nonconformity it is not necessary to distinguish elaborately between Congregationalists and Independents, Baptists and Anabaptists, the Bear and the Boar and the Wolf and the Fox of Dryden's *The Hind and the Panther*. But there is a rather special place for the Quakers—mystical, practical, and inextinguishable. Defoe himself had little interest in the Quakers until some characteristic kindnesses shown to him in prison caused him to speak well of them. In the manuscript just referred to he says that the Dissenters as a whole in the reign of Queen Anne were 'divided and impolitic; they are not formed into a body; they hold no correspondence among themselves. Could they have been brought to do so, their numbers would have made them formidable.'

Yet formidable in several senses they were, despite divisions and disabilities. Their considerable strength in the towns was increased, after Louis XIV's Revocation

[1] In the Harleian MSS. in the British Museum. First printed by Professor Sutherland as appendix to his *Defoe*, 1937.

of the Edict of Nantes, by refugee craftsmen. They
were associated both with middle-class economic enterprise and with a certain sturdy mob-temper which
ministries could not ignore. As the party system developed,
Dissent was commonly an ally of the Whigs—the 'faction' of Samuel Johnson's brief and celebrated dictionary
definition. Its power in the City was as important when
parliamentary government needed money as it had been
when monarchy tried to raise it without recourse to
parliament. Its mercantile vigour can be partly traced,
no doubt, to the exclusion of Dissenters from other
callings, and partly also to the characteristic virtues of
the Puritan sects—thrift, industry, and seriousness.
With Baxter and Steele (the divine, not the essayist)
that very word 'calling' takes on a special significance
and popularity, applied alike to business and to devotion.
This is a theme—the religious aspect of the development of capitalism and the middle-class—which has
been much studied and disputed in our own day, and
Defoe illustrates it abundantly.[1] Just because he was
less prejudiced than others, because his own Dissenting
position was a matter of conscience and commonsense
and not of political or theological passion, we can learn
a good deal from the personal history of the man who
wrote not only *The Shortest Way With The Dissenters* but
also *The Compleat English Tradesman* (and almost on his
deathbed, be it added, *The Compleat English Gentleman*).

*   *   *

The father of Daniel Defoe (we are now going back to
the tyranny of Cromwell's last years and the nervous

[1] For detailed argument in this field there is a 'Pelican' edition of R. H.
Tawney's *Religion and the Rise of Capitalism* (16th and 17th centuries). See also
publications therein mentioned, especially Miss E. D. Bebb's *Nonconformity and
Social and Economic Life, 1600–1800.*

uncertainty that followed them) was a Dissenter, and
no more a Republican that the saintly Richard Baxter.
For his royalism there is evidence, and his son was proud
of it. James Foe was a tallow-chandler of Cripplegate,
afterwards a butcher and member of the Butchers'
Company—his son succeeded to this privilege and was
later commemorated in a stained glass window (since
destroyed by bombing) in Butchers' Hall. Henry Morley
imagined Defoe's father 'bringing cattle from their
grazing-grounds to the London meat-market'; and here is
Defoe's own note on the gentle countryside about Oundle
(tranquil even today though the open-cast desert creeps
towards it from Corby) where the family, before the
Civil wars, had been substantial yeomen:

'Here again there is a most beautiful range of meadows,
and perhaps they are not equall'd in England for length;
they continue uninterrupted for above thirty miles in
length, from Peterborough to Northampton, and, in
some places, are near to two miles in breadth, the land
rich, the grass fine and good, and the cattle, which are
always feeding on them, hay-time excepted, number-
less.'

That is from the *Tour Through the Whole Island of Great
Britain* (1724-6), based as the author says upon seventeen
different journeys through the country. But there is no
reference in it to his ancestral village of Etton,[1] where
the parish register records the marriage of his grandfather Daniel Foe. Defoe was a townsman, a great
Londoner who apparently had no close interest in his
farming forebears. He does tell us somewhere that his
(presumably maternal) grandfather kept a pack of hounds.

[1] Confused by some earlier biographers with Elton, in the north-west corner
of Huntingdonshire.

Elsewhere he claims descent from Sir Walter Raleigh, and there is a discovery in the *Tour* of 'an antient Norman family of the name of De Beau-Foe . . . retaining the latter part of their surname, but without the former to this day.' The Foes in point of fact came to England, not with the Conqueror but as Protestant refugees from Flanders in Elizabeth's reign. But Daniel was a business-man looking for a coat-of-arms. This he legally acquired in 1706, having in the meantime added to his father's name the prefix which posterity, more kind than some of his contemporaries, has agreed to incorporate. Defoe's human vanity was not the sort to demand con-cealment of 'the Middle Way of Life.' On the contrary, his lifelong pride and interest in the commercial calling speaks to us in his old age, in *The Compleat English Trades-man*:

'King Charles II, who was perhaps that Prince of all the Kings that ever reign'd in England, that best under-stood the country and the people he govern'd, used to say, *That the Tradesmen were the only Gentry in England.* His Majesty spoke it merrily, but it had a happy significa-tion in it.'

The monarch thus complimented had come unto his own again at just about the time that Daniel Defoe was born. There is no record of the birth, since like other children of Dissenters he was not baptized. This circumstance left gaps in the parish registers which rendered the guesses at population figures made by Defoe and others liable to considerable inaccuracy. It now appears that the births of his two elder sisters were nevertheless entered by the Dissenting Minister of St. Giles, Cripplegate; and this has guided us towards a date between July and December 1660 as Daniel's probable birthday. The actual day has been guessed as September 30, because of the importance given to that date not only in *Robinson Crusoe* (it was the day of Crusoe's casting upon the Island) but in several of the other novels as well. It may be so.

England, since the merry month of May, was once more a monarchy. The change had been accomplished 'without one bloody nose,' which was to Richard Baxter a sign of divine direction. To James Foe the Restoration must have been equally welcome after the insecurity of affairs under Richard Cromwell and the army. Charles Stuart, after all, had been prepared to take the Covenant when the Scots had crowned him before his exile. When he landed at Dover on 25 May 1660, it was not the controversial Book of Common Prayer but a Bible that he accepted, declaring (as Pepys records) that 'it was the thing he loved above all things in the world.' Loyal Protestants of several sects were delighted. James Foe was no more to know that Charles's natural tolerance would yield to the political forces preparing for the exclusion of Dissenters than he was to foresee those other visitations of the Plague and the Fire.

But Charles, intelligent and broad-minded and perhaps even understanding his subjects as Defoe declared, was in no position to resist the reactionary zeal of his first Cavalier Parliament. It was his grandfather who had said drily 'No Bishop, No King.' Now Kings and Bishops were back, the Puritans were out and it was intended that they should remain so. One of the Dissenting Ministers dispossessed of his pulpit by the 1662 Act of Uniformity was Dr. Samuel Annesley of St. Giles, Cripplegate, where James Foe and his wife Alice had worshipped. Forthwith he founded a Dissenting chapel in Bishopsgate, and the Foes staunchly attended his services, even after the Conventicle Act of 1664 had made such attendance a severely punishable offence. We have seen that there was latitude—there had to be —in the execution of laws aimed, especially in London, at a numerous and orderly population. But the family atmosphere of Defoe's infancy and childhood can be imagined as one of quiet resistance, and vigilance, and waiting upon the Lord.

One voice had prophesied, indeed, that liberty and righteousness would be cast away, with all that had been gained by the Great Rebellion, if Parliament and people turned once more to court a King. John Milton, next to the actual regicides, had most to fear from the son of Charles I. Andrew Marvell, M.P. for Hull, saw to it that Milton should be forgiven in the Act of Oblivion which spared all but a few; but the blind poet was dismissed from office, arrested, released on payment of fees. When Daniel Defoe was three years old Milton, having married his third wife, came to live in the same parish, in the house in Artillery Row, Bunhill Fields, where he stayed quietly if not happily for most of his remaining years, dictating the noblest poem in the language. When he died in 1674, Defoe was fourteen or so. It is tempting to think that the boy must have seen him, sitting as Jonathan Richardson had heard 'in a grey coarse cloth coat at the door of his house, near Bunhill Fields, without Moorgate, in warm, sunny weather, to enjoy the fresh air;' or led by Millington the bookseller down Grub Street; or at length borne to his burial in the parish church of St. Giles.

But the question that had most earnestly engaged those who have tried to chronicle Defoe's early years is provoked by those awesome occurrences, the Plague and the Fire. For the librarian it comes to this: is the

Journal of the Plague Year, published fifty-seven years after the event, to be catalogued as history, or to go on the fiction shelves, or into the class called 'biography and memoirs'? In the end it turns out to be a wholly characteristic accomplishment, a piece of that creative journalism, dextrously woven of fact and fiction, for which we really need a new name—or an old name if we could find one. So great has been the influence of this vivid narrative that a modern historian of the Plague of London must ignore almost everything written since Defoe's time and return to such original sources as survive. Yet at one time the chief interest in attempting to fix the date of Defoe's birth was the hope of providing him with personal recollections of the Plague that was at its worst in the streets and alleys about his parents' home in Cripplegate, and of the Fire which stopped short thereabouts at London Wall. We can suppose now that he was in his fifth year in 1665, but we have no means of knowing whether the family braved the horrors of the Plague in Cripplegate or fled to the country like thousands of others—like Milton himself. The *Journal of the Plague Year*, of course, is properly given out as 'Written by a Citizen who continued all the while in London. Never made publick before.' But the citizen (signing himself 'H.F.' and for that and other reasons sometimes traced to a certain Henry Foe who was probably Defoe's uncle) makes no great show of his own fortitude. He carefully debates the problem of whether to escape or to remain, and he does not in general blame those who chose the former course. One *might* infer that Defoe's parents in fact took him and his two elder sisters out of the stricken city. There are hints that would lead us both ways. We remember also that his father was a brave and godfearing man, and that the parish of St. Giles was distinguished, during the ignominious absence of its Anglican Minister, for the devotion of a vicar and several Dissenting church-wardens.

Let us for a moment look at the other end of the matter, at Defoe in his phenomenally busy sixties, in the year 1722 that opened with the publication of *Moll Flanders* and closed with that of *Colonel Jack*. Throughout the previous year Marseilles and Provence had been ravaged by a plague so virulent that there was a lively fear of its being carried to England. The authorities took some precautions. The subject was news. Defoe did a job on it. His *Due Preparations for the Plague, as well for Soul as Body* was on the bookstalls early in February. Five weeks later it was followed by the famous *Journal*; and this, it may be noted, is interlarded with lessons to be drawn from the visitation of 1665 and suggestions for prudent behaviour in face of the 'visible approach' of another pestilence. Happily they were not needed, but the motive and the occasion are interesting. Even if Defoe remembered the calamities of his childhood (and he claims elsewhere to have done so) he felt no compul-, sion to use them as literary material until this topical opportunity presented itself.

His method thereupon is fairly clear. Working at his usual speed, he got hold of a copy of 'Orders Conceived and Published by the Lord Mayor and Aldermen' for dealing with the Plague. These are graphic in themselves, with their institution of examiners and watchmen, their directions for sequestration of the sick and disposal of the dead, for shutting up of infected houses, cleaning of streets, airing of hackney-coaches, control of beggars, taverns, assemblies for bear-baiting, ballad-singing, and the like. The assumption that all such orders were carried out is a rash one. But from them, nevertheless, with imagination and scraps of witness, the horrid incidents could be strung together, the individual dramas garnished with circumstance. And by their printing at length in the early part of the *Journal*, they press upon the reader a belief which is only slightly suspended on the discovery that the Orders copied out by Defoe were in fact issued for an earlier epidemic, and that he himself added the signatures of the Lord Mayor and Aldermen of 1665.[1] No citizen in that dreadful time could have witnessed everything, as the author reminds us, nicely balancing what he says he saw with what he says he heard, and leaving some things properly open to conjecture or to doubt. Defoe must have had contemporary memoirs to draw upon,[2] and one that has since been traced happens to support him in the single incident which his more literal-minded admirers have taken leave to discredit: that of the sleeping piper taken up for a corpse and hooked into the dead-cart where, coming to his senses, he was said to have played his pipe to attract attention.

It is not impossible that Henry Foe did leave a diary which his nephew used when he needed it. And if Defoe himself had childhood memories, what could they be? Not, obviously, the perambulation of the streets, the conversations in the taverns, the visits to the river. Not the frightful burial-pit at Aldgate (the location has since been plausibly confirmed), where no father could have allowed a five-year-old child to watch the disposal of infected cadavers. Perhaps the little boy could have seen from a window, or in his father's shop, the surviving customers who placed their money in pots of vinegar.

[1] See W. G. Bell's *The Great Plague in London*, 1924.
[2] The 'Everyman' edition of the *Journal of the Plague Year* includes some contemporary accounts.

He might have caught sight of the wild figure of Solomon Eagle striding naked down the street with a glowing brazier on his head, calling for repentance. 'I remember, and while I am writing this story I think I hear the very sound of it . . .' That is Defoe's device, but even a child might store in his memory those 'incessant roarings,' 'loud and lamentable cries,' 'terrible shrieks;' and yet more terrible, perhaps, the silences, with only the bell of St. Giles tolling over Fore Street, until that too fell silent with its ringer.

'Passing through Tokenhouse Yard, in Lothbury, of a sudden a casement violently opened just over my head, and a woman gave three frightful screeches, and then cried, "Oh! death, death, death!" in a most inimitable tone, and which struck me with horror and a chillness in my very blood. There was nobody to be seen in the whole street, neither did any other window open, for people had no curiostiy now in any case, nor could anybody help one another, so I went on to pass into Bell Alley.'

We may leave it at this: that whether James Foe's small son spent that grim summer in London or outside it, there would be enough in his recollections and the later conversation of his elders to associate him personally with the topic which, when the occasion arose, he turned into a near-masterpiece. There would be enough for him to say to himself: 'This, but for the grace of God, might have been my family.' And 'This might be I' is exactly what he wanted his readers to say as they contemplated their own peril in 1722. It sold his book.

The second judgment, as the pious saw it, fell upon London in September 1666, that week of fire and fear when, as Defoe says, 'the power of man was baffled and

E

brought to an end;' the week that destroyed the old walled city and left Samuel Pepys footsore, unshaven and troubled with bad dreams. The pious would perhaps have done well to keep their notions of judgment to themselves, for their sermons gave colour to the rumours that it was the Dissenters (or Papists, or French agents) who had fired London. Defoe, when he came to put together his *Tour* nearly sixty years later, would still not commit himself as to whether it had been accident or treachery; 'yet nothing was more certain, than that as the city stood before, it was strangely exposed to the disaster which happen'd, and the buildings look'd as if they had been form'd to make one general bonfire, whenever any wicked party of incendiaries should think fit.' Among Dissenting ministers who preached in the open-air among the ruins, none being at leisure to molest them, was that Dr. Annesley whom the Foes had followed from the pulpit of St. Giles. The French Defoe-scholar, Paul Dottin, has unearthed a sermon of his:

' . . . A mighty city turned into ashes and rubbish . . . the merciless element where it raged scarcely leaving a lintel for a cormorant or bittern to lodge in, or the remainder of a scorched window to sing in. A sad and terrible face was there in the ruins of London: in the places where God had been served, nettles growing, owls screeching, thieves and cut-throats lurking. The voice of the Lord hath been crying, yea, roaring in the city, of the dreadful judgment of plague and fire . . .'

Defoe's obituary tribute to Samuel Annesley, 'the best of Ministers and best of Men,' is a good example of the pedestrian level of most of his large output of verse. It was commissioned by John Dunton and published in

1697, one of the earliest of Defoe's known works. The following fragments may suggest the quality:

> His native Candour and familiar Style,
> Which did so oft his Hearers' Hours beguile,
> Charmed us with godliness, and while he spake,
> We loved the Doctrine for the Teacher's sake.
> While he informed us what those Doctrines meant,
> By dint of Practice more than Argument,
> Strange were the Charms of his Sincerity,
> Which made his Actions and his Words agree
> At such a constant and exact a rate
> As made a Harmony we wondered at . . .
> How much Celestial Vision comprehends,
> Whether to Human Actions it extends,
> Whether he's now informed of things below,
> Is needless as impossible to know.

Annesley had been Defoe's first tutor, when he was quite a child, and the acquaintance was clearly prolonged into his adult years. And there is one respect in which the tutor may have helped to form the style of the author of *Robinson Crusoe*. The Bible would in any case have been the best-known book in the Foe family; but the restrictions in favour of the Established Church, and then the darker rumours of returning Romanism, filled the Dissenters with such alarm that they took to copying the Bible in some sort of shorthand lest it should be confiscated and proscribed. Under Annesley's guidance Defoe not only read God's word in Jacobean English, but had some early practice in his prodigious penmanship. In his *Review* he afterwards recalled that 'I myself then but a boy, worked like a horse, till I wrote out the whole Pentateuch, and then was so tired I was willing to run the risk of the rest.'

The final point of interest in Dr. Annesley is that he

had two daughters. One of them was to marry John
Dunton, journalist and publisher, and the other, as the
wife of Samuel Wesley, became the mother of Charles
and John, the founders of Methodism. Both John Dunton
and Samuel Wesley were educated, as has been mentioned, at the Academy at Newington Green to which
Daniel was sent at the age of twelve or thirteen. Other
names of schoolfellows, besides Crusoe, found a corner
of Defoe's memory: 'Kitt, Battersby, young Jenkyns,
Hewling . . . that, had they lived, would have been
extraordinary men of their kind.' They died at the
judgment of the Bloody Assizes after the defeat of
Monmouth's rebellion in the West.

Charles Morton's Academy was evidently a flourishing
institution when Defoe attended it at Newington, some
three miles north of his home in Cripplegate through
open country. The headmaster was a Dissenter who had
been dismissed from his fellowship at Wadham under
the Act of 1662. Most of Morton's pupils, including
Defoe, were intended by their parents for the Ministry,
and the fact that such Academies long continued to be
publicly discussed both by Dissenters and their opponents
caused Defoe to draw more than once in his writings on
his recollections of Morton's establishment. Theology
and the arts of argument were naturally prominent in
the teaching, but the curriculum seems to have been
surprisingly modern. It included the French, Dutch,
Italian, and Spanish languages, natural science, geography,
astronomy, and shorthand. Defoe mentions a laboratory
with some equipment. He also comments thus in a
paper on *The Present State of Parties in Great Britain* (1712):

'At Newington the master or tutor read all his lectures,
gave all his systems, whether of Philosophy or Divinity,

in English, and had all his declaimings and dissertations in the same tongue. And though the scholars from that place were not destitute in the languages, yet it is observed of them, they were by this made masters of the English tongue, and more of them excelled in that particular than of any school at that time.'

Practical subjects, geography, mastery of the English tongue: it all seems just what we should look for in Defoe's education. Yet he was not a University man, and in later life his enemies did not forget it. In return he sometimes castigated pedantry for its neglect of useful knowledge; as in the character of the reputed scholar (in a contribution to *Applebee's Journal*) who 'knew Saint Cyprian and Saint Augustine, but not whereabouts they lived, nor whether Africa was divided from America by water, or by land . . . and perhaps could read half the Polyglot Bible, but knows nothing of the world.'

It is obvious, however, that the taunts of an inferior education, among all that he received in the quarrelsome exchanges of journalism, were the ones that hurt. Swift, poor himself but correctly connected with University and Church, called him 'illiterate' and left it at that. Defoe replied angrily and too often. He described, in contrast to the false scholarship that he exposed, that of a man too modest to give his name, yet given to translating from learned Latin, Spanish, and other authors, familiar with the new astronomy and philosophy, and having in geography and history 'all the world at his fingers' ends.' He vainly challenged one of his critics (Tutchin, in 1705) to a translating competition, back and forth, between Latin, French, Italian, and English for twenty pounds each book. 'And by this he shall have an opportunity to show the world how much Defoe, the hosier, is inferior in learning to Mr. Tutchin, the Gentleman.' The last sentence gives the key. Defoe could read and write Latin, and he had also learned at Newington to read Greek. But if he could 'acknowledge myself blockhead enough to have lost the fluency of expression in the Latin, and so far trade has been a prejudice to me,' he was never going to acknowledge that a tradesman could not be as good as a gentleman.

*   *   *

Tim Crusoe and many another of Defoe's Newington schoolfellows became Dissenting Ministers like their headmaster—Sam Wesley among them, though he later conformed to the Anglican Church and made his brother-in-law Dunton 'very maggoty.' Daniel crossed his parents' intentions by taking a different road. 'The pulpit,' he observed much later in his *Review*, 'is none of my office;' a remark which was taken drily by his critics, who found his tendency to preach in print was little to their taste. Sermons, as it happens, were among the most popular of all printed works in the early eighteenth century. If a number of people did not relish them from Defoe it was because he was not a divine but a business-man, a journalist and a political pleader. His moral dissertations, Charles Gildon implied, were fit reading for foolish old women, who would bequeathe their copies of *Robinson Crusoe* to their children 'with the *Pilgrim's Progress*, the *Practice of Piety* and *God's Revenge against Murther*.'

There could be, and have been, different answers to the problem of what proportion of Defoe's sermonizing was sincere. A short answer might be that he believed his own dictum: 'An upright man does not play hide-

and-seek with the Almighty.' There is surely significance in the stand that he made against 'Occasional Conformity'—the practice of taking the Anglican Communion on occasion so that a Dissenter might comply with the letter of the law and so obtain office or advantage otherwise denied him. Had Defoe been merely the time-serving opportunist, Occasional Conformity would have suited him very well. Under the sands that sometimes seemed so shifting, there was certainly this rock of belief. He believed in the God to whom his parents had taught him to pray, and even if he declined to enter the Ministry he had no thought of abandoning the simple forms of worship in which he had been reared. He believed also in the Devil, of whom he wrote at the end of his life a readable History. He had no difficulty in meeting from time to time the public appetite for apparitions, miraculous cures, prodigies, signs and marvels; but his own attitude to all such things was seriously thought out. He accepted for himself only such supernatural phenomena as he found well attested by his own experience or the tried evidence of others. One of his favourite private superstitions was grounded in coincidences of dates and numbers. And he heard voices. He tells us so himself, and Crusoe speaks the author's conviction when he reflects:

'. . . how when we are in (a *quandary*, as we call it) a doubt or hesitation, whether to go this way, or that way, a secret hint shall direct us. . . . A strange impression upon the mind, from we know not what springs, and by we know not what power, shall overrule us to go this way. . . . And I cannot but advise all considering men, whose lives are attended with such extraordinary incidents as mine, or even though not so extraordinary, not to slight such secret intimations of Providence, let them come from what invisible intelligence they will, that I shall not discuss, and perhaps cannot account for; but certainly they are proof of the converse of Spirits, and the secret communication between those embody'd and those unembody'd; and such a proof as can never be withstood.'

It would not be cynical to suppose that the voices which counselled Defoe as a youth not to enter the Ministry were giving him something of a professional tip; for he makes it clear that the 'unembody'd' guidance was commonly of a practical sort. It may be, as Paul Dottin concluded, that he was offended by the republican rowdiness of his fellow-pupils. It is not, however, a loss of faith that is in question but the choice of a calling. Defoe must have had ambition. He intended to be a gentleman, he intended to make money and live well and enjoy sophisticated company. Since he also intended to retain the faith of his fathers there was only one course open to him, and that was to go into trade. The pulpit was none of his office. Had he been of age at the time, he would not have been found preaching among the smoking ruins of the Great Fire. He would have been investigating the fire-fighting system and devising schemes of insurance.

Business enterprise obviously suited his inclinations. But according to his own testimony he began writing for publication in Charles II's reign with a tract against the Turks. This pamphlet of 1683 has not been identified; but the Turks being then at the gates of Vienna, and the English Dissenters ready to wish them well as the scourge of the Catholic Hapsburgs, Defoe evidently found himself early at odds with the extremists of his party. Having read the history of the Turks, he considered that they had no business breaking into Christendom, and said so: 'which,' he relates, 'was taken very unkindly indeed.'

Vienna was saved by John Sobieski, and however that famous relief may have been viewed in the City of London, the Protestant Dissenters were not to profit long from the fierce wave of anti-Catholic feeling which had been provoked in England by the Popish Plot. Defoe before long saw through the inventions of Titus Oates. At first, like everyone else, he believed them; and indeed in the secret clauses of the Treaty of Dover there was substance enough. With remarkable address King Charles remained the clandestinely Catholic and authoritarian monarch of an increasingly Protestant and parliamentary nation. He good-humouredly ignored the vilifications of Oates, waited till the imprudent Whig leaders had committed themselves to supporting the allegations of conspiracy; and when these were exposed he was able to break the Whigs and dissolve Parliament. With the same stroke he defeated the movement to dis-inherit his obviously Catholic brother, James, Duke of York, in favour of the illegitimate Duke of Monmouth. And when Charles died in 1685 to be succeeded by James, the Dissenters could not doubt that fresh tribulations were in store for them. The imprisonment and trial of Richard Baxter, old and ill (whom Charles had sufficiently esteemed to offer him, vainly, a bishopric) provided a celebrated clash with Lord Chief Justice Jeffreys. Among the Dissenters who left the country for America within a year of James II's accession was Defoe's old headmaster Charles Morton, who became the first vice-president of Harvard and left among his writings a book on the migration of birds, delightfuly titled:

Whence come the Stork and the Turtle, the Crane and the Swallow, when they Know and Observe the appointed Time of their Coming? This was a topic, by the way, which did not escape the large curiosity of Dr. Morton's pupil. In the *Tour through Great Britain* there are observations of the swallows on the Suffolk coast which are rather more scientific than Dr. Johnson's acceptance, a generation later, of the notion that swallows sleep through the winter at the bottom of rivers.

There were old schoolfellows from Morton's Academy riding with Monmouth in the ill-managed rebellion in the West that followed the accession of James. It was the right sort of company, no doubt, for one of Defoe's upbringing, and he later said that he was there. He had seen the handsome Duke of Monmouth (we learn from the *Tour*) at the races on Quainton Meadow near Aylesbury. But what part Defoe really took in the final and fatal gamble from Lyme Regis to Sedgmoor nobody knows. Since he escaped the doom of his comrades in the Bloody Assize, it seems likely that he stayed on the fringe of events, and that he found himself there more or less by chance when riding through the West Country on business. It is only by scattered and sometimes dubious references that we can get at the Defoe of this period: in sum they seem to present us with a rising young business-man, full of energy and curiosity, placing himself with alternate political prudence and recklessness in a position to profit by the gathering storm that King James had no capacity to ride. The King made the necessary mistakes and his son-in-law William of Orange chose the right moment to accept the invitation as a liberator. Others—the most famous being John Churchill, later Duke of Marlborough—had to make their own decisions and leave it to history to argue about treachery.

Defoe was already in the appropriate camp. Whether or not he had been out with Monmouth, he certainly rode to the Court of King William III, some months after the double coronation, in a troop of volunteer horse sent by the City merchants to escort William and Mary to a Guildhall banquet. It is the historian Oldmixon who notes, among the finely appointed cavalry, 'Daniel Foe, the hosier in Freeman's Yard, Cornhill.'

*   *   *

The hosier of Freeman's Yard was still under thirty. He had prospered quickly, not by selling stockings across a counter—a taunt which he always resented—but in the general way of commission business, importing and exporting as well. When he rode to Whitehall in the escort of City gentlemen he was helping to assert that correspondence between commerce and government which was to become his pride and interest. In the latter part of his strange career, when he published his descriptive *Tour*, he was able to point to the advance of London's prestige and wealth and power in his own lifetime. Formerly, he said, there had been jealous attempts by the Court to humble and restrict the City, but 'the city has outliv'd it all.'

'The city, I say, has gained the ascendant, and is now [1724] made so necessary to the Court (as before it was thought rather a grievance) that now we see the Court itself the daily instrument to encourage and increase the opulence of the city, and the city again, by its real grandeur, made not a glory only, but an assistance and support to the Court, on the greatest and most sudden emergencies.

'Nor can a breach be now made on any terms, but

the city will have the advantage; for while the stocks, and Bank, and trading companies remain in the city, the center of the money, as well as of the credit and trade of the kingdom, will be there.'

In the 1680's this satisfactory state of affairs was still in the making. The 'great article of publick credit' which sustained eightenth-century governments in peace and war, was not yet well established, and even under William and Mary the raising of funds had often to be accomplished at exorbitant interest. But Defoe could hardly have chosen a more propitious moment to enter upon a commercial career. The re-building of London was accommodating a much increased population and reflecting a rapid advance in the volume of trade as well as significant improvements in its organization. There were new facilities for private finance, a new Exchange, the first insurance companies, a Penny Post operating in and around London several times daily (and unique in Europe), new coffee-houses with the news-sheets which Defoe was to be so prominent in develop-ing. A Londoner whose eyes and ears missed nothing, Defoe was excited by the physical impact of this new London, whose splendours, indeed, he was quite ready to exaggerate at the expense of more stately capitals. As a topographer he was to prove himself not merely industrious but extraordinarily lively, and the topo-graphical aspect of his narrative style is famous. Not least among the pleasures for the modern reader of *Colonel Jack*, for example, are the atmosphere and the very lay-out of Defoe's London which the first part of it conveys: the glass-bottle factory where the young vagabonds slept at night among the warm ashes, the streets and fair-grounds where they learned to pilfer,

the brisk business in the long room at the Custom
House where the first substantial pocket was picked—
these are not so much described as animated. The
characteristic inventories of the thieves' booty have
their own eloquence, whether they are the small
possessions of country visitors and shopkeepers' trifles
(item, 'a jointed baby, and a little looking-glass, stolen
off a traveller's stall in the fair'); or the pocket-book of
some mercantile gentleman too quickly prosperous to
be careful, with its bearer bills in large sums payable on
demand, 'some under men's hands, some goldsmiths',
and some belonging to insurance offices, as they call
them,' or bills of foreign exchange, or a paper of loose
diamonds. The haul secured, the pace quickens familiarly
across the street-plan:

" 'Run, Jack," says he, "for our lives," and away he
scours, and I after him, never resting or scarce looking
about me till we got quite up into Fenchurch Street,
through Lime Street, into Leadenhall Street, down St.
Mary Axe to London Wall, then through Bishopsgate,
and down Old Bedlam into Moorfields. By this time we
were neither of us able to run very fast, nor need we
have gone so far, for I never found that anybody pursued
us. When we got into Moorfields and began to take
breath, I asked him what it was frightened him so.
"Fright me, you fool!" says he, "I have got a devilish great
bag of money." "A bag!" said I. "Ay, ay," said he, "let
us get out into the fields where nobody can see us, and
I'll show it you.' So away he had me through Long
Alley and Cross Hog Lane and Holloway Lane, into the
middle of the great field, which since then has been
called the Farthing Pie-House Field. There we would
have sat down but it was all full of water; so we went

on, crossed the road at Anniseed Cleer, and we went
into the field where now the great Hospital stands. And
finding a by-place, we sat down, and he pulls out the
bag. . . ." '

The hosier of Cornhill, one might assume from his
warnings, kept his wallet in an inside pocket, and was as
hawk-eyed in defence as were in attack the rascals whom
he drew for an avid public in a later phase of his existence.
It was high-life that he aimed at as a young man, but his
characterization of low-life in the novels of his full
maturity must have been fed from abundant springs of
observation, man and boy, in this city where 'nothing is
more remarkable than the hurries of the people.' In
imagination, and with his wide reading of geography and
travels, Defoe could circumnavigate the globe without
forgetting London (where most of his readers were to
be sought). Crusoe, the York-born mariner, remembers
at need on his Island the basket-makers whom he had
watched as a boy 'in the town where my father lived':
are they not rather the London basket-makers whose
working quarter was hard by Cripplegate?

The known facts of this first and not unimportant
period of Defoe's career are few: that he ran a haber-
dashery business, for a time in partnership with two
other merchants; that he married on 1 January 1684,
Mary Tuffley, of a mercantile and dissenting family, who
brought him the considerable dowry of £3,700; that he
must at this stage have undertaken some of the journeys
through Britain which he later referred to in the *Tour*;
that he was admitted a liveryman of the City of London
in 1688; that his commercial enterprises were many
and diverse; that he published two poems in 1691 and
failed disastrously in business in the following year.

There is a strong presumption that between 1680 and 1683 his affairs took him abroad, probably to France and Spain, possibly also to Holland and Italy. We are unlikely ever to know what proportion of his far-ranging familiarity with other nations, with ships and travel, was acquired at first hand, but it cannot have been large. For the variety of his business activities at this time, however, the evidence is of an interesting kind. Not only hose and stuffs, but tobacco, snuff, wine, beer and spirits were among a cargo shipped by him to Belfast, on which in 1690 he sought to recover import duty. And between 1688 and 1694 there are records of a number of lawsuits in which he was involved, concerning among other matters trading voyages to Portugal and to the American colonies, the patent of a Cornish inventor for a diving-engine, a York merchant's bill of exchange, and finally the remarkable affair of a civet-cat farm at Newington which was to give his detractors an even more amusing term for him than that of sock-seller.

If these and other scraps of evidence reflect in some degree the exhilarating climate of the late seventeenth-century boom, with its fertility in commercial and scientific ideas, good and bad, its 'projectors' on every hand, its stock-jobbers, its bubble-blowers, they also raise the broad question of Defoe's technical and ethical notions of trade relations. And here curiosity pursues him not only in his own person but as the vocal representative of a class and a community.

A good many allowances would have to be made to presume Defoe innocent of double-dealing in all the suits brought against him, though he may have been wronged often enough himself. The connection that any student of Defoe is tempted to make is between these ambitious and sometimes equivocal practices (so far as they can be ascertained) of the young city man fresh from the pious instruction of Dr. Morton, and the elderly reflections of *The Compleat English Tradesman*, of which the first volume appeared in 1725, when Defoe was sixty-five, and the second two years afterwards. Are we to share Lamb's moral indignation at advice based upon the proposition, now more easily accepted, that 'business is business'? Baxter had admonished in 1678: 'Be wholly taken up in diligent business of your lawful callings, when you are not exercised in the more immediate service of God.' His colleague Steele declared in 1684, in the first years of Defoe's establishment as a merchant: 'Next to the saving of his soul, his (the tradesman's) care and business is to serve God in his calling, and to drive it as far as it will go.' Defoe, looking back forty years later upon a life of extraordinary vicissitudes, held that religious duties 'ought not by any means to be thrust out of their places, and yet they ought to be kept in their places too.' The Quakers, founders of successful commercial traditions, had particular views on vexed questions of business morality. They held, for instance, that bargaining was dishonest, that one should not ask more than the minimum price acceptable. 'Time and the necessities of trade,' observes Defoe airily, 'made them wise.' These necessities of trade impelled the young aspirant to remember, hypocritically if you like, that the customer is always right and that the progress of the business comes first. Such counsels have been picked out from the considerable body of Defoe's recommendations to the merchant, much of which is unexceptionable.

The Compleat English Tradesman, as the wisdom of a lifetime's chequered experience, has also been carefully examined by Defoe's biographers for indirect light upon his own commercial career. Some of the light, indeed, is direct: he reproduces his own cash-book for January 1725. This special interest has rescued the work a little, but only a little, from neglect. It deserves a new edition for what it is, a treatise on the business life and methods of the time and the inland trade of England in a style which seldom graces such works: a little repetitious, no doubt, and with its prolix passages; but for the most part a familiar, personal, pleasantly jogging style, coloured with anecdote, dialogue, and interjection; in short, the style of Defoe's maturity, if not among its first examples.

'A true-bred merchant,' said Defoe in his *Review*, 'is a universal scholar.' He repeatedly stated his belief in the superiority of experience over study. But clearly he gave time to both, which perhaps partly accounts for the commercial failures that he suffered and survived as well as for the second place that he had to take in the company of scholars. The darts that he aimed at the Wits had doubtless a feather or two of envy on them; and one of the warnings in *The Compleat English Tradesman* that suggest personal remorse is that against intellectual diversions. 'A Wit turned Tradesman' is an incongruity. ' 'Tis in vain to lock him in behind the compter, he's gone in a moment; instead of journal and ledger he runs away to his Virgil and Horace.' Apart from the uncertain first pamphlets, Defoe's earliest published works are the verse-lampoon *A New Discovery of an Old Intreague*, and an *Ode to the Athenian Society*, both issued in 1691 when he was 'something in the City,' and both bearing the mark of the dilettante. Neither was anything to be proud of, but in his *Essay upon Projects*, his first work of real merit, Defoe speaks of himself with satisfaction as an 'Athenian.' John Dunton was the chief founder of the Athenian Society, a literary club as he liked to think,

F

but really the editorial board (including Sam Wesley) of a curious journalistic venture. In the *Athenian Gazette*, begun in 1690 and soon changing its title to *Athenian Mercury*, we see the first lively and successful example of non-political journalism. It devoted itself, in a manner that raised hosts of imitators, to 'resolving weekly' (later twice a week) 'all the most nice and curious questions proposed by the ingenious.' The modern addiction to question-and-answer radio features does not qualify us to be contemptuous of this publication, which ran into twenty volumes and numbered Sir William Temple among its fascinated readers and Swift among its contributors. While William III laboured to build a system of collective security against the ambitions of Louis XIV, while Wren rebuilt London, and Newton perfected his *Principia* and Locke established natural philosophy, the coffee-house tables were regularly supplied with the answers to these among other questions:

Whether the torments of the damn'd are visible to the Saints in Heaven? And *vice versa?*

Shall Negroes rise at the Last Day?

Whether 'tis lawful for a man to beat his wife?

What is Platonic love?

Why a horse with a round fundament emits a square excrement?

*   *   *

The Athenian Defoe, it would seem, was cutting a dash. He had a reputation, if not in the most exalted circles, as a talker, a poet of the fashionable manner, a quoter of Rochester's frivolous verse and of Butler's mordant *Hudibras*, neither of which can he ever have read in his good father's house. He says that he was fond of music in his younger days, and 'was accounted no despicable performer on the viol, and lute, then much in vogue.' He may have sat to Kneller, like all the best people.[1] He traded in wine and drank it, lamenting the days that brought gin to popularity with the interruption of the French commerce. While he worked in London or travelled the country, he is thought to have rented a house for his wife and first children at Tooting, thus emulating the wealthy merchants whose residences were beginning to ring the metropolis: in his *Tour* he afterwards described such a way of life with happy admiration, letting us know that business-men travelled daily in the summer season from as far as Epsom; 'for 'tis very frequent for the trading part of the company to place their families here, and to take their horses every morning to London, to the Exchange, to the Alley, or to the warehouse, and be at Epsom again at night.'

The extent of Defoe's trading activities may be guessed from the fact that when he failed in 1692 it was to the tune of £17,000. He must have gone on raising credit and losing it, hoping and risking and trying every sort of strategem—'things which like a slow poison infallibly destroy the vitals of the tradesman.' Like the man he describes in *The Compleat English Tradesman* he must have said:

'I'll try my utmost, I'll never drown while I can swim, I'll never fall while I can stand. Who knows but I may get over it? In a word, the poor man is loth to come to the fatal day; loth to have his name in the *Gazette*, and see his wife and family turn'd out of doors, and the like. Who can blame him? or who is not, in the like case, apt to take the like measures? for 'tis natural to us all to put

[1] If we accept the description, in *Notes and Queries* (1882), of a portrait now lost.

the evil day far from us, at least, to put it as far off as we
can . . . but at last the dead warrant comes down.'

Looking back in his old age, his word to those whose
trading position was deteriorating dangerously was
'BREAK, GENTLEMEN, for God's sake!' But bankruptcy in Defoe's day, as he shows in several moving
passages, was a terrible thing to face. His property and
his person could be seized. Flight itself could be a felony
in the first degree. The loopholes were few but recognized. There were temporary sanctuaries—the South
London quarter called the Mint was one—where mis-
creants of all sorts mingled with insolvent tradesmen in
a vicious asylum which later on Defoe trenchantly
exposed. Possibly he went to ground in this way to
bargain with his creditors, and if so he made an early
acquaintance with robbers, debauchees, and mere un-
fortunates—whom fate a decade later gave him another
opportunity of studying in Newgate Gaol. It is generally
said, but has not been certainly established, that he then
got away to Bristol where he lived at an inn from which
he emerged only on Sundays, being on that day safe from
arrest.

Defoe's name occurs in the list of merchants who, by
a bill introduced in the Commons in February 1694, were
to be compensated for their losses in the war of King
William's Grand Alliance against France. The Bill failed
in the Lords, but at least it partly substantiates Defoe's
own repeated explanation of the chief cause of his ruin.
Others had suffered, no doubt even more disastrously,
for it was a very lively market that the war interrupted.
And a substantial tradesman, 'like a great tree in a thick
wood, if he falls, he is sure to crush a great deal of the
underwood which lies within the reach of his boughs

and branches.' Thus the *Review*, and the *Compleat Trades-man* hints at an unwise exuberance shared by Defoe with other speculating tempers of his age:

'I think I may safely advance, without danger of reprehension, there are more people ruined in England by over-trading than for want of trade; and I would, from my own unhappy experience, advise all men in trade to set a due compass to their ambition.'

The litigation of these years probably steepened the path to disaster. It culminated in April 1692 with the case of the seventy civet-cats, bred for their valuable perfume, in which Defoe attempted a profitable invest-ment. The cats passed from hand to hand in some evidently shady transactions, in the course of which the desperate Defoe appears to have defrauded his mother-in-law, if nobody else. Is it of the Newington cat-farm alone that he is thinking as he writes later in the *Review?*

'I freely name myself with those that are ready to own that they have in their extremities and embarrassments in trade done those things which their own principles condemned, which they are not ashamed to blush for, which they look back on with regret, and strive to make reparation for, with their utmost diligence.'

Whatever the chief causes of the crash, the con-sequences followed him all his life. Some have thought that it made him into an author, but the development was not so sudden as that would suggest. 'The English Tradesman,' we are not surprised to hear from him, 'though unfortunate, is a kind of phoenix, who rises out of his own ashes.' Defoe rose again and again, but in the particular part he had played up to now he was

finished. He never forgot the failure, and the ideal of
the successful tradesman, the merchant-gentleman, the
man he might have been, was always somewhere in his
vision. The virtuous Crusoe and the unvirtuous Roxana
are alike in this, that all goes well with their commercial
ventures. In the agonizing injury to a sanguine tempera-
ment may be seen, perhaps, the beginning of Defoe's
habit of squaring with his Protestant conscience such
shifts as might preserve him in the future, and avert
from his family the awful threat of expropriation. And
on the other side his enemies found in his bankruptcy,
that crime against a material society, the first firm
ground of attack.

Debt itself, rather than the manner of contracting it,
is the intolerable condition to mercantile man. Defoe
felt this, and even the briefest view of his code would
be incomplete without a reference to his heroic return
to solvency. From his refuge, and through the media-
tion of his wife and friends, he succeeded in compound-
ing with his creditors. But this was not enough for his
pride and peace of mind. In his subsequent labours he
set himself to pay off his debts in full. There is a much-
quoted testimony from an opponent, John Tutchin, in
his *Dialogue between a Dissenter and the Observator*, of 1702:

'I must do one piece of justice to the man, though I
love him no better than you do: it is this—that meeting
a gentleman in a coffee-house, when I and everybody
else were railing at him, the gentleman took us up with
this short speech, "Gentlemen," said he, "I know this De
Foe as well as any of you, for I was one of his creditors,
compounded with him, and discharged him fully.
Several years afterwards he sent for me, and though he
was clearly discharged, he paid me all the remainder of

his debt, voluntarily and of his own accord; and he told me that, as far as God should enable him, he intended to do so with everybody. When he had gone, he desired me to set my hand to a paper to acknowledge it, which I readily did, and found a great many names to the paper before me; and I think myself bound to own it, though I am no friend to the book he wrote no more than you." '

The book was *The Shortest Way With the Dissenters*, the occasion of Defoe's second catastrophe.

Chapter Three

THE SHORTEST WAY TO THE PILLORY

WITH few great writers are life and work so in-
tricately, so intriguingly bound up as with Defoe. Incomplete as is our knowledge of what happened to him
at several stages of his long activity, most of what we do
know, or can infer, is of value in the appreciation of his
writings. The elements of his exclusion have been seen
in his upbringing as a Dissenter, and to a smaller degree
in his bent for business. But it is going too far to imagine
an intellectual solitude comparable to the physical
solitude of Crusoe. He was too constantly committed
to his own and his nation's business to be thought of in
brooding isolation. 'Time,' he observed pointedly in
his old age, 'is no more to be unemployed than it is to be
ill employed.' If the tinge of melancholy that we find in
his greatest work (but seldom elsewhere) was a reflection of his own disposition, then it must seem that he
appeased it as Crusoe did, by action. Buoyancy and
vigour, courage at its best and bounce at its worst, are
what we encounter repeatedly in Defoe's reaction to
circumstance as well as in the flow of polemics and
journalism that began in right earnest in his thirty-
seventh year.

Of the crises that played their part in the direction of
his energies, the first was the bankruptcy of 1692.
Within two years of that considerable catastrophe he
was on the fringe, at least, of the Court of William and

Mary. Within six years he had published his first important pamphlets as well as the *Essay Upon Projects*, and held a Government appointment. By 1702 he had prospered afresh, this time as a manufacturer and employer of labour—when King William's horse stumbled upon the fatal molehill to provoke another climax in Defoe's affairs. In the second year of Queen Anne's reign he was in prison and the pillory, his business in pieces, his house and coach and library sold up. But it was after this experience that he stepped into the confidential service of Robert Harley and the new Government. This time, though he would still take commercial chances when they came to him, his fortunes were finally committed to his pen.

The period at which Defoe found himself in royal favour was of some general interest in literary history. Since he speaks of 'attending' Queen Mary when she was planning the garden of Kensington Palace (Wren having just built the south front and one wing), his emergence from disaster and disgrace had indeed been phoenix-like; for the Queen died in December 1694, two years after his crash. The Revolution led to significant changes in the situation of English writers, in their professional prestige and in their sources of income. The foreign king was not himself, by inclination or knowledge, a patron of letters. 'Charles II loved literature without paying for it,' says Professor Beljame; 'James II paid for it without loving it; William III neither loved nor paid.'[1] But William's first Ministers included men who did love literature; moreover the new political climate, in which public opinion was a factor of some significance and conciliation a constant need, gave writers a social and

[1] Beljame, ed. Dobree: *Men of Letters and the English Public in the 18th Century*; 1948.

political value that was worth paying for. It is at this time that government appointments, not always sinecures nor always very lucrative, begin to figure in the literary biographies. Matthew Prior was an Ambassador and a Gentleman of the Bedchamber; the essayist Steele secured a succession of posts; the philosopher Locke was a Commissioner of the Board of Trade, Isaac Newton Director of the Mint, William Congreve Commissioner of Hackney-Coach and Wine Licences; and Daniel Defoe was Commissioner of the Glass Duty during the four years of its operation from 1695 to 1699.

This does not mean that Defoe was one of the literary élite, although John Dunton mentions him in the same sentence with Swift and the Poet Laureate Tate. He was never a member of the Kit-Cat Club, where poets and playwrights, often of middle-class origin, met the new Whig aristocracy on familiar terms. But he had his contacts in political society (Sutherland suggests that his patron was Charles Montagu, Earl of Halifax, to whom there is a letter of Defoe's in the British Museum). And he must have made those contacts, at this stage, as a business man with financial and political ideas. He had friends who stood by him, no doubt, while he was striving to compound with his creditors, and he had prepared himself to take advantage of the first chance that should arise to gain the ear of the powerful. At Bristol or wherever he took refuge, he had begun work on a series of proposals on public affairs which was finally published in 1698 as *An Essay Upon Projects*.

It was, he says, the losses and depredations which the war with France at first brought with it (to himself among others) which caused such a proliferation of ideas good and bad, on every hand, directed to the raising of money. But he goes back to 1680, and to a few earlier instances including Noah's Ark, to trace 'the art and mystery of projecting' and 'the projecting humour.' He distinguishes between 'new inventions and projects . . . improvements of manufactures or lands, which tend to the immediate benefit of the public and employment of the poor,' and on the other hand the innumerable fantastic but exciting ideas that were current in his day. Yet he allows that the latter, when occasionally successful, enter the serious category, as for instance Sir William Phipps' salvage of £200,000 in silver from a sunken Spanish ship. He also exposes dishonest projects, and makes the first of many protests against the excesses of stock-jobbing. This latter craze, he says, 'was at first only the simple occasional transferring of interest and shares from one to another, as persons alienated their estates; but by the industry of the Exchange brokers, who got the business into their hands, it became a trade, and one, perhaps, managed with the greatest intrigue, artifice, and trick that ever anything that appeared with a face of honesty could be handled with.' One may suspect that Defoe had himself been bitten.

There are other complaints in the book of malpractices and business disadvantages of various kinds under which the author had perhaps laboured. But there is a wind of enterprise blowing through it, an exhilarating sense of what it may have felt like to live in a society confident of having more to look forward to than to look back upon. It gave the *Essay Upon Projects* appreciative Victorian readers who saw the springs of their own civilisation glimmering through its pages. In our own day it has still the appeal of freshness and intelligence, and a considerable personal interest; for in any attempt to condense an 'essential Defoe' from the formidable mass of his writings, the *Essay Upon Projects* demands to be included.

The book has separate papers on banking, insurance, the bankruptcy laws, the highways, education, and other matters; and there are proposals or 'projects' for an income-tax, a pension-office, a charity lottery, and a system for registering, almost for nationalizing, all seamen. The extent to which Defoe was really an innovator in these 'particular thoughts' has been disputed; but the force of the writing, the mingling of shrewdness and daring, are certainly striking. Some of his ideas were obviously already in the air in this speculative period. Other projectors had caught up with him here and there during the four or five years between first composition and publication, and the Bank of England was established while his mind ran on such an institution—or rather on an improved version. Elsewhere he shows himself ahead of his time; for example in his demand for a system of good highways to replace the muddy lanes over which he had ridden on his business; in his recommendation for the more humane treatment of the insane (the new Bethlem Hospital had been opened at the south end of Moorfields in 1676); in the idea (scarcely likely to endear him with the new rich) of a close investigation of private estates to make taxation more fair and less evadable; and certainly in the plea for feminine education in the chapter *Of Academies*.

In this chapter Defoe has three proposals to make, and none of them without interest. The first is for a society or academy under royal patronage to vie with the celebrated Academy established in France, so that the English tongue should be polished and refined to appear no whit behind the French, but 'as it really is, the noblest and most comprehensive of all the vulgar languages in the world.' The Defoe who writes thus seems to stand somewhere between the youthful aspirant to polite literature and the creator of the 'homely plain English' of his later and greater period. He wants to introduce 'purity and propriety of style,' but he is wary of the pedantry and affectation that such a project might in its turn produce—'hard words, and long unusual coupling of sentences, which sound harsh and untunable to the ear, and shock the reader both in expression and understanding.' These are the faults of scholars, and he would exclude also from his society such specialists in speech as clergymen, physicians, and lawyers. He had, one would think, an idea of what he was after, but no very clear plan of getting it.

Defoe's second educational proposal lays down the organization, expenditure, and curriculum for a Royal Academy for Military Exercises. He notes the changes since the Civil Wars in the military art and practice, 'which now differ as much from what they were formerly as long perukes do from piqued beards, or as the habits of the people do now from what they were then.' Always in Defoe we meet this feeling for change. 'It is evident,' he says of his own times, 'what an improvement the English nation has made during this seven years' war.' But the costly length of warfare, with its encampments and sieges and waiting upon the foe, might be reduced by better training and a more efficient state of national readiness. He would like also to see musketry as much a natural exercise for youth as archery was formerly. He wants experimental grounds for ordnance and new inventions. He wants the English gentry to take a lead in training themselves and others. How often since Defoe's day have we heard words like these:

'It is a great hindrance to this nation, especially where standing armies are a grievance, that if ever a war

commence, men must have at least a year, before they are
thought fit to face an enemy, to instruct them how to handle their arms: and new-raised men are called raw soldiers.'

The third educational design, that for an Academy for
Women, is notable not so much for Defoe's sketch of
the form of a suitable establishment (one college 'at
least in every county in England, and about ten for the
City of London'), as for his advocacy of feminine
education itself. His arguments are ingenious, amusing,
and unanswerable. How much worse, he wants to know,
is a wise woman than a fool? 'Does she plague us with
her pride and impertinence? Why did we not let her
learn, that she might have had more wit?' Every
objection he smites, lightly but decisively. Eleven years
before Dick Steele started his happy idea of *The Tatler*,
touching graceful heights with his tribute to Aspasia
(Lady Betty Hastings), Defoe had in his own mind the
novel possibility of a woman whom to love might be a
liberal education, provided that was what she had already
been given. One need not dispute the sparkling achievement of the *Tatler*, nor the reformation in manners
consolidated by Addison and the *Spectator*, to appreciate
the significance of Defoe's short and early essay. The
first forthright words state his case:

'I have often thought of it as one of the most barbarous
customs in the world, considering us as a civilized and a
Christian country, that we deny the advantages of learning to women. We reproach the sex every day with
folly and impertinence, while I am confident, had they
the advantages of education equal to us, they would be
guilty of less than ourselves.'

The product of feminine education is presented in
contrast with its horrid opposite:

'A woman of sense and manners is the finest and most delicate part of God's creation; the glory of her Maker, and the great instance of His singular regard to man, His darling creature, to whom He gave the best gift either God could bestow or man receive . . . Her society is the emblem of sublimer enjoyments; her person is angelic and her conversation heavenly; she is all softness and sweetness, peace, love, wit and delight. . . . On the other hand, suppose her to be the very same woman, and rob her of the benefit of education, and it follows thus:

'If her temper be good, want of education makes her soft and easy. Her wit, for want of teaching, makes her impertinent and talkative. Her knowledge, for want of judgment and experience, makes her fanciful and whimsical. If her temper be bad, want of breeding makes her worse, and she grows haughty, insolent and loud. If she be passionate, want of manners makes her termagant and a scold, which is much at one with lunatic. If she be proud, want of discretion (which still is breeding) makes her conceited, fantastic and ridiculous. And from these she degenerates to be turbulent, clamorous, noisy, nasty and the devil.'

'It is but an essay at the thing,' says the projector, looking 'to those happy days, if ever they shall be, when men shall be wise enough.' And here is his final tribute to the sex:

'I cannot think that God Almighty ever made them so delicate, so glorious creatures, and furnished them with such charms, so agreeable and so delightful to mankind, with souls capable of the same accomplishments with men, and all to be only stewards of our houses, cooks and slaves. Not that I am for exalting the female government in the least; but, in short, I would have men take women for companions, and educate them to be fit for it.'

This sketch of perfected womanhood emerging from the license and cynicism of a male society comes from the pen which, twenty to thirty years later, was to give us those lively and unidealized portraits: Crusoe, independent of women; the gaol-bred Moll Flanders, 'debauched from her youth, nay, even being the offspring of debauchery and vice;' Colonel Jack, who 'was five times married to four whores;' and the Fortunate Mistress Roxana, who was in fact elegantly trained and 'set out into the world having all the advantages that any young woman could desire to recommend me to others and form a prospect of happy living to myself.'

*   *   *

Defoe's concern with reform, as suggested by his plea for women's education, chimed well with the spirit of this time. That, no doubt, was one reason why it found expression. It responded also to the influence of the King and Queen. Kensington Palace itself might be thought of as a modest rural retreat after Whitehall with its urban freedom of manners; and the choice of the more grandiose Hampton Court as another royal residence was again in some sense a flight from London and the playhouse and the associations of a licentious society. After describing the progress of gallantry in previous reigns in his *Poor Man's Plea*, which appeared a few weeks after the *Essay Upon Projects*, Defoe proceeds:

'The present King and his late Queen, whose glorious memory will be daer to the nation as long as the world stands, have had all this wicked knot to unravel. This

Robinson Crusoe, 1719

Defoe pilloried and at large

was the first thing the Queen set upon while the King was engaged in his wars abroad. She first gave all sorts of vice a general discouragement, and on the contrary, raised the value of virtue and sobriety by her royal example. The King having brought the war to a glorious conclusion and settled an honourable peace, in his very first speech to his Parliament proclaims a new war against profaneness and immorality.'

The peace was the Peace of Ryswick, concluded with France by England and her allies at the end of 1697, and it lasted—but only just—until the death of William and the accession of Anne in 1702. It was a period in Defoe's life when we should have said, did we not know what was to come, that he reached with remarkable speed the height of his achievement: a period upon which he himself looked back as one of unbounded hopes. In his devotion to William's memory, sometimes eloquent and touching, sometimes tedious, there is naturally an element of nostalgia for the good days when he walked with the highest in the land. Some writers have imagined a bond of deep sympathy between Defoe and the King, both slow to make friends, both men of the middle way, not altogether trusted by Whig or Tory, both Protestant in temper, disliking domestic strife most of all on religious issues but declared foes of 'the Devil, the Pope and Louis XIV.' In fact there is evidence of contact only, not of intimacy; and although Defoe speaks of attending the Queen, it may not have been until the publication of the *True-Born Englishman* some six years after her death that he actually met the King. It is at least probable that some of his ideas were listened to by the King as well as by the politicians, and it is certain that all his writing during these years

G

was devoted to causes which were William's causes also.

The reformation of society was one of them, but it was not the monopoly of Whigs and Dissenters. Jeremy Collier, whose famous *Short View of the Immorality and Profaneness of the English Stage* appeared in the same year as Defoe's *Essay Upon Projects* and *A Poor Man's Plea*, was neither. He was not only a Tory churchman but a fierce opponent of the Revolution and King William, and this gave additional force to his vituperations against the stage and its supposed influence. Like Defoe, he had his experience of Newgate, but the same passionate words in the mouth of a Dissenter would have failed of their immediate effect, which Collier's did not. Defoe had been brought up to regard the Restoration theatre as an abomination, and later on he gave space in his *Review* to the usual sort of railing against the contemporary stage. But it is not literary criticism, and the drama obviously had singularly little interest for him, one way or the other. The brief reference in the *Tour* to the monument of 'old Shakespear' appears to be the conventional exception: 'the famous poet . . . whose dramatick performances so justly maintain his character among the British poets; and perhaps will do so to the end of time.' And though there is much to show that Defoe could write presentable dialogue, he was not (as was Fielding) trained in the theatre but in journalism. In the conflict precipitated by the *Short View* he was in no position to take sides, either with so rude a rebel as Collier or with the distinguished Wits who joined issue with him. The immorality and profaneness on which he preferred to turn his pen at this point were those of real life. The assault on intemperate language in particular is one of Defoe's recognisably Puritan activities; but the

Puritan dress (at that time often seen as the uniform of a regicide or an anarchist) seldom fitted him very well. He was not wearing it when he wrote the *Essay Upon Projects*. He was garbed as a business-man, a man-about-town, an official adviser, His Majesty's Commissioner of the Glass Duty. His views on women, as we have seen, are nearer to those of the *Tatler* and the *Spectator* than to any meeting-house moralizing; and the digression on bad language, in the same book, has a similar flavour. He prettily eschews the pulpit manner:

'I am not about to argue anything of their being sinful and unlawful, as forbid by divine rules; let the parson alone tell you that, who has, no question, said as much to as little purpose in this case as any other; but I am of the opinion that there is nothing so impertinent, so insignificant, so senseless and foolish as our vulgar way of discourse when mixed with oaths and curses; and I would only recommend a little consideration to our gentlemen, who have sense and wit enough, and would be ashamed to speak nonsense in other things, but value themselves upon their parts, I would but ask them to put into writing the commonplaces of their discourse, and read them over again, and examine the English, the cadence, the grammar of them, then let them turn them into Latin, or translate them into any other language, and but see what a jargon and confusion of speech they make together.'

This literary view of profanity, though it leads him into pedantry, is interesting in Defoe; no less so when he gives, as an example of what is to be avoided, a piece of conversational small change from the mint of the future storyteller:

' "Jack, God damn me, Jack, how do'st do, thou little dear son of a whore? How hast thou done this long time, by God?" and then they kiss; and the other, as lewd as himself, goes on:

' "Dear Tom, I am glad to see thee, with all my heart; let me die. Come, let us go take a bottle; we must not part so; prithee let's go and be drunk, by God." '

Swearing, drunkenness, and sundry other mis- demeanours were scheduled for suppression through the magistrates and justices. The King proclaimed the policy, and in return a loyal Parliamentary address called for the example to be set in high places. Defoe supported this with considerable verve in his *Poor Man's Plea* of 1698. It is a good radical piece on the theme of one law for the rich and another for the poor: 'the small flies are catched, and the great ones break through.' Magi- strates themselves, complains the 'Poor Man,' are often found wanting in virtue and manners, and 'punish a man for drunkenness, with a *God damn him, set him in the stocks!*' Though Defoe, as usual, did not sign this pamphlet there was probably no secret of its authorship, and he acknowledged it a few years later by including it in his first collected volume. He stands in this instance in the somewhat dangerous character of a man of the people:

'My Lord Mayor has whipt about the poor beggars, and a few scandalous whores have been sent to the House of Correction; some alehousekeepers and vintners have been fined for drawing drink on the Sabbath-day; but all this falls upon us of the mob, the poor *plebeii*, as if all the vice lay among us: for we do not find the rich drunkard carried before my Lord Mayor, nor a swearing lewd merchant fined, or set in the stocks.'

The plebeian who thus talked was later to be rewarded by the mob with a kind reception in the pillory. On the other hand such treatment of the officers of justice may have opened up a short road for getting there. Six years later, in 1702, Defoe was still more outspoken with his verse satire *The Reformation of Manners*, in which individual justices, magistrates, and clergymen were indicted for viciousness in stinging terms and under the thinnest of disguises.

The effective reform of society was carried out, as it had to be, under the influence of men free from the suspicion of Dissent. But Defoe returned to this rôle from time to time, and more particularly (as we might expect) in his old age. To his late maturity as a writer belongs that pious and once popular domestic manual, *The Family Instructor*, which found a place not only in humble homes up and down the land but also in the nursery of the children of George I. This appeared four years before *Robinson Crusoe*, which gave a whole sequel to moralizing. Close upon *Moll Flanders*, in 1722, came the dialogue treatise on *Religious Courtship*; and in Defoe's sixty-seventh year, in 1727, when he was writing on trade, apparitions and approaching war, he produced not only the theological dialogues of *A New Family Instructor*, but also 'a treatise concerning the use and abuse of the marriage-bed' under the resounding title of *Conjugal Lewdness, or Matrimonial Whoredom*. Again in the following year his *Augusta Triumphans*, a new and elderly essay upon projects, numbered among its proposals the proper care of unwanted children, the prevention of street robberies in London, the reduction of the immoderate consumption of gin, 'clearing the streets of impudent strumpets, suppressing gaming-tables and Sunday debauches.'

We shall come to these books later, and to the great human stories of which Charles Lamb, searching for the moral element, was satisfied to declare:

'In no other book of fiction, where the lives of such characters are described, is guilt and delinquency made less seductive, or the suffering made more closely to follow the commission, or the penitence more earnest or more bleeding, or the intervening flashes of religious visitation, upon the rude and uninstructed soul, more meltingly and fearfully painted. They, in this, come near to the tenderness of Bunyan.'

The question of Defoe's moral sincerity as revealed in his writings has been endlessly debated. It was raised often enough in his own lifetime, and before he had written his tales of thieves and molls. What, said his critics, about the lay-preacher's private life?

Defoe pointed out more than once that 'the man who has been sick is half a physician,' and he was prepared in serious moments to acknowledge himself not only in error but at fault. But against the imputation of some of the weaknesses that he castigated he did on one occasion openly defend himself. In 1703, in the preface to one of his reforming satires, he declared:

'But if I must act the Pharisee a little, I must begin thus: God, I thank thee, I am not a drunkard, or a swearer or a whoremaster, or a busie-body, or idle, or revengeful, etc., and I challenge all the world to prove the contrary.'

At the time of this challenge, one who later called himself Benjamin Norton Defoe was in his infancy. If we are to believe the story, he was the bastard of an oyster-wench.

Nobody can be quite sure now whether that story is true. Pope helped to give it circulation, but it came from Richard Savage, the disreputable or perhaps tragic character to whom Samuel Johnson later gave fame in

one of his first works. Defoe was nearing seventy before
the matter was aired, and it may be more than a coincidence that his *Augusta Triumphans* (1728) had just
then made what was taken for a reference to Savage in
its proposal for a Foundling Hospital—Savage having
given himself out as the needy love-child of an earl.
Smarting, perhaps, under what was intended as a
charitable solicitude, Savage may at this point have
retorted with the story of the oyster-girl and baby
Benjamin. Benjamin Norton Defoe, a hack-journalist,
certainly existed, stuck to the name and passed it down
to a grandson who was hanged at Tyburn for highway-
robbery towards the end of the century. If this male-
factor really had in him the blood of Daniel Defoe,
chronicler of his kind, then Daniel Defoe had two sons
called Benjamin; for his good wife Mary bore him a boy
who was thus named. He was her second son, the first
having been called Daniel. There were also four
daughters, Hannah, Henrietta, Maria, and Sophia. Two
other little girls, Mary and Martha, seem to have died
young.

It is only in his later years that his household relationships are known to have afflicted Defoe. It must,
presumably, have cost him more than a few cares to
bring up a family, but we know nothing of them in
detail, nor whether he showed himself the wise and
affectionate parent whose portrait he drew in family
manuals. His constant activity, his restlessness, are well
enough understood; and therefore there may be a note
of personal regret in his later advice to the young tradesman: 'If he has a family, he will make his excursions up-
stairs, and no further.' That he made many excursions
with oyster-women hardly seems likely—indeed the
reiteration of this lowly but useful occupation throws a

little suspicion on his detractors. One such excursion, it might be thought, would be refreshingly human in so human a writer. But to dismiss Defoe briefly as 'uxorious,' as a modern biographer of Steele has done, is the wildest guess-work.

*   *   *

The episode of the furtive liaison, if liaison there were, is assigned to Defoe's second period of comparative prosperity, when he had bought back his carriage and horses and paid off most of his debts beyond the agreed amount. This time he was an employer, the owner and manager of a brick and tile factory at Tilbury. It was on the north side of the Thames just in front of the Fort, then a large and strong construction 'which may justly be looked upon,' says Defoe in his *Tour*, 'as the key of the river of Thames, and consequently the key of the city of London.' In the same book he describes the marshy tracts where his brickfields were established as 'held by the farmers, cow-keepers, and grasing butchers who live in and near London,' so his property here may possibly have been a family inheritance. His bricks and tiles, at all events, were good bricks and tiles, if we accept the testimony of his enthusiastic Victorian biographer Lee, who picked up some specimens in the railway workings of 1860. They had to be good to make their way against the Dutch product in the rebuilding and extension of London; and we know of at least one public contract, for Greenwich Hospital, which Defoe's political position no doubt helped him to secure. There are references in the *Review* and elsewhere to this enterprise, trouble with the workmen, and so on, and from these we learn that Defoe was keeping a hundred artisan families and making at one time a profit of £600 a year.

Into his new business went his salary as Commissioner of the Glass Duty, and such presents as he received from King William. The King may not have ranked high as a literary patron, but Defoe had other services to offer. It may well be that his journeys through the country in this reign served the same purpose as they certainly did in the next one, that of collecting confidential information on the state of opinion. There are hints, tantalizing enough, of a high advisory standing, beginning with the 'eminent persons' with whom Defoe had been concerned so soon after his bankruptcy, 'in proposing ways and means to the Government for raising money to supply the occasions of the war.' Somewhat later, being of opinion that trade should be re-opened with France despite the war, he 'had the honour [he recalled much later in the *Review*] to defend this opinion, and give my reasons for it, before the House of Commons and before the Privy Council in the late reigns.' He insisted that the Glass Duty Commission was given him without any solicitation in 1695. In the same year, in October, *The Post-Boy* carried his name, previously Daniel Foe, for the first time as Daniel De Foe, in the capacity of managing trustee of a royal lottery—an assignment suggesting already some public standing.

But there *were* literary services to the King—some of the best that Defoe ever rendered to anyone. After the Peace of Ryswick in 1697, the cry was at once raised that William's experienced army must be disbanded. The old fear of a standing army as a danger to civil liberties was then relatively new and powerful. We can see its symbolic effects today in the fact that the Navy and the Air Force are in name 'Royal', but not the Army. In the sixteen-nineties there were people living who had seen the Stuart armies in the field, and many who had resented the military power of Cromwell. William had needed troops behind him before the new constitution was settled. Once settled, it was for Parliament to consider when an army should be raised for foreign service. The militia, it was urged, was sufficient for home security without a mercenary army quartered upon the land.

Defoe, calmly and reasonably, cut this and other contentions to pieces in his *Argument showing that a Standing Army, with consent of Parliament, is not inconsistent with a Free Government*. This, and a lesser pamphlet on the same subject, (*A Brief Reply to the History of Standing Armies in England*), appeared in 1698, the year of *The Poor Man's Plea* and the *Essay Upon Projects*—in the latter of which, as we have noticed, he had had things to say about military training. No less modern in their ring were the words in which he now showed that the fruits of victory on the Continent would be thrown away if England disarmed herself on a point of principle while France prepared for the next campaign.

'Some people talk so big of our own strength, that they think England able to defend herself against all the world. I presume such talk without book; I think the prudentest course is to prevent the trial.'

Defoe was not the only advocate of a small regular army with parliamentary authority. Nor, this time, was he the first in the field. A battle of pamphlets had preceded his own, and he was on the winning side. Nevertheless, this is a work not to be forgotten. Two years later he pleaded, in a poem called *The Pacificator*, by no means above his usual level of versifying, for a truce in the literary conflict between the Men of Sense and the Men of Wit. In the best of his hundreds of pamphlets—and

the *Argument for a Standing Army* is among the best as well
as among the first—Defoe exhibits himself as a Man of
Sense, a compatriot of Locke, his senior by twenty-
eight years. There is nothing passionate in it, and there
is nothing involved. But the quiet skill in the contrivance
of telling answers to exactly those objections which
would be sincerely raised; the air of detachment, of talk
for its own sake about an interesting and topical subject;
the plain man's thought in the plain man's language:
these and other qualities led William Minto to write in
1887:

'To persuade the mass of the freeholders was his
object, and for such an object there are no political
tracts in the language at all comparable to Defoe's. He
bears some resemblance to Cobbett, but he had none of
Cobbett's brutality; his faculties were more adroit, and
his range of vision infinitely wider. Cobbett was a
demagogue, Defoe a popular statesman. The one was
qualified to lead the people, the other to guide them.
Cobbett is contained in Defoe as the less is contained in
the greater.'

The plain man spoke again in November 1700, in a
tract lucidly entitled: *The Two Great Questions Consider'd.
I. What the French King will do, with respect to the Spanish
Monarchy. II. What Measures the English ought to take.*
These two great questions, which had to be 'further
consider'd' by Defoe just over a fortnight later, in reply
to the objections which in those days got so rapidly into
print, were occasioned thus: The King of Spain died
childless, and in a death-bed will bequeathed his throne
to the Duke of Anjou, second grandson of Louis XIV.
Louis was pledged by treaty to make no claim upon the
Spanish monarchy either for himself or his heirs, and had

agreed to a different arrangement. The first question, therefore was whether he would break his pledge. If he did so, the coalition so patiently built up by William to preserve the balance of power in Europe would either collapse or have to fight again, and that was the second question. If the French King accepted this legacy for his grandson, must there be a War of the Spanish Succession?

The Tories, at this time steadily gaining influence, said no. There was the last war still to be paid for, and England should now be kept out of foreign entanglements and rely upon the protection of her fleet. Defoe, staunch for William's statecraft, saw France and Spain uniting under one ambitious monarch to dominate the world, 'when a French garrison is planted at Cadiz and the French fleet brings home the plate from Havana,' with England's American colonies cut off while the French 'have a free commerce from Quebec to Mexico behind ye;' and French 'pirates' in the Channel ports from Brittany to Flanders. His eyes were on the overseas trade, which was not, as a rule, the first interest with the Tories; and when he tried another approach in the following January it was again unimpressive to the extreme opponents of the war policy, a few of whom were Jacobites and saw in Louis XIV the protector and supporter of the exiled Stuarts. For this time, in *The Danger of the Protestant Religion Consider'd*, Defoe talked of a religious war and dropped mundane argument for challenging appeal. No man, he said, had the right to remain neutral in this great struggle.

If William and his supporters spent sleepless nights contriving checks on the aggrandisement of France, Louis XIV was no less concerned with his Ministers in escaping the death-grip of the alliance that threatened

France's northern and eastern frontiers, and in saving his navy and his trade from the maritime menace symbolized by a Dutch King on an English throne. Divided counsels in England helped him. Though William had secured his standing army, it was much reduced from effective strength and the question of parliamentary supplies for a new war (a question which did not, of course, trouble Louis) was in grave doubt. Elections were due in February 1701, and Defoe prepared for them by addressing 'the good people of England' in his *Six Distinguishing Characters of a Parliament Man*. But the tide was still running the other way. Louis disposed of a whole series of undertakings and recognized his grandson in the Spanish succession. The new English Parliament, undismayed, pressed William to do the same. French troops took the offensive by occupying fortresses over the border of the Spanish Netherlands and holding their Dutch garrisons to political ransom. It was dismissed as the business of the Dutch. So confident was the newly elected Tory majority that when five gentlemen of Kent brought to Westminster a constitutional petition on behalf of the freeholders of their exposed county they were arrested.

This was the famous Kentish Petition, imploring Parliament 'to have regard to the voice of the people' and vote supplies for the defence of the realm 'before it is too late'. It may have been a party manœuvre, but it had secured popular backing, and it was certainly high-handed to take the spokesmen into custody. A fortnight later the protests took shape in another deputation to the House of Commons. Its leader, 'guarded with about sixteen gentlemen of quality' presented the Speaker with a paper and the party withdrew. The Speaker was Robert Harley, later Earl of Oxford. The

leader of the deputation was Daniel Defoe. The paper
was *Legion's Memorial to the House of Commons*.

Of several different accounts of this dramatic business,
there is the one provided by Defoe's own *History of the
Kentish Petition*, published in August of that year 1701
and hardly likely to distort an event that had so many
witnesses. It was a brief encounter between Defoe and
the man for whom he was later to employ his pen so
busily. And the *Memorial* itself, in a style of indignant
and extremely daring eloquence rare with Defoe, may
well have stuck in Mr. Speaker Harley's memory. In
the House at large, according to one witness, it struck
terror. In this document that *required and demanded* a
change of policy, we do not hear merely the voice of
Whigs out of office and skirmishing to get back. The
Kentish Petitioners had been seized for much less, and
Legion's Memorial proposed that the thanks of the House
should now be given to them for their gallant appearance
'in behalf of their country.' Looking at it historically,
it is at this moment in behalf of his country that Defoe
appears, and in a character different from the tolerant,
pacifying, sensibly persuasive rôle that he so often played
politically. Suddenly, dangerously, even nobly, he is a
fanatic. 'You are not above the People's resentments,'
he declares to a House elected in virtue of his respected
Constitution yet tainted by the 'corruption' and 'stock-
jobbing' which he denounced in other pamphlets at this
time. And finally:

'For Englishmen are no more to be slaves to Parliament than to a King. Our name is LEGION, and we are
many.'

Not long afterwards, the House having risen and the
Petitioners being free, Defoe was a guest at a banquet

given to them by the citizens of London, before their triumphal journey back to Maidstone. The Tories had undoubtedly been shaken. By September King William was in a position to conclude his Grand Alliance with the United Provinces and Hapsburg Austria. It was signed for him by Marlborough, whose military genius was almost alone to save the combination from disaster. And the next thing that happened was the death on 16 September of the former King James II. This was a moment of critical importance in Jacobite politics, and Defoe was at once ready with a tract on *The Present State of Jacobitism Considered*. Louis XIV, alarmed by the coalition, took a step by which he must have hoped to widen the split in England, but in fact it was to unite the people in support of William's war policy. On the very day of James's death, Louis recognized James's son, the Stuart Pretender, as lawful sovereign of England. And in October came a pamphlet from Defoe, his last service in William's lifetime, of which the irony is sufficiently indicated in the title: *Reasons against a War with France; or an argument showing that the French King's Owning the Prince of Wales (the Pretender) as King of England, Scotland and Ireland, is no Sufficient Ground of a War*. It consists, of course (in that inverted manner of which Defoe was a master) of the demonstration of reasons *for* a war with a foreign despot who presumed to arrange the succession to the English throne. And one of these reasons, pleasantly insinuated, was that such a war would prove profitable, since it offered a chance of laying hands on the riches of Spanish America. The division of the Spanish colonies, as Louis had for some time expected, had been written into the treaty of the Grand Alliance. 'All the news from England and Holland,' Louis had written in February 1701, 'points to the fact that the chief design of the two nations is to undertake enterprises in the New World.' The Tories at that time, who designed nothing but to stay in their tight little island, would have been indignant to hear it. But the French King himself was helping to push matters to the point at which, in February 1702, Defoe could lay before William a detailed plan for attacking the Spanish possessions in America, embellished with his own widely-gathered geographical knowledge. How much in the change of mood in England had been contributed by Defoe's pamphleteering cannot be known. It may have been, as it seemed to him to be, very little. It was Louis XIV's insulting support of the Jacobites that had enabled William to dissolve Parliament and to find the next one belligerent at last. 'Of all the nations in the world,' observed Defoe, 'there is none that I know of so entirely governed by their humour as the English.'

The work that brought Defoe into familiar terms with William has not yet been described. This was the celebrated *True-Born Englishman*, a long poem which appeared in January 1701, ran into nine editions in the same year and was frequently reprinted—not only by Defoe but in pirated editions which he calculated lost him the proceeds of 80,000 copies. Over nearly all of Defoe's verse time has drawn a charitable veil. *The True-Born Englishman* scored its great success in a reign in which Dryden was old and Pope a child, a time of innumerable and barbarous pseudo-pindarics, with Nahum Tate the laureate and Prior the only poet who has survived. The verse is rough, but it has lines that startle by their point and vigour, and it is sustained by a shrewdly provocative central idea. Defoe in this poem springs to the defence of his hero the Stadtholder-King against the whispers and the publications of a rising xenophobia.

London market scene, c. 1720

R. Review

Of ye State of ye Brittish Nation. Saturday
Decbr 31 1709

I think the Jacobites have no reason to be angry att this paper at all, nor is any thing
written so pointedly against yor Qua Jacobites — as at an other sort of people, whom I cannot
I confess, speak of without some warmth, I meane Such as take ye Oathes, abjure ye Pretr.
and all his forreigne race. That Sit down among us, worship wth us, nay Some pretend to teach
us, and yet on all occasions, shew their enmity to the Government and their hearts joyning with
its worst Enemies. I remember, when I asked once, what I shou'd call these, own'd I wanted
a name for them, ye late Mr. Rehearsal, to excuse them, esteemed them to a Sort of Men,
which he allowed to be, in his opinion, the worst out of Hell. I will not go his length, but I'm
ptd to say anything too Severe, for Such people. To See a Justice of Peace (as I at Christmas
take ye Abjuration, and Swear to ye Ann: or visibly own ye Interest of R: Jame. And
whiles he is taking ye Oath bid G — to D — n him if he keeps it.

to hear a Minister, yt has taken ye Abjuration, & all necessary oaths to a Government, which
Government is built on ye principles of resisting and deposing ye K: upon his Mal administration — so his people. That ye very pillar on wch our Gov: stands, is founded upon
the steady belief the Subjects obligation to an absolute & unconditional obedience to ye Supream
power, and ye utter illegality of resistance upon any pretence whatsoever.

To See these paradoxes in practice, & hear these contradictions is enough to move any
mans patience. If these are not Traitors to ye Revolution, if these are not betrayers of ye
God, and mockers of Oaths, if these are not ye K. Enemies, and ye Churches Judas's, the
betters of Liberty, and ye Destroyers of ye present Constitution, then we have no rule
to judge right & wrong by.

Defoe's handwriting

He had what God could give or man desire
Till pity roused him from his soft repose,
His life to unseen hazards to expose;
Till pity moved him in our cause t'appear;
Pity! that word which now we hate to hear.
But English gratitude is always such,
To hate the hand which doth oblige too much.

The poem was occasioned by a satire by John Tutchin, a journalist who was to have more than this one brush with Defoe. Tutchin had roundly stated that it was 'intolerable for a true-born Englishman to be governed by a Dutch King.' Defoe flared up with the withering enquiry: what is a true-born Englishman?

A Turkish horse can show more history
To prove his well-descended family.

The proudest of the English nobility could trace their pedigree only to some French soldier who came over with the Norman bastard to conquer an already 'amphibious ill-born mob.'

These are the heroes that despise the Dutch,
And rail at new-come foreigners so much,
Forgetting that themselves are all derived
From the most scoundrel race that ever lived;
A horrid crowd of rambling thieves and drones,
Who ransacked kingdoms and dispeopled towns,
The Pict and painted Briton, treacherous Scot,
By hunger, theft and rapine hither brought;
Norwegian pirates, buccaneering Danes,
Whose red-haired offspring everywhere remains,
Who, joined with Norman-French, compound the
    breed
From whence your true-born Englishmen proceed.
And lest by length of time it be pretended
The climate may this modern breed ha' mended,

H

> Wise Providence, to keep us where we are,
> Mixes us daily with exceeding care.
> We have been Europe's sink, the jakes where she
> Voids all her offal outcast progeny.

Proceeding with his catalogue of miscegenation, in
language which his opponents weakly replied he must
have learned from some 'Billingsgate Amazon', Defoe
had no difficulty when he reached the reign of Charles II.

> The royal refugee our breed restores
> With foreign courtiers and with foreign whores,
> And carefully repeopled us again,
> Throughout his lazy, long, lascivious reign . . .
> This offspring, if one age they multiply,
> May half the house with English peers supply;
> There with true English pride they may contemn
> Schomberg and Portland, new-made noblemen.

In the defence of William, he must also defend the
favourite counsellors whom the King brought over with
him, such men as Frederick de Schomberg, made Duke
of Schomberg, and William Bentinck, made Earl of
Portland.

It is all laid on with a will, and Defoe's own admiration
for a fluid society is turned inside out to make his point.

> Wealth, howsoever got, in England makes
> Lords of mechanics, gentlemen of rakes:
> Antiquity and birth are needless here;
> 'Tis impudence and money makes a peer.
> Innumerable City knights, we know,
> From Bluecoat Hospital and Bridewell flow;
> Draymen and porters fill the city Chair,
> And footboys magisterial purple wear.
> Fate has but very small distinction set
> Betwixt the counter and the coronet.
> Tarpaulin lords, pages of high renown,

Rise up by poor men's valour, not their own.
Great families of yesterday we show,
And lords whose parents were the Lord knows who.

The English 'humour' that was to change confusion into resolve at a slight from the King of France, took a swift and enormous fancy to the derisive couplets of their very English countryman. There was a shower of ripostes, of course. Defoe, writing anonymously as usual, had taken care to make it clear that he was not a Dutchman. Fame made his authorship well known, and his resounding attack on English incivility was met by the assertion that he was 'the spawn of both nations, a loathsome thing, shap'd like a toad with spots and scabs' —the mole on Defoe's chin being a favourite item with the caricaturists of the pen. But this was part of the common exchange of literary and political London. What mattered was that everybody read *The True-Born Englishman*, thousands praised and quoted it, Dunton advertised Defoe's name with those of Swift, Tate, and Le Motteux, as 'the great writers of the age!' King William sent for him, recognizing the value of a wildly popular lampoon aimed at his detractors. When Defoe came to publish his first collected writings in 1703, they were put out as those of 'the Author of *The True-Born Englishman*.' For long it was his proudest title.

The King had need for such support. Whatever his qualities, the gift of popularity was not among them. Defoe was near the truth in suggesting that the sense of obligation in the nation that had summoned him made William disliked—chiefly, as was to be expected, by the Tories who were given leisure and security to regret the sacrifice of principle whereby they had acquiesced in the Glorious Revolution; but even the Whigs felt uncomfortable sometimes in the presence of their nominee, reserved but strong of will, dark and proud and brooding. Beyond the parties there was, of course, a general national acceptance, disturbed only when some sectional interest, the Dissenters or the City of London, seemed to be claiming William as their own. Defoe had no doubts about it. He was Defoe's King, the Protestant King, the honest, hard-working, god-fearing monarch of all Englishmen who were the same. The quality of Defoe's pamphleteering in these years owes something, at least, to the fact that his basic views and loyalties were broadly engaged. That February day in 1702 when William's horse stumbled at the gallop on a molehill in Hampton Court Park, fatally throwing its rider, became for Defoe sacred to an immortal memory. Throughout the publication of his *Review* the day was marked each year by an article of praise and gratitude. 'Can an Englishman go to bed or rise up without blessing the very name of King William?' One, at least, could not.

But when William died, with war just round the corner though not yet joined, there were sundry trueborn Englishmen who toasted, not the architect of the Grand Alliance but the horse which had thrown him and 'the little gentleman in black velvet' that had provided the opportune molehill. Defoe rounded on them, and the seven editions in twelve months of his satire *The Mock Mourners* suggest that he was not alone in his hero-worship.

*   *   *

One of the ornaments of William's reign, in Defoe's eyes, had been the Act of Toleration. By the Tories and the Anglican interest, however, the Dissenters were still, and for long to come, seen as a potential danger to Church and State, and most public offices were denied to them. By the letter of the law, the holding of office required occasional conformity—that is, the taking of Communion now and then—with the rites of the Established Church. Some Dissenters began to take advantage of this soon after the Revolution, quietening their consciences, for professional reasons, towards an occasional appearance in Church. Defoe's conscience, elastic in some ways, was notably rigid on this point, and when in 1698 a Dissenting Lord Mayor of London drew attention by attending an Anglican service one Sunday morning and a Dissenters' conventicle, in full regalia, the same afternoon, there shortly appeared on the bookstalls *An Enquiry into the Occasional Conformity of Dissenters in Cases of Preferment*. Apt as always with scriptural quotation, Defoe found his text in the challenge: 'If the Lord be God, follow Him, but if Baal, then follow him.' Reading the tract now, it seems a vindication of logic as much as of belief—the Man of Sense again. It was not the true Dissenters, for they would not for any reason take Communion, whom he sought to expose: it was the fellow-travellers of Dissent, those politically rather than religiously inclined, those indeed whose existence justified a measure of exclusion in the laws. Such appears to have been Defoe's attitude, but his tract opened a breach between himself and the community in which he had been reared.

That was in January 1698, before the appearance of Defoe's first great political pamphlets. There was no immediate reply to the *Enquiry into Occasional Conformity*. Its offence to Dissenters, many of them upright and able men, who had thus 'played hide-and-seek with the Almighty,' was in the publicity it gave to the practices; and they were probably disinclined to invite any more of the limelight. In 1702, just after Queen Anne had come to the throne, Defoe reprinted his pamphlet.

But with the accession of Anne the wind was blowing the other way. She fulfilled William's foreign policy by maintaining the Grand Alliance and declaring war against France within a fortnight of her accession. But in the new House of Commons Tories outnumbered Whigs by more than two to one. The Lords were still packed with the late King's friends, but Tories and High Churchmen knew that they had the Queen's favour, which indeed she had indicated in her speech from the throne—a mistake which Defoe respectfully but repeatedly pointed out. She had missed a great opportunity he held, of uniting the nation. Despite her formal undertaking to maintain the Act of Toleration, it was at once put about that 'now we had a Church of England Queen, and the Dissenters must all come down.' The celebrated 'High-Flier' Dr. Sacheverell said as much in a sermon at Oxford, and the House of Commons prepared severe legislation against all office-holders who had taken the Sacrament for the purpose and afterwards attended any non-Anglican service or meeting.

Occasional Conformity was the practice that Defoe had attacked. Now came a Bill against it, tension between the Commons and the Lords, fierce feeling whipped up throughout the country, intemperate speeches and sermons, the burning down of conventicles, and the foreign war almost unregarded in the excitement. Defoe's contribution was to publish anonymously, in December 1702, his celebrated pamphlet *The Shortest Way With The Dissenters*. This time it was no poor man's plea but the righteous indignation of a High Tory seeking to be rid at last of an intolerable nuisance.

'No, gentlemen, the time of mercy is past, your day of grace is over; you should have practised peace, and moderation, and charity, if you expected any yourselves.

'We have heard none of this lesson for fourteen years past. We have been huffed and bullied with your Act of Toleration; you have told us that you are the Church established by law, as well as others; have set up your canting synagogues at our church doors, and the Church and members have been loaded with reproaches, with oaths, associations, adjurations, and what not. . . .

'You have butchered one king, deposed another king, and made a mock king of a third, and yet you could have the face to expect to be employed and trusted by the fourth. . . . Your management of your Dutch monarch, whom you reduced to a mere King of Clouts, is enough to give any further princes such an idea of your principles as to warn them sufficiently from coming into your clutches; and God be thanked the Queen is out of your hands, knows you, and will have a care of you.'

Of course it is ironical, but why should it appear so at the time, when the politico-religious feud was being prosecuted every day in similar, or even more violent, terms? Even today, did we not know the author and the circumstances, we might find ourselves temporarily impressed by the sustained argument. The Dissenters had claimed they were a numerous part of the nation. Here are the answers:

'1. They are not so numerous as the Protestants in France, and yet the French King effectually cleared the nation of them at once, and we don't find he misses them at home. . . .

2. The more numerous the more dangerous, and therefore the more need to suppress them. . . .

3. If we are to allow them only because we cannot suppress them, then it ought to be tried whether we can

or not; and I am of opinion it is easy to be done, and could prescribe ways and means, if it were proper; but I doubt not the Government will find effectual methods for the rooting the contagion from the face of this land.'

The ways and means that Defoe would find, in the character of the author of this remarkable work, are presented in a series of bloodcurdling innuendoes. 'I do not prescribe fire and faggot,' he announces, but shortly afterwards observes:

'Moses was a merciful, meek man, and yet with what fury did he run through the camp, and cut the throats of three-and-thirty thousand of his dear Israelites that were fallen into idolatry. What was the reason? It was mercy to the rest to make these examples, to prevent the destruction of the whole army.'

The legislative proposals that had caused such a commotion were mere trifling, 'foolish handling of them by mulcts, fines etc.' If the Government armed itself with really severe powers, says the author contemptuously, most of the Dissenters would be frightened into obedience.

'If the gallows instead of the counter, and the galleys instead of the fines, were the reward of going to a conventicle, to preach or hear, there would not be so many sufferers. The spirit of martyrdom is over; they that will go to church to be chosen sheriffs and mayors would go to forty churches rather than be hanged.'

'If one severe law were made and punctually executed, that whoever was found at a conventicle should be banished the nation and the preacher be hanged, we should soon see an end of the tale.'

And with a highly disturbing allegory he approaches his peroration:

'Alas, the Church of England! What with Popery on one hand, and schismatics on the other, how has she been crucified between two thieves!

'Now let us crucify the thieves. . . .'

This is Sacheverellism run mad. But Sacheverellism was in fact running mad at the time. The irony was too thin to be perceived at first (the frequent references to Her Majesty's responsibilities have a most engaging subtlety). *The Shortest Way With The Dissenters* is superb in its species, and a mental refreshment in our own heresy-hunting age. In Defoe's day it may in the end have done much to blunt the face of the intended intolerance: and that, naturally, was Defoe's object; for though he could tease his fellow-Dissenters on the score of Occasional Conformity, the smell of real persecution made him a different being. But from his own point of view, *The Shortest Way* was the rashest thing he had ever penned. It raised for him two sets of enemies like the two thieves of his Biblical simile. Once his authorship was known, the frightened Dissenters who had already been peppered by him with one charge of shot concluded that he had gone over to the enemy's camp: or if, on reflection, this could not be so, there yet must remain a suspicion of so brilliant, volatile, and unaccountable a pen. The High Tories, on the other hand, at first applauding the anonymous blasting of the Dissenters and then, discovering the audacious hoax upon their own excesses of intolerance, had the best of all reasons—humiliation—for hating its author.

In a sense Defoe had placed himself aptly between the extremists. The Defoe that we know, with his whole work before us, the sensible, moderate, civilized man who is there under so many disguises, here makes a gesture as convincing as it was imprudent. More than that, the personal crisis which this publication precipitated was in some degree the means of producing the riper author who is still loved and read. Professor Trent went so far as to say that without it the world would not have had *Robinson Crusoe*.

That being so, the rewards of research into these years 1702 and 1703 must be great. The facts that have so far been yielded can be briefly summarized. *The Shortest Way* appeared on 1 December 1702. On 3 January 1703 a warrant for the arrest of Defoe was issued by the Earl of Nottingham, one of the Secretaries of State, and on 10 January the *London Gazette* carried a notice offering £50 reward for information leading to the arrest of the 'middle-sized man, about forty years old' who has been itemized at the beginning of this book—a description which perhaps deliberately omitted any reference to Defoe as an author. Four days later an order was issued for seizing the manuscript and all stocks of the pamphlet from the printer, Croome. On 24 February *The Shortest Way* was declared seditious in the Assizes, and ordered to be publicly burned by the hangman. On 20 May Defoe was arrested in the house of a French weaver of Spitalfields and taken to Newgate Gaol (the informer's claim to his £50 reward has been preserved).

Defoe had been in hiding for four and a half months. The veil on one incident of that period was lifted by John Tutchin shortly afterwards when he described an encounter of Defoe in Hackney Fields with an unnamed man who recognized him. Instantly Defoe drew his sword, forced the man to his knees and made him swear 'that if he ever met him again he should shut his eyes till

he was half a mile off him.' More is revealed in letters
written by Defoe from his refuge, from April onwards,
to his friend William Paterson—the correspondence is
among the Portland MSS published in 1897 by the
Historical Manuscripts Commission. Paterson, one of
the founders of the Bank of England, became Defoe's
secret intermediary with the moderate Tory Robert
Harley, then rapidly coming to the fore in politics.
But Defoe had already been appealing to Nottingham
himself, pleading 'a body unfit to bear the hardships of
prison and a mind impatient of confinement . . . the
cries of a numerous ruined family, the prospect of a long
banishment from my native country.' He wished to
throw himself upon the Queen's mercy, and offered his
military services, without payment, in any troop of
horse in the Netherlands; 'and without doubt, My Lord,
I shall die there much more to her service than in a
prison.' To such and more abject (though not unreason-
able) pleas Defoe later said that his wife added her own,
gaining admittance to the Earl of Nottingham only to be
offered a bribe (which she refused) to betray her
husband.

Reading these vain appeals, one remembers the man
who two years before had marched into the House of
Commons with a document infinitely more provocative,
on the face of it, than *The Shortest Way With the Dissenters*.
The triumph of *Legion's Memorial* and the favour of King
William in the last thirty years may both have un-
balanced Defoe. With William dead and his memory
slighted, the author of *The True-Born Englishman* had
drawn boldly on the most powerful resources of his
irony in the preservation of fair comment and of the
late king's Act of Toleration; and now he fully recognized the fury of the storm that he had raised. He knew

what threatened him. The pillory, Sir W. Besant has recorded, 'was sometimes as fatal as the gallows, and far more terrible.' Ear-cropping had been abandoned (which makes Pope's later dig at 'earless' Defoe gratuitous), but the pilloried man was at the mercy of the mob. Defoe may have seen Titus Oates taken down nearly dead after his first day of the punishment, and in known cases after his time it proved fatal. In the Portland MSS we find these frank and moving words in one of Defoe's letters to Paterson:

'Gaol, pillories and such like, with which I have been so much threatened, have convinced me I want passive courage, and I shall never for the future think myself injured if I am called a coward.'

Dreadful as was the menace of the pillory, one is tempted to think that the 'numerous ruined family' may have been an equal anxiety to Defoe, who did not lack active courage. And perhaps the 'mind impatient of confinement' provided the most brooding anxiety of all through those months of hiding that were ended by the denunciation in the weaver's house.[1]

From his arrest until his trial in July, Defoe had seven weeks in which to consider his defence and enlist what support he could. His legal adviser William Colepeper (he had been one of the five Kentish Petitioners)

[1] It is curious how the shade of William Cobbett dogs that of Defoe. Cobbett's 'most famous and seditious libel' of more than a century later, though furiously sarcastic where Defoe was subtle, was likewise an exaggerated distortion of an actual excess—the flogging of the Ely mutineers. Defoe had to hide: Cobbett merely retired to the country, but to await with equal misgiving a sentence which would not include the pillory. Cobbett had shown himself bold enough in Pennsylvania. At the prospect of Newgate and a heavy fine he was prepared for almost any concession if he could have avoided martyrdom. 'Indeed,' remarks his most recent biographer, W. Baring Pemberton, 'it is arguable whether any man upon whom a family depends, is justified in playing such a rôle.'

counselled him to admit the authorship of *The Shortest Way*, plead guilty, and throw himself upon the Queen's mercy (as Defoe was to argue thereafter, if his pamphlet were seditious, then so were the sermons and speeches of Sacheverell and the High-Fliers whom he had parodied). But this played straight into the hands of his accusers, who wanted only this confession to proceed to an exemplary revenge. The precise complaint against the offender is a little obscure; Sir Simon Harcourt, the Advocate-General, described Defoe as 'paving his way with the skulls of Churchmen,' a quaint inversion of the literal sense of the tract; but the punishment was all that had been threatened. Defoe was sentenced to pay the crippling fine of 200 marks, to stand three times in the pillory, to be lodged in Newgate during the Queen's pleasure and thereafter to find sureties for his good conduct during another seven years.

Somebody was after Defoe's blood, and many attempts have been made to explain who, and why. In part, no doubt, it was a wild blow at the Dissenters themselves, little as they relished Defoe's complex intellectual exercise on behalf of Toleration. It was certainly also a High Tory attempt to destroy a dangerous man, a champion of Dutch William, a supposed tool of the Whigs, a man with too popular a pen who had offered affronts more direct than that of which he stood accused. But there was another and an important element in this vindictiveness which has been little noticed until recently,[1] though John Dunton's contemporary *Life and Errors* had offered a useful hint. In this book Dunton says of Defoe:

'The world is well satisfied that he is enterprising and bold; but alas! had his prudence only weighed a

[1] See, for example, J. R. Moore's *Defoe in the Pillory* (Indiana University Publications, Humanities Series, No. 1).

few grains more, he would certainly have wrote his
Shortest Way a little more at length. . . . Had he written
no more than his *True-Born Englishman*, and spared some
particular characters that are too vicious for the very
originals, he had certainly deserved applause. . . . '

There are no 'particular characters' in *The Shortest
Way*. There are some in the *True-Born Englishman*.
There are plenty, and vicious enough, in that verse-
satire *The Reformation of Manners*. *The Poor Man's Plea* had
broadly appealed for the reform of those who ad-
ministered justice. *The Reformation of Manners* had been
peopled with judges and aldermen, named or nearly so,
and charged in a picturesque vocabulary with in-
temperance, profanity, corruption, lechery or—worse
still—the would-be lechery of the senile. It was an
exercise, no doubt, in a fashionable manner. But even
in a free-spoken age, the man who has dealt thus with
the officers of justice would do well not to have to appear
before them.

The savage sentence passed, a struggle began to
mitigate or avoid it, and in these manoeuvres the
prisoner's political importance developed significantly.
For one thing Robert Harley was now considering the
approach made to him by Paterson on Defoe's behalf,
and Harley was a rival for the power of the Earl of
Nottingham. Harley, Nottingham, the Lord Treasurer
Godolphin, the Quaker William Penn, Colepeper,
Queen Anne herself, all were involved in the case of the
seditious pamphleteer. Nottingham visited him in prison,
vainly trying, it seems, to uncover the confidences of
the late King and the Whig Party. Defoe himself was
taken to Windsor for examination. Opinions on the
Queen's part in the whole affair vary, but Defoe certainly

never bore her a grudge and was afterwards perfectly loyal.

The pillory was not to be avoided, but it could be cheated. The famous episode of Defoe's popular reception in the instrument of shame and torture makes an even better story when we realize that he had prepared for it, though his success may have outrun his expectations. The agile mind and the indefatigable pen that had got him into the worst situation in his life were briskly engaged to get him out of it. While in hiding from Nottingham's men he had written and printed two pamphlets, one a 'brief explanation' of what had been intended in *The Shortest Way With The Dissenters*, the other *King William's Affection to the Church of England Examin'd*. Neither had saved him. In the middle of that month of July when his fate hung on the comings and goings of Ministers and their intermediaries, Defoe published from prison a 'satyr upon himself' in a thousand lines of verse called *More Reformation*. And by more than a coincidence the day finally fixed for his appearance in the pillory, 29 July, was the publication day of two other works, *The Shortest Way to Peace and Union* and *A Hymn to the Pillory*: Copies of these and other writings were on sale in the nearby streets and at the very foot of the pillory where their author was exposed. Both were revised later on when Defoe made up his collected volumes; and this gave him the chance of putting his accusers in the wrong by pointing out that they did not proceed against him for the defiant *Hymn to the Pillory* when they had him fast in their power. It is gallant doggerel, this *Hymn to the Pillory*, but it rises in passages to more than that, displaying both dignity and wit as Defoe first honours the 'hieroglyphic state machine' for the virtuous men that had stood in it before him, and

then proposes a catalogue of those who might more fitly
be punished. It ends with the celebrated lines:

> Tell them the Men that placed him here
> Are scandals to the times,
>   Are at a loss to find his guilt,
>   And can't commit his crimes.

Of this audacious broadsheet Professor Sutherland says
warmly: 'It is the declaration of a man who expects fair
play, and who believes that he will get it from his
fellow-citizens if it is denied him in the courts of law.'
From his fellow-citizens, as he stood there with head
and arms locked, Defoe got flowers and friendliness
instead of abuse and unsavoury missiles. According to a
contemporary reference, they 'halloo'd him down from
his wooden punishment, as if he had been a Cicero that
had made an excellent oration in it, rather than a Cataline
that was exposed and declaimed against there.' The
demonstration was repeated at his second exhibition,
and on the third day it reached extraordinary enthusiasm,
with garlands and toasts and all the acclamation of a hero.
This was at Temple Bar: and Fleet Street, which owes
so much to Daniel Defoe, should remember it.

The mob that thus helped him to turn the tables upon
his enemies was the same that had riotously attacked
Dissenters' meeting-houses and was ready to cheer Dr.
Sacheverell and the bigots of the High Church party.
That Defoe captured them for three days may have been
partly due to the work of Whig politicians, discreetly
whipping up opinion in relief at Defoe's refusal to betray
their secrets and in hopes of discomforting the Tory
Government. Yet however brief, it was a personal and
not an artificial triumph. The reckless appeal of the
Hymn to the Pillory must have made its impression. At

the bottom of the whole business, it was doubtless realized, lay the joke that had been played on those in high places. And if such papers as the *Poor Man's Plea* were among the works of Defoe being hawked through the crowd, then it is not difficult to imagine the mood in which a plain, outspoken and plucky citizen was saluted.

Certain contemporaries saw more than that in the business. In the following year Nottingham was out and Harley was in, and the rumour went about, *post hoc ergo propter hoc*, that the enigmatical Defoe, of whom almost anything came to be believed, had been for some time past in Harley's counsels, and his pay: indeed that the whole sequence of sedition, trial, and punishment had been precipitated, if not engineered, for the purpose of raising a hornet's nest about the Government. The correspondence in the Portland MSS, however, with Defoe seeking patiently to secure Harley's interest, makes this impossible to believe. It also disposes of the idea that *The Review* was started in Newgate—as maintained by his nineteenth-century biographers and, less excusably, by some recent writers. Defoe was free by November 1703, little more than three months after he had stood in the pillory, and *before* Nottingham was replaced by Harley as Secretary of State. How much he actually composed in prison is uncertain, though he did assemble some of his writings into the *True Collection of the Writings of the Author of the True-Born Englishman*. What matters more, surely, is first that Newgate gave him the scenes and the people, perhaps the ideas also, that later inspired *Moll Flanders* and other human narratives of the unrespectable; and secondly that his experience throughout this whole year, the rank injustice of his usage and the shifts that were necessary to resist it, left a mark upon him. He

I

had been in the jungle and had learned some of the cunning of the hunted.

The man who saved him from his prison sentence was, as we shall come to understand, a man whom Defoe could have served even had he not been under the necessity of rescue. After the vain attempt to placate the inveterate Nottingham, Defoe had shown good judgment in turning, or trying to turn, to Robert Harley. That Harley's good offices required considerable wooing was in part due to the complex animosities of the political situation, and in part to Harley's own intelligence. The man who was to assemble the Harleian Library of books and manuscripts was certainly among the first to recognize the political value of recruiting able pens; but the choice of Defoe, a Whig, a Dissenter, possibly eccentric, probably dangerous—was not an obvious one. Harley proceeded cautiously, and by means calculated to ensure an obligation to which Defoe might remain loyal. It was first necessary to convince the Lord Treasurer Godolphin (whom Defoe, incidentally, had lampooned in the *True-Born Englishman*) that the writer would on the whole be safer as friend than as enemy. When that had been accomplished, Harley sent to Defoe in Newgate, by word of mouth, the non-committal message: 'Pray ask that gentleman what I can do for him.' Defoe's reply was equally discreet: 'Lord, that I might receive my sight.' Perhaps, at this moment of exhilarating decision, he had opened his Bible and pricked a text, if we may use so sceptical an expression, at random.

Memorably it should have ended there. But there was still the Queen's pardon to secure; and since there was a danger now of Defoe's fine being paid for him by others, Harley stood to lose his gratitude if he did not finish the matter off. Once Godolphin had talked the

Queen to the point of pardon, she was generous. She settled Defoe's fine and the costs of his discharge and she also sent a liberal present to his family. They needed it, for the brick and pantile business was in ruins with the collapse of Defoe's credit. He estimated that this meant a loss of £4,000 to him, which may have been an exaggeration. But it did mean that from now on he was to live mainly by his pen.

Chapter Four

THE GREAT POLYGRAPHER

BETWEEN November 1703, when the middle-sized man with the hooked nose, the sharp chin, and the grey eyes walked out of the prison of Newgate, and April 1719 when *Robinson Crusoe* appeared from the sign of the Ship in Paternoster Row, some two hundred and fifty separate publications came from Defoe's hand. Many of them, it is true, were quite short; and one of the shortest—the *Apparition of Mrs. Veal*—has lasted among the best. Some were reprints of his newspaper articles, or old material re-worked. But others, *Jure Divino* for instance or the *History of the Union*, were formidable productions. Within this period he produced additionally, from 19 February 1704 to 11 June 1713, nine volumes of his *Review*, writing a dozen printer's pages of copy each week even when he was away— sometimes far away—from London. The speed and freshness of composition can be judged from the fact that one of the rare manuscript copies of the *Review* (31 December 1709, in the British Museum) exhibits only two erasures. And after the *Review* came to an end Defoe was actively connected, in one way or another, with half a dozen other journals.

It is a period which has fascinated biographers: Minto, lacking much material that has since been uncovered, gave nearly half his short book to these sixteen years. To the controversies over Defoe's character and his journalistic integrity they offer plenty of material for both sides, and still leave something to conjecture. These are the years which produced some of Defoe's sharpest personal conflicts, and they are the years which subsequent admirers have tried to unravel, to explain, and where necessary to excuse. Defoe was in the thick of journalism, the keen journalism of Queen Anne's reign, dealing out blows as fast as he received them. But he was also, or quickly became, an acknowledged leader in the new profession—'the first,' as Dunton was ready to say, 'that deservedly leads the way.' Because of this eminence, of which he was not unaware; because of the political backing and protection which for a time he secured; and also because his character inclined him to it, Defoe's style of controversy has undoubtedly more marks of good sense and good temper upon it than that of his rivals. The *Review* especially is notable for a peculiar type of urbanity which is Defoe's and no one else's, an air of friendly confidence in the intelligence of the 'gentlemen freeholders' whom he chiefly addressed, an enjoyment of the surprises of paradox, a delight in the exercise of debating skill, a cool assurance of superior reason which maddened his opponents and caused the High-Tory editor Charles Leslie to burst out:

'The insolence of the *Review* is intolerable! He studies to provoke in the most affronting manner he can think of. And then he cries: "Peace and Union, Gentlemen, and lay aside your heats!"'

The High Tories—Highfliers as they were often called —were always fair game for Defoe. There were times when the Whigs, on the other hand, did not know in whose pocket to look for him. The foremost living historian of the period calls Defoe 'the typical man of his day;'[1] and one of the commonest apologies for Defoe's shifts of ground, his impersonations, his readiness even to write for his opponents in order to destroy their arguments, is the explanation that in the early eighteenth century party divisions had not yet assumed the character of rival sets of principles contending for the favour of the electorate and the responsibilities of government. The politicians whom Defoe served were shrewd and able, careful calculators of their own and their country's profit. If anything, they were less idealistic in the business than he was himself. It is in the perspective of history that he appears as a typical man of his day, not in the immediate pattern of politics through which he found a path with a devious mixture of rashness and skill, and with something else that we should remember —a patriotism both staunch and sanguine.

Queen Anne, like William of Orange throughout most of his reign, thought of her Cabinet as a collection of Ministerial advisers chosen with no special regard to party or to the composition of the House of Commons. Defoe prefaced the seventh volume of his *Review* with the statement:

'For my part, I have always thought that the only true fundamental maxim of politics that will ever make this nation happy, is this—that the Government ought to be of no Party at all. Would this Ministry, or any Ministry that shall succeed them, pursue this principle, they would make themselves immortal. . . . Statesmen are the nation's guardians. Their business is not to make sides, divide the nation into parties, and draw the factions into battle array against each other. Their work ought to be to scatter and disperse parties, as they would

[1] G. M. Trevelyan: *Blenheim*.

tumults; and to keep a balance among the interfering interests of the nation, with the same care as they would the civil peace.'

Defoe felt himself to be a constitutionalist, a good Parliament man, and even his near-rebellion as author of *Legion's Memorial* he took pains to justify by dwelling more than once on the right of petition—notably in the pamphlet of 1701 examining *The Original Power of the Collective Body of the People of England*. His theory of a government above party was not what would be called today democratic theory, yet the popular vote can lead us to a situation where even now Defoe has something to say to us. He was obviously speaking his thoughts when he thus expressed his 'fundamental maxim.' He was also anxious, in the conduct of the *Review* for Harley's policies and his own ideas, to effect an air of impartiality. He seems, moreover, to have become increasingly chagrined by the extremities of party strife, even though Swift in 1710 could 'hardly find one material point in difference' between Whig and Tory. What Defoe thought of as the fruits of good government can be seen in his annual eulogies of the late King William.

'When you sit down to eat, why have you not soldiers quartered in your house, to command your servants and insult your table? 'Tis because King William subjected the military to the civil authority, and made the sword of justice triumph over the sword of war. When you lie down at night, why do you not bolt and bar your chamber to defend the chastity of your wives and daughters from the ungoverned lust of raging mercenaries? 'Tis because King William restored the sovereignty and dominion of the laws, and made the redcoat world servants to those that paid them. When you receive your rents, why are

not arbitrary defalcations made upon your tenants,
arbitrary imposts laid upon your commerce, and
oppressive taxes levied upon your estates? . . . 'Tis
because King William re-established the essential security
of your properties, and put you into that happy condition,
which few nations enjoy, of calling your souls your own.'

The England that Voltaire and Montesquieu so much
admired in the 1720's, where 'the Englishman goes to
heaven by the road he pleases,' where 'there are no
arbitrary taxes' and where 'the sovereign is unable to
inflict any imaginable harm to anyone,' did not happen
entirely by accident; nor was it so perfect a society as
enraptured foreigners supposed. A Liberal historian has
pointed out that 'the Whigs, exulting in their Revolution
Settlement, were too apt to think that it had settled
everything.'[1] Defoe spent much ink in defending what
had been gained by, for instance, the Act of Toleration;
in advising the Dissenting sects to unite if they hoped
for justice; in attacking the corruption of elections and
the partiality of the Courts. In his important work for
the Union of the Scottish and English legislatures he did
as much as any one man to place the coping-stone on the
structure laid by the Revolution Settlement of 1689.
He was at the same time quite prepared to exploit a
situation for his own advantage or that of his political
patron. His assertions of independence were often
evasions of the truth, to be adjusted to his moral
principles by the considerations, first that the ultimate
ends he kept in view were honest ones, and second that
Harley usually and very sensibly allowed him a free hand.

Both Harley and Defoe seem to have learned something
from the Great Trimmer Halifax; and the coalitions, or

[1] H. A. L. Fisher: *A History of Europe.*

governments resembling coalitions, which were often (though uneasily) maintained under William and Anne suited Defoe's taste for the 'middle way.' When the *Review* was supporting the Whigs in a parliamentary election that returned the Tories, Defoe could write that so long as the new members 'act upon the Revolution principle, keep within the circle of the law, proceed with temper, moderation, and justice, to support the same interest we have all carried on . . . they will be Whigs, they must be Whigs; there is no other remedy, for the Constitution is a Whig.' The Protestant succession was the main thing, and as it happened the accession of George I was to usher in the Whig Supremacy. Changing sides when necessary, calling Tories Whigs and Whigs Tories so long as the 'hot' ones were excluded, Defoe could tell himself that it was a government rather than a party that he was serving— and still more, a constitutional sovereign. Robert Harley had accurately judged the character of the loyal Dissenter when he saw to it that Defoe's deliverance from Newgate should appear to be as much a gift from the Queen as from the statesman.

The generation of journalists in which Defoe so quickly assumed prominence was the first to enjoy relative freedom from an oppressive literary censorship. The resounding appeal of Milton's *Areopagitica* (1644) had had little practical effect until the end of the century, when the last Licenser of Printing, Edmund Bohun, was removed. Pursuit for libel or sedition, variously interpreted, was still an occupational risk—a risk taken, it would seem, with much gusto by the writers of the day, and one which encouraged the widespread use of anonymity, allegory, and literary disguise. The lapse of the licensing acts which encouraged a proliferation of news-sheets and coffee-house journals had, however, another effect. It introduced the book pirate, from whose activities Defoe suffered with his contemporaries. Addison describes the book pirates in the *Tatler* (1 December 1709) as 'a set of wretches . . . who print any book, or poem, or sermon as soon as it appears in the world, in a smaller volume, and sell it, as all other thieves do stolen goods, at a cheaper rate.'

There were also, for the writer, occupational risks. Against arrest and proceedings such as he had already suffered Defoe had the protection of Harley—a protection often vouchsafed, like the financial support from the same source, at the last possible moment. But there was a danger from which secret compacts with the powerful could not protect him, a danger real enough in his own day, though we may conclude that he feared it less than enclosure within four walls and the ruin of his household. This was the danger of physical assault. Cudgellings, nose-slittings and the like were not uncommon, either at the hands of those who felt themselves or their views attacked in print, or else by hired bullies. John Tutchin, the extreme Whig of the bi-weekly *Observator* (and author of the tract which had roused Defoe to the *True-Born Englishman*), died after a merciless beating in September 1707. It is to him and the life-preserver which he carried that Defoe refers in a reply to his own enemies in the second volume of the *Review*:

'I move about the world unguarded and unarmed; a little stick not strong enough to correct a dog supplies the place of Mr. O——r's great oaken towel, a sword sometimes perhaps for decency, but it is all harmless to a mere nothing; can do no hurt anywhere but just at the tip of it, called the point. And what's that in the hand of a feeble author? . . . Let him alone, gentlemen, and have patience, you'll all come to be of his mind ere long; and then if you had killed him you would be sorry for it.'

He was 'often waylaid,' he says, 'and often dogged into dark passages' by agents of the High Tory faction. But in the spirit of Samuel Johnson's retort to the author of *Ossian*—'what I cannot do for myself the law shall do for me'—he reminded menacing and anonymous correspondents:

'Gaols, fetters and gibbets are odd melancholy things; for a gentleman to dangle out of the world in a string has something so ugly, so awkward, and so disagreeable in it, that you cannot think of it without some regret.'

Some of this may be set down to bravado, but not all of it. One cannot read far in Defoe without realizing that for him (as for Johnson) the contemplation of death was serious and terrible. Yet he took risks with his life. He had adventures. The element that has sometimes been overlooked is that of his enjoyment of them. He relished the power of his pen, the political disguises he assumed, a sudden disappearance when he was wanted, a sudden appearance where he was least expected, the challenging and the mystification of foes, the forwarding of clandestine causes. 'I act the old part of Cardinal Richelieu,' he once boasted to Harley in a letter from Scotland explaining his methods of obtaining information. But it might not have worked. There could easily have been an accident. Had his connections been known, says a Scottish witness, 'the mob of Edinburgh would have torn him to pieces.' And that, Trevelyan reminds us in a glance at destiny,[1] was at a time when 'the most

[1] *Ramillies and the Union with Scotland.*

utterly friendless and forgotten of all Queen Anne's subjects'—Alexander Selkirk—was still on his island: and Crusoe not yet in the imagination.

*   *   *

The age of Anne, with its military triumphs and its backstairs politics, has left us with an unforgettable group of portraits: the Queen herself, the great Duke of Marlborough, his Duchess Sarah, his ally Godolphin, of whom Charles II had said that he was 'never in the way and never out of the way;' the enigmatical Robert Harley; and that calculating waiting-woman Abigail Hill (almost a Defoe character), who as Mrs. Masham brilliantly supplanted Sarah Churchill in the royal affections, established herself in the little house by the gate of Windsor Castle, and thence gave Harley and his friends secret access to the Queen. Thereby hangs the oft-told tale wherein the chameleon Ministry dominated by Marlborough, Godolphin, and Harley at last began to break up, Harley moving towards the extreme Tories with the Queen, Marlborough and Godolphin reluctantly forced towards the Whigs. Beside these personalities, whose characters and relationships were of such import to the nation and its developing forms of government, Daniel Defoe remains a shadow. At times he seems completely out of place. The mark of prosecution and pillory was still on him and Harley never received him openly as he received Swift, whom he also employed. Defoe might get what satisfaction he could from the excitement of secret compacts, but for the most part he must forego that other satisfaction (which he would have appreciated) of conversing in exalted company.

Yet he has his place: as the eyes and ears of Harley, the best-informed statesman of his time; as the tireless if

often unrecognized exponent of the three prime issues
of the reign—Peace (domestic), Union and the Protestant
Succession; and in the smooth change of masters after
Harley's fall he has his place in history also. For if
Godolphin's reputation is to have established the tradition
of the permanent civil service, it was Defoe who so
notably, and to the fury of his foes, accepted that
professional principle. Of the political significance of
his work in these years, little more than a hint can be
given here. Its literary significance is to be found in the
character of the *Review* and its technical influence on
periodical writing; in examples of controversial style
selected from the ceaseless flow of his pamphlets; and
in a few other works which we may glance at next,
partly because more than one of them foreshadow the
narrative writer who in his sixtieth year hit at last upon
the rich vein that was awaiting him.

Late in November 1703 a fierce and memorable storm
struck London and a great part of the country, the same
which was in Addison's mind in the poem commissioned
from him on the victory of Blenheim, wherein Marlborough *Rides in the whirlwind and directs the storm*.
Defoe also put the storm to use in a poem employing the
characteristic Dissenter's device of exhibiting the wrath
of God visited upon the nation for certain specified
offences. What is more to our purpose, he compiled in
prose an account of the calamity which Minto set down
as 'the first of his works of invention.' That judgment,
however, arose from the illusion that Defoe was still
within the four walls of Newgate when it was written.
In fact he had just been released when the trumpet-
voice of heaven spoke with the whirlwind which may
well have had a personal significance for him. *A Collection
of the most remarkable Casualties and Disasters which*

happened in the late Dreadful Tempest, both by Sea and Land is a piece of very sound journalism. Through correspondence with people known to him, and also through an advertisement inserted in some of the London periodicals, Defoe collected a variety of noteworthy anecdotes and observations of the storm and its effects, by land and sea. He rode through Kent to sample the damage for himself, and relates that he stopped counting ruined houses and farm-buildings when he reached the figure of 1,107. He got hold of the official reckoning, melancholy enough, of naval vessels lost or damaged. He added a couple of essays on storms in general and English storms in particular; and from the whole it would no doubt be possible for a meteorologist to reconstruct the course of the phenomenon, for Defoe was particular as to times and dates. He disclaims any embellishment of the reports he put together, but in the very nature of the enterprise Defoe the storyteller and Defoe the topographer can be discerned. And indeed he is there himself with his own experiences, as autobiographical as his later characters, narrowly escaping falling masonry as the wind rises to gale force in London; astounded the next evening by his barometer, lower than he had ever seen it, 'which made me suppose the tube had been handled and disturbed by the children;' spending a night of fear and wonder with his family about him while outside the wind roared through the town and buildings split and crashed; and at length, after nearly a week of disturbance, setting forth to talk to his neighbours and assess the wreckage. In one item of his investigation there is some irony, for he remarks that the price of roof-tiles rose after the disaster from twenty-one shillings a thousand to over six pounds. If only he had still had that pantile factory at Tilbury!

The storm of 1703 was no nine days' wonder. It lived in the memory of all who had been through it, and Defoe returned to it more than once when he came to put together his *Tour Through England and Wales*. The first Eddystone lighthouse, for instance, disappeared completely on the terrible night of November 27, and its builder Winstanley with it ('but there is now another lighthouse built on the same rock,' adds the alert chronicler of projects). Still further west, at Helford in Cornwall, a ship loaded with tin was blown out to sea and driven in seven hours to the Isle of Wight, with but one man and two boys aboard her: and the full account of this adventure which Defoe set down in the *Tour* reads like a page from *Robinson Crusoe*. Indeed the first storm in that tale, when young Crusoe got his baptism of the sea off the mouth of the Humber, has been seen to correspond with Defoe's notes of the 1703 storm in those waters; where—as he tells us in detail in the *Tour*—colliers and other vessels plying between Northumberland and London often ran into trouble in the dangerous open stretch between Flamborough Head and Winterton Ness.

The account of the storm appeared in July 1704. In 1706, among a mass of other writings, Defoe issued a very short work which quickly earned a popularity that doubtless surprised him. He would have been more surprised, and certainly gratified, if he could have known that a little more than two centuries after his death the University of London Council for Psychical Investigation would select a copy of this work, with six other pieces from his hand, for a display illustrating the treasures of its library of twelve thousand volumes. The full title under which it was shown in this 1934 exhibition was: *A True Relation of the Apparition of one Mrs Veal, the next day after her death, to one Mrs. Bargrave at Canterbury, the 8th of September, 1705. Which Apparition recommends the Perusal of Drelincourt's Book of Consolations against the Fears of Death.* This slender production has thus a place not only in the documentation of psychical phenomena but also in the history of the literary puff. The advertisement for Drelincourt was regarded by nineteenth-century admirers of Defoe as the chief if not the only motive for writing about the ghost of Mrs. Veal; and Sir Walter Scott, whose enthusiasm began the modern reputation of the work, deemed it a superb early example of Defoe's circumstantial invention.

It was Aitken in 1895 who demonstrated that what Defoe was actually doing was the reporting of 'a ghost story which was attracting notice at the time.' There *was* a Mrs. Veal and there *was* a Mrs. Bargrave, and Mrs. Bargrave did declare that she had spoken with Mrs. Veal on a certain day, not knowing that she had died the day before. And Defoe, who had a personal quite as much as a professional interest in the supernatural, went down into Kent to cover the story. The title-page of the *first* edition of his account does not refer to Drelincourt. But among the religious works which in life Mrs. Veal would often read with her friend, the one that she (or her apparition) most esteemed was this particular discourse. Not only did it get into the title-page thereafter, but in subsequent editions it is often found bound in with Defoe's little work. And no wonder, for what better recommendation could Charles Drelincourt have for his *Defence against the Fears of Death* than praise from one already dead? He himself, however, had died before his work was published in England (the original was in French); and all that was some forty years before the quiet paths of the two ladies crossed the busy turnpike of

Daniel Defoe. The booksellers were ready to accept the advertisement for a work that must in any case have been fairly well-known—a work which was, in fact, just the sort of thing which Mrs. Bargrave and Mrs. Veal, as they appear in Defoe's narrative, would have upon their shelves.

That we cannot accept *The Apparition of Mrs Veal* as the ingenious *jeu d'esprit* it was once thought to be, does not lessen its simple and compelling narrative appeal. It is Defoe in miniature, a well-constructed short story founded on careful reporting. In the following extract the details—the stuff of Mrs. Veal's gown, the fits, the day and time and sequence—are all material to the 'matter of fact' which the author is conveying to possibly sceptical readers:

'Talking at this rate, Mrs. Bargrave thought that a fit was coming upon her, and so placed herself in a chair just before her knees, to keep her from falling to the ground, if her fits should occasion it (for the elbow-chair, she thought, would keep her from falling on either side); and to divert Mrs. Veal, as she thought, took hold of her gown-sleeve several times and commended it. Mrs. Veal told her it was a scoured silk, and newly made up. But for all this, Mrs. Veal persisted in her request, and told Mrs. Bargrave that she must not deny her, and she would have her tell her brother all their conversation when she had an opportunity. "Dear Mrs. Veal," said Mrs. Bargrave, "this seems so impertinent that I cannot tell how to comply with it; and what a mortifying story will our conversation be to a young gentleman? Why," says Mrs. Bargrave, "it is much better, methinks, to do it yourself."

' "No," says Mrs. Veal, "though it seems impertinent to you now, you will see more reason for it hereafter."

K

Mrs. Bargrave then, to satisfy her importunity, was going to fetch a pen and ink, but Mrs. Veal said, "Let it alone now, but do it when I am gone; but you must be sure to do it;" which was one of the last things she enjoined her at parting. So she promised her.

'Then Mrs. Veal asked for Mrs. Bargrave's daughter. She said she was not at home, "But if you have a mind to see her," says Mrs. Bargrave, "I'll send for her." "Do," says Mrs. Veal. On which she left her, and went to a neighbour's to see for her; and by the time Mrs. Bargrave was returning, Mrs. Veal was got without the door into the street, in the face of the beast-market, on a Saturday (which is market-day), and stood ready to part. As soon as Mrs. Bargrave came to her she asked her why she was in such haste. She said she must be going, though perhaps she might not go her journey until Monday; and told Mrs. Bargrave she hoped she should see her again at her cousin Watson's before she went whither she was going. Then she said she would take her leave of her, and walked from Mrs. Bargrave in her view, till a turning interrupted the sight of her, which was three-quarters after one in the afternoon.'

This is the sort of writing, designed in this case to convince rather than to beguile, which led Sir Leslie Stephen to deny that Defoe's later stories (apart from *Crusoe*) 'can fairly claim any higher interest than that which belongs to the ordinary police report, given with infinite fullness and variety of detail.' The account of Mrs. Veal's apparition *is* a report, though not a police-report; and the reporter's talent is certainly an ingredient, but certainly not the only one, of the novelist's maturer power. The very circumstance that Defoe's heroes and heroines, for reasons at which we have already glanced, present their own stories, and in so doing come alive in their own right, marks out Moll Flanders and Captain Singleton and the rest from the snapshot of Mrs. Veal and Mrs. Bargrave. Defoe's fiction transcends the fact which it imitates.

A very much bulkier curiosity than *Mrs. Veal* had appeared among Defoe's publications of the previous year, sandwiched between tracts both direct and ironic concerning the liberty of conscience and the quarrels of the sects. This was *The Consolidator; or Memoirs of Sundry Transactions from the World in the Moon. Translated from the Lunar Language. By the Author of the True-Born Englishman.* It was published (like *Mrs. Veal*) by the bookseller Bragg, on 26 March 1705, with a second and enlarged edition in November. *The Consolidator* is in the vein of satirical allegory which Swift made his own. Swift's *Tale of a Tub* had appeared in the previous year (after lying for several years in manuscript) and Defoe took something from it. In his turn Swift took something from *The Consolidator* when he came to write *Gulliver*; but the degree of such exchanges is arguable. In any comparison in this style of writing Defoe comes off second best, but although a good deal of *The Consolidator* has more bark than bite it is still interesting to those who enjoy their history; and it also casts a reflected light upon the personal history of its author, his relation to the politics of his time, and his views on some of his contemporaries, including fellow-authors. The ever-present issue of Dissent is transferred to the lunar world in the thinnest of disguises; and here is the philosopher (for whom we need not look far) counselling the Crolians (Dissenters) on their dealings with the High-Church Solunarians:

'He had been but scurvily treated by them in his troubles, and so universally abandoned by the Crolians, that even the Solunarians themselves insulted them on that head, and laughed at them for expecting anybody should venture for them again. But he, forgetting their unkindness, asked him what it was they desired of him.

'They told him they had heard that he had reported he could put the Crolians in a way to secure themselves from any possibility of being insulted again by the Solunarians, and yet not disturb the public tranquility nor break the laws; and they desired him, if he knew such a secret, he would communicate it to them, and they would be sure to remember to forget him for it as long as he lived.

'He frankly told them he had said so, and it was true he could put them in a way to do all this, if they would follow his directions. "What's that?" says one of the most earnest inquirers. "It is included in one word," says he—"Unite." '

If we are to follow the philosopher of *The Consolidator*, what Defoe meant when he urged the Dissenters to unite was that they should use the commercial power they possessed to put themselves in a superior position by setting up their own banks, monopolising the trade and reducing their opponents to beggary. Perhaps the suggestion, which in any case fell on deaf ears, was not seriously meant. There was a typical devilry in it, nonetheless; and in the same spirit he proceeded to expose various contemporary devices for getting rich at other people's expense, including stock-jobbery, 'paper societies, linen societies, sulphur societies, copper societies, glass societies, sham banks, and a thousand mock projects to hook unwary people in.' It only remains to add that the Consolidator itself was conceived as a machine made of feathers for flying to the moon where these events took place, and in the allegory it represents the House of Commons.

One more considerable publication of Queen Anne's reign shows the strange polygrapher (as Saintsbury called Defoe) in yet another guise, as author of a long politico-philosophical poem. *Jure Divino* refutes in twelve books the doctrine of the Divine Right of Kings sustained by the Jacobites, but it also draws the positive picture of a good sovereign derived from the writings of Locke as well as from Defoe's admiration of William III. Professor Sutherland looks forward in this connection to Bolingbroke's *Idea of a Patriot King*, written in 1738 but not published until 1749 when Jacobitism was no more; and Trevelyan finds in the *Patriot King* many of the ideas of Robert Harley. Defoe's enormous verse-project had been begun in prison. It was announced when he left Newgate in November 1704, and sub-scriptions were invited, a course which brought the author into conflict with the booksellers and gave hostile pamphleteers the opportunity of doubting whether the subscriptions would ever be honoured. It duly appeared for the subscribers on 20 July 1706, and on the same day an incomplete, defective, and cheaper edition was on sale in the streets, the booksellers (Bragg among them) having got their own back on him by piracy and a conniving printer. Literary piracy, as much practised as attacked (and sometimes by the same individuals), was in its dishonest way a sort of tribute. There was a public for Defoe's poem, and what is more, a popular public; for a subsequent act of piracy produced *Jure Divino* in chap-book form for the pedlars' packs, in single half-sheets at a halfpenny each with another six-pence for stitching the parts together when completed.

The symbol of Defoe's popular renown was still the pillory, if we are to judge by the cover of the chap-book edition, a naive but telling woodcut in which he appears in that engine wearing his own hair and with the mole on his lower left cheek clearly shown. There is much less charm, and how much likeness we cannot say, in the richly bewigged portrait (again not omitting the mole) which Defoe prefixed to his own edition of *Jure Divino*, an engraving by Van der Gucht after an unknown painting by Taverner. For once he was giving himself full and proud publicity, with his name, 'Daniel De Foe, Author of the *True-born Englishman*,' and the coat of arms which he had succeeded in legally acquiring. When he was released from prison two or three years earlier he had published an *Elegy on the Author of the True-Born Englishman* in which he suggested that his mouth had been stopped, at any rate from political expression.

> To seven long years of silence I betake,
> Perhaps by then I may forget to speak.

Whatever this may have meant, and there have been some odd interpretations put upon it, he certainly kept no kind of silence save that of anonymity. And the ambitious, if uneven *Jure Divino*, an important work in its time, dropped even that thin disguise, though he had been warned that it might get him into fresh trouble with the Highfliers. A second volume of his collected (or rather selected) writings, running to some five hundred octavo pages, had appeared in 1705; and each year there was a bound volume of the *Review*, of which he was well known to be the author. Here he is, no longer the civet-cat merchant nor the dislocated hosier, but a new sort of viper to his enemies, replying in his *Review* to the charge of being a mercenary writer:

'Oh! but 'tis a scandalous employment, to write for bread! The worse for him, gentlemen, that he should take so much pains for bread, run so many risks, make himself so many enemies, many hazards, flouts, banters and scurrilous treatment for bread, and not get it neither. . . . But, after all, suppose you say true, that all I do is for bread, which I assure you is very false, and what are all employments in the world pursued for, but for bread? What do you sell, run, fetch, carry, stoop, cringe, build, pull down, turn, and return, what is it all but for bread? And what do you sail, travel, fight, nay, without offence, what preach for? Is it not bread? I hope there are other ends joined in the sacred office, or else I should break in upon my charity, but that office would be thinly supplied if bread were not annext to it.'

*   *   *

Much praised and little known, Defoe's *Review* has never enjoyed the re-editing as a classic that has fallen to its famous successors, the *Tatler* and the *Spectator*. There is indeed no absolutely complete run of the journal in existence, but there are five relatively so, the best in the British Museum and the others in America; and from these five, in 1938, an entire fascimile edition was at last produced at the Columbia University Press. The index to this, completed in 1948 by Professor W. L. Payne, is in itself a catalogue of the topics, serious and less so, of the reign of Queen Anne. The *Review* was a commentary rather than what we should now call a newspaper, a journal of opinion through which the turns of history can be descried; and one has some sympathy when 'The Author,' as he justly styles himself, being at the time in Scotland, tells his readers that 'it cannot be but that sometimes his conjecture of things will be a little out of time, and ought to be taken as the state of affairs were when he wrote it.' One such conjecture was shown up by the wonderful victory of Ramillies, for which neither Defoe nor anyone else was prepared. He atoned for it with a poem of a hundred lines or so in commemoration of the battle—written, he told his public, in three hours.

The coffee-house public and the subscribers in the provinces no doubt condoned lapses in news-gathering so long as the editorial grip and quality were maintained. Coffee-house distribution considerably enhanced the influence of such a paper as the *Review*, which seems never to have had a large circulation and yet was known even among common and unread folk to whom its contents were transmitted by gossip. London had already a very large number of coffee-houses, among them the first of the clubs, when Defoe launched his project in 1704; and 'what attracts enormously in these coffee-houses,' wrote a Swiss visitor about twenty years later, 'are the gazettes and other public papers. All Englishmen are great newsmongers.'[1] The half-century in which the coffee-house habit had taken hold had marked also the real beginning of newspapers.

If we are to recognize a single predecessor for Defoe in this field, the Cavalier journalist Sir Roger L'Estrange, industrious and controversial, best fits the part: even to such correspondences as persecution and imprisonment, the brief satisfaction of royal patronage, and some enduring excursions into literature, in L'Estrange's case through translation.[2] The political paper of the extreme Right which L'Estrange kept going in the last years of

---

[1] César de Saussure, quoted in *The Visitors' Book* (Ballam & Lewis).

[2] Defoe used his version of an Aesop fable to introduce *The Shortest Way with the Dissenters*.

Charles II's reign and then under James II through the year of the Monmouth Rebellion and the Bloody Assize, was called the *Observator*. Defoe may often have seen it in his first merchant-days, but when he emerged from prison it was a different *Observator*, that of John Tutchin (himself a victim of Jeffreys and the Assize) which was running successfully. This extreme Whig organ, which came out twice a week, had borrowed from its Tory forebear not only the title but the rather awkward form of a constantly renewed dialogue between *Observator* and *Countryman*. On the High Tory side was Charles Leslie's *Rehearsal*, which did not last long but provided Defoe with another vitriolic opponent and, as it were, a second steering-point for his own course of moderation and centre-party government. There were several other papers appearing two or three times a week, including the semi-official *London Gazette*, the *Flying Post*, the *Post Boy*, and the *Post Man*; and there was already one daily paper, the *Daily Courant*. The exchange of abuse between most of these was doubtless the accepted form of exercise for preventing sluggishness and maintaining circulation. The very fact that lines of purely party divergence were still far from clear seemed to sharpen the personal animosities of politics. In the midst of the flailing fists stood the author of the *Review*, never backward in castigation of his enemies but by his own protestation 'a sincere lover of the constitution of my country; zealous for liberty and the Protestant interest; but a constant follower of moderate principles, a vigorous opposer of hot measures in all parties.'

That is from the remarkable *Appeal to Honour and Justice* of 1715—remarkable because even now, when some of Defoe's statements in his own defence have been shown to be highly questionable, it is difficult not to call it, at first reading, a noble document. The *Appeal to Honour and Justice, Though it be of his Worst Enemies,* carries out the intention of the title, as well as its verbal felicity, from first to last. In a sense it reads like the appeal to posterity of the Defoe of these years, for he presents himself as ill and tired and with a premonition of death: 'very near to the great ocean of eternity, and the time may not be long ere I embark on the last voyage.' It seems almost a pity that posterity should have evidence of certain things that Defoe was intent on glossing over, in regard both to the *Review* and other journalistic work: the fact that he *was* subsidized, for instance, and the fact that he did sometimes consult Harley on specific points before making his comments. Defoe was advocate in his own cause, feeling himself ill-used and well aware of his own forensic persuasiveness. If there are evasions and downright untruths that time has exposed, the *Appeal to Honour and Justice* fascinates, nevertheless, by some of the same qualities as made the *Review* outstanding among the journals of his day. If bad luck and spiteful treatment (for he had had plenty of both) had brought out the casuist in the Puritan, it had not revealed a misanthrope or a coward. It might be said, indeed, that appreciation of Defoe's spirit and adroitness as a writer gains what an excessive moral reverence loses when the *Appeal* is closely examined.

There is still scope for an unwritten thesis on Defoe's temperamental relish and faculty for debate. His brilliance in argument—at its best it is that—rests largely on his uncommon ability to talk from all points of the compass: to present the views of his opponents, before demolishing them, more cogently than they could do themselves. His fictional characters are for ever weighing up their conduct in a manner which only this curious gift of the author preserves from tedium. Often they reach a point in such deliberations where the reader is well satisfied that the course resolved upon is sensible and even virtuous, only to inform him that this was the subtle prompting of the devil to a vicious character. Crusoe communes with himself and with God; Roxana exhausts every attitude in consulting with her faithful maid Amy whether or not to go to bed with her protector; Singleton and the Quaker William closely debate the propriety of retaining the profits of piracy. Defoe and his Protestant conscience must, one feels, have had many similar bouts. With such variety in attack, it may be that he won them all—but often, against such a conscience, only in the last round.

But we must have some facts. The first number of the *Review* was dated 19 February 1704, little more than three months after Defoe's release from Newgate. Ostensibly independent, its reflection of the views of Harley and Godolphin was not difficult to recognize, and when Harley became First Secretary on the fall of Nottingham Defoe was an important supporter of this moderate Government. The *Review* began as a penny weekly of eight quarto pages. With the fifth number it changed to four pages in smaller type; after the seventh it was issued twice a week; and after the eighth, except for one short period, there were three issues weekly for more than nine years. At first sight one of the oddest things about the new publication was its title: *A Review of the Affairs of France, Purged from the Errors and Partiality of News-Writers and Petty Statesmen of all Sides.*

Why the affairs of France? Because, replied Defoe, the affairs of France are those of all Europe. He wished to concentrate attention on 'the powers of the French money, the artifice of their conduct, the terror of their

arms' as something that Englishmen must study, understand and resist. England and her allies were at war with
the France of Louis XIV, and for Defoe it was a service
of patriotism to produce a commentary on French
affairs, to relate the affairs of England, or Poland, or
Sweden, to the dominating fact of French expansionist
policy. It was also a twist that offered occasion for
paradox, irony, and that startling presentation of events
which suited his talents. At times his paper was frankly
educating its readers in the elements of French strength.
At others the same approach was used to expose a weakness
or a fault, as in his little essay on 'the wonderful benefit
of arbitrary power' to the régime that had abandoned
religious toleration and governed without appeal to the
people. 'If any man ask me what are the benefits of
arbitrary power to the subject,' he concluded, after
describing the absolute monarch's advantages, 'I answer
these two, poverty and subjection.' It was in such
generalizations from the particular that Defoe engaged
English readers for 'the affairs of France,' as well as with
his remarks on the war itself. In volume two, however,
(the series was collected annually), the title was extended
'with some Observations on Transactions at Home,' and
volume three was called decisively *A Review of the State
of the English Nation*. With the twelfth number of volume
four this became, most significantly, the *British* nation:
the Act of Union having just been passed, Defoe was as
active in publicizing it by the use of the new terms as he
had been in preparing the way for it. A hint as to the
widespread influence of the *Review* (its numerical
circulation is not certainly known) is provided by the
appearance in the sixth year of a special edition printed
in Edinburgh for Scotland, the North of England and
Ireland—mainly, but not entirely, a reprint of the

London numbers. On more than one occasion during the earlier stages of the *Review* the 'last' issue was regretfully announced. But there were always 'some gentlemen' or 'charitable persons' who would not let it die.

Critics have given much attention to a feature of the paper which for us today is probably the least readable. This was its fourth page, headed *Mercure Scandale, or Advice from the Scandalous Club, being a weekly history of Nonsense, Impertinence, Vice and Debauchery*—a magazine-section which in the second year became a *Supplementary Journal* and finally was separated altogether into the popular *Little Review*. Its reputation is really due to the improvements on Defoe's idea that came from other hands, notably from Steele, who had the official appointment of editor of the *Gazette* when Defoe's paper first appeared on the coffee-house tables. The medley of gossip, anecdote, *personalia*, scandal and reproof was in some degree the jam with the *Review's* political medicine. Steele saw that the public had a taste for jam and began, in the *Tatler*, to mix it with his individual and skilful hand.

Not that Defoe's hand was as heavy with this sort of thing as one might have expected from a Dissenter. He accepted (or invented) questions and correspondence, now and then over a feminine signature. And in the latter stages of his miscellany he exploited the appetite for odd enquiries and replies which had made such a success, in the first days of his journalism, of Dunton's *Athenian Gazette*. Dunton had since followed up the *Gazette* with a *Monthly Oracle* of a like nature, and this was evidently put out of business by Defoe's quicker turnover. 'It is strange,' wrote the good-natured Dunton in his *Whipping-Post*, 'that such a first-rate author as Daniel De

Foe should be so barren of new projects that he must
needs interlope with mine.' This first-rate author, who
put his hand to almost every current form of writing
before inventing his own, had no misgivings about entering the market for *facetiae*. The topical fun of his
Scandalous Club may have evaporated, but taking the
Review as a whole it is still remarkable that Defoe, being
what he was, could be as entertaining as he was. The
influence on society which he hoped to exert in the rôle
of a Juvenal was inevitably limited, as compared with that
of Steele, by the taint of a Puritan origin. But he was
manifestly not the stock Puritan, looking down a long
nose at all levity. From even the best of his novels to
those of Fielding, with their Hogarthian sense of the
comic, there is doubtless a step to be taken. Nevertheless, Defoe has salt as well as substance. Not all the
lighter side of his great journalistic venture has withered.
Coleridge thought that he could 'select from Defoe's
writings a volume equal in size to Addison's collected
papers, little inferior in wit and humour, and greatly
superior in vigour of style and thought.'

Matters of trade, and Defoe's opinions thereon, have
probably sent more students back to the *Review* (and too
few at that) than either its politics or its chit-chat.
Since economics might be said by now to have replaced
theology as a field of controversy, there is a partisan
colour about some of the reassessments of Defoe's
economic views. It can at least be shown that within the
framework of the mercantile system of his age he saw
endless scope for improvements; and his own country
he thought so well placed for prosperity under liberal
and orderly government, 'that if ever this nation were
shipwrecked and undone, it must be at the very entry
of her port of deliverance.' His politics and his economics

hang pretty well together, and in the *Appeal to Honour and Justice* he was eager to refute charges of inconstancy in both. At the end of the war, when the *Review* had ceased publication, he supported in the *Mercator* Bolingbroke's plans for encouraging trade with France. He had said much the same thing after Blenheim, with the precaution of advocating a tariff policy manipulated to Britain's advantage. 'It was not thought criminal to say so then,' he reminded his Whig accusers. 'How it come to be villainous to say so now, God knows; I can give no account of it.'

He stuck to his long-cherished proposal that Britain should succeed to the waning power of Spain in the West Indies, and he wrote a whole series of articles in the *Review* on trade to Africa. He welcomed—not only as a lover of liberty but as a calculator of his country's good—the refugees from political or religious persecution on the Continent. 'Every labouring man,' he believed, 'however poor, increases the public wealth;' and he proposed the establishment in the New Forest of colonies of subsistence villages for the peasants and craftsmen of the Palatinate who had fled from Louis XIV's troops. In the financial aspects of commerce he continued to keep a wary eye upon stockjobbers and bubble-projects—he prophesied, in the same year as he wrote *Robinson Crusoe*, the tremendous French crash which followed the operations of John Law; and he urged restriction of credit to avoid the dislocation caused by local or seasonal over-production.

More important than any single theory or attitude is Defoe's broad recognition of the part that trade must play in the destinies of his country, and his realistic eagerness to get at the facts of the matter. 'I am a professed opposer,' he was to write in his *Plan of the*

English Commerce, 'of all fortuitous calculations, making estimates by guess-work.' He poured scorn on those who hazarded hypotheses without statistical evidence. In a memorable phrase in the first year of the *Review* he set forth his passionate design to penetrate 'the dark gulph of general negoce, this hidden mystery, this half-known thing called trade.' More than seventy years before Adam Smith, Defoe chose the same pre-eminent subject of investigation:

'The power of nations is not now measured as it has been, by prowess, gallantry and conduct. 'Tis the wealth of nations that makes them great.'

One of the subjects on which he did *not* prophesy correctly was the future of the American colonies. He went wrong because he expected mutually advantageous trading arrangements in which the settlements would find their own interest perpetually bound up with that of Britain. It was the converse of his proposition that worked itself out. And perhaps one of the reasons why Defoe is today so thoroughly studied in American universities may be read in the phrasing of this argument. Here is a passage from the *Review* of 1704, fifty-six years before Burke's famous speeches in the House of Commons:

'If they die, we decay; if we decay, they die; if we cannot support them, they fall; if they fall, we must in proportion sink. . . . To fear to make our Colonies too great is as if a father, in the educating his child, should fear to make him too wise, or to give him too much learning; or in feeding him, should be afraid of making him too strong, or too tall, or too beautiful; for the Plantations being our own children, the offspring of the Commonwealth, they cannot, politically speaking, have too much care taken of them, or be too much tender'd by us.'

In the first year of the *Review*, towards the end of 1704, Defoe enlarged in one of his many pamphlets some of the ideas on trade, industry, and employment which make his paper so much more interesting than its contemporaries. The pamphlet was (to shorten its elaborate title) *Giving Alms no Charity*. It was occasioned by a Bill to prevent unemployment, introduced in the House of Commons by Sir Humphrey Mackworth, one of the earliest industrialists who had been a founder at the same time (1698) of the Corporation of the Mine Adventurers of England and of the Society for Promoting Christian Knowledge. Mackworth's Bill, which survived the Commons but met its death in the Lords, proposed to set up in every parish factories supported by public funds and provided with raw materials. Defoe's criticisms of this method of relieving poverty (he repeated them years later in the *Compleat English Tradesman*) were those of an experienced manufacturer as well as a market-observer. Intelligent planning of output and distribution by employers, and honest industry from workmen, were all that was needed (he held) to absorb the unemployed and raise the material status of the poor; and he had plenty of fault to find with both management and labour. To establish parish industries, he argued, would tend to promote self-sufficient local units and thus endanger the whole movement of trade. The tract has that flavour which generations of changing economic thought have each found 'modern,' and it is highly readable when we have all but forgotten Sir Humphrey Mackworth and his ideas. Trade, 'the whore he doated

L

upon,' had for Defoe so deep and constant a fascination
that when he wrote upon it, even repetitiously, he could
hardly ever be dull. We see the coaling vessels straining
through the gales off East Anglia; we see the woman of
Berwick-on-Tweed described in the *Compleat English
Tradesman*, her items of clothing representing a circulation of trade throughout the country and beyond it; we
hear the musket-shot from Gravesend that warns the
merchantmen to heave to for the visit of the customs;
we attend the provincial fairs and markets pictured in
the *Tour*, and watch the vast flocks of geese and turkeys
being driven up from Norfolk on the London road.
'This half-known thing called trade' comes alive.

*   *   *

It may be that Defoe was never happier than when he
took to the road himself. If we had anywhere a statue
of him, which we have not, it ought to be an equestrian
figure. He loved horses, horse-fairs, and horse-races: at
Epsom he delighted in 'the racers flying over the course,
as if they either touch'd not, or felt not the ground they
run upon; I think no sight, except that of a victorious
army, under the command of a Protestant King of Great
Britain, could exceed it.' He had a keen eye for a horse's
quality, and for a groom's quality as well. When he
praised the breeding in North Yorkshire and Durham he
added a considered explanation of his judgment that
those parts produced 'gallopers that will outdo for speed
and strength the swiftest horse that was ever bred in
Turkey, or Barbary, take them both together.' Now and
then he may have made a long journey in a wheeled
vehicle, but he lived before the real coaching age, in an
England where even a good horseman was well advised
to avoid the roads in winter, and where a town like

Liverpool was almost unknown except to travellers by sea (Defoe was carried ashore from the Mersey ferry, most uncomfortably, on the back of a countryman). The reader of the *Tour through Great Britain*, published twenty years after the political travels on which it was partly based, finds no clue to the 'we' whose routes in wild or settled country are described. Often Defoe rode alone, sometimes with a companion— his friend Christopher Hart on one journey, his brother-in-law Robert Davis on another: but these are dim figures, not easy to bring to life from scattered references in Defoe's letters. His own presence is vivid enough on these journeys during the first busy years after his release from Newgate. In each town he had contacts, meetings, plenty to do and see and talk about, messages waiting for him, his own and Harley's business to be done. In Coventry he found electoral corruption and a High Tory majority; in the newly incorporated industrial towns of the north (the term can be used as early as this) there was as yet neither parliamentary representation nor political passion; in Exeter or in Bath (which he did not like) there was the coffee-house life in which 'Mr. Review' was well qualified to engage; in the West Midland towns there were strong Dissenting interests ripe for political education. In the first months of the *Review's* circulation Defoe was evidently not so well known in the provinces as to be unable to travel *incognito*. Here and there his enemies detected him and made trouble, but it was with the agreed pseudonym of Alexander Goldsmith that he made out his confidential reports for Harley.

In two tours, in 1704 and 1705, Harley's agent covered more than a thousand miles on missions which the new Secretary of State considered just as important as the production of the *Review*. Defoe sounded out opinion for him, providing him with information which no Minister had previously had at his disposal, and probably few had sought. At the same time he forwarded the Government's policy wherever it could be done by discreetly turned propaganda. There are grounds for believing that it was Defoe himself who had put into Harley's receptive mind the idea of a secret intelligence service reporting on the disposition of the people. And in political manoeuvre Defoe's sagacity can be illustrated by his advice to Harley, in November 1704, to arrange unobtrusively for the notorious Bill against Occasional Conformity to be brought in again at that juncture. Whether Harley in fact followed this hint has not been established, but it was a shrewd one. The Bill, at any rate, *was* revived by the High Church party, it was imprudently 'tacked' to a financial measure, defeated by an increased majority with a hue and cry after the tackers and so cast back (at least for a time) upon the heads of its promoters. Had Defoe's prompting of Harley in this sense been known among his fellow-Dissenters they would have been more than ever suspicious of him. Throughout Queen Anne's reign, in dozens of tracts and controversies, he continued to busy himself, enrage his opponents and perplex posterity with his treatment of the issues of Dissent. Yet on the face of it his double allegiance is comprehensible and indeed honourable. The form of faith and worship in which he had been brought up was something on which he declined to compromise; but *political* Dissenters might beware of his pen, for he was no less staunch in his loyalty to the Revolution Settlement. That Settlement had secured constitutional primacy to the Anglican Church, with toleration for the sects that had challenged it. The battle of toleration had to be fought over and over again, but Defoe intended to fight it within the constitution.

The stone that was still wanting in that constitutional edifice was the Union of the Scottish and English Parliaments. Defoe's hero William of Orange had dreamed of it, and Anne and her Ministers recognized that the Union and the Protestant succession were as important to the realm as Marlborough's victories over the Bourbon patron of the Pretender. Harley, having tried out Defoe in the business of secret agent at large, decided in the summer of 1706 to send him north on an errand as congenial as it was momentous. Defoe was very much dependent upon Harley at this time and would scarcely have refused such an assignment; but it is equally certain that his heart and mind were with the Union that was then in the vital stages of negotiation. He waited with some impatience for his marching orders, while Harley made his own arrangements to ensure that Defoe himself should be kept under secret observation. He also had the sense to secure for his envoy the honour of an interview with the Queen. 'In less than half a year,' Defoe wrote, he had 'tasted the difference between the closet of a King and the Dungeon of Newgate;' and here he was, two years later, in a royal presence again. On 13 September he took the long road for Edinburgh.

He went to Scotland as Daniel Defoe, 'on your own business and out of love to the country' said Harley distinctly in his instructions. His own business involved him in a variety of rôles, and to conceal his real mission he had sometimes to conceal his identity, sometimes to be as obviously Defoe as possible. At different times and places in his Scottish sojourn he showed interest in a salt-mine, a glass-factory, a fishery and a linen-factory— the last of these he did in fact acquire and run on his own account, so that he was able when the time came to offer tablecloths worked with the arms that symbolized Union. He also employed the disguise (thin indeed) of a fugitive from rapacious London creditors; and it is worth bearing in mind this almost boyishly energetic adoption of one character after another or several at the same time; for this was the man who was to write himself into the clothes of a castaway, a gentleman of fortune, a pirate and explorer, a dozen sturdy opportunists of either sex.[1] It was, in truth, as a business-man that he could best influence the Scots, dissecting and correcting their prejudices, for the most visible Scottish gain from a United Kingdom would be in improved trading opportunities. While the Edinburgh mob stormed the streets, breaking windows, crying 'No Union!', assaulting southrons and only just failing to get their hands on Defoe himself, his job was persuasion by means straight or devious. Daniel Defoe, merchant and market expert, could translate Union into terms of 'general negoce.' Daniel Defoe, Dissenter, was equally well equipped to urge upon the Presbyterians that the Kirk stood in no danger. And Daniel Defoe, writer and editor of the *Review*, would find plenty of attacks on the Union to answer (and some to suppress quietly at the printer's). Harley's secret correspondent, in the meantime, remained secret.

We have space only for Daniel Defoe the writer. His *Essay at Removing National Prejudices against a Union with Scotland* was a serial affair, Part I appearing anonymously in London in May 1706, four months before the author transferred himself to Scotland. Further parts were

---

[1] 'Moll Flanders, Captain Singleton, Colonel Jacque and the rest are Defoe in masquerade; Robinson Crusoe is Defoe in the part that came most natural to him, the part that he would have sustained with entire credit.'—Ernest Baker: *History of the English Novel*, Vol. III.

thereafter printed in Edinburgh, where the argument naturally took the form of 'removing national prejudices against a Union with *England*.' Thus it proceeded, interpolating replies to objectors, up to a sixth Essay in January 1707, the month in which the Union of the Parliaments was ratified. Pamphlets and some satirical verse had kept the fight going in favour of Defoe's purposes, and in that first month of 1707 there was printed in London a subscription edition of *Caledonia*, a poem of about a thousand lines (and many pages of notes) already issued in Edinburgh 'in honour of Scotland and the Scots nation.' The letters to Harley (*Portland MSS*) apprise us of these and other literary activities of the indefatigable agent, and throw more than a little doubt on the sincerity of the verses with which he honoured the Scots nation. 'Proud and barbarous,' 'a fermented and implacable nation,' 'a terrible people,' are the words he uses to Harley, possibly to leave no doubt that his task was formidable. But with *Caledonia*, he tells him when composing it, 'my end will be answered. . . . All conduces to persuade them I am a friend to their country.' There have been worse motives, before and since Defoe, for the panegyric manner. He did make a mark in Scotland, both for himself and for his country; and to the literary historian *Caledonia* is a rarity in English letters of the time—rare in the first place because it deals with Scotland, in the second place because it does so favourably.

Ecclesiastical affairs in Scotland engaged Defoe's particular study, partly from his own bent and partly from their relevance to the political issue of Union. His accounts of the persecution of Episcopalians by the Presbyterian Church, whether accurate or not, were

freely copied by later writers, and many of his subsequent pamphlets on Protestantism, Dissent, and toleration took the wider view justified by the Union of the
two countries. That Union, for long after the Queen's
assent in March, 1707, required to be explained and
defended, and Defoe did both—on one occasion in reply
to an attack by Swift.[1] There were also, of course,
articles on the Union in the *Review*, whose London
printers received their material regularly even when
Defoe was touring Scotland; and there was the traveller's
information that he gathered in the Lowland towns (and
even, adventurously, the Highland fringes) for the later
Tour through Great Britain. But the most solid and
distinguished production of his Scottish mission was the
History of the Union, published in Edinburgh in 1709 and
in London two years later. It is still valuable.

There remain the letters to Harley, never collected
with Defoe's works but much studied by biographers
and historians since their publication by the Historical
Manuscripts Commission revealed the importance of the
relationship between the two men. Here is an extract
from a Defoe dispatch dated 10 March, 1707, the day
on which the news of the royal assent reached Edinburgh:

'I have now I hope the satisfaction of seeing the fruit
of all this mischief, the effect of all the labouring,
fighting, mobbings *etc. viz.* Union; and while I write
this the guns are firing from the Castle and my man
brings me up the Queen's speech. Methinks *Nunc
Dimittis* comes now into my head, and in writing to you
I should say:—Now let me depart from hence for my
eyes have seen the conclusion. I confess I believe I might
be serviceable here a long time yet. But everybody

[1] *The Scots Nation and Union Vindicated from the Reflections cast on them in an
infamous Libel entitled The Public Spirit of the Whigs.* (1714)

is gone up to solicit their own fortunes, and some
to be rewarded for what I have done—while I depending
on your concern for me and her Majesty's goodness am
wholly unsolicitous in that affair.'

The last sentence is a figure of speech. What Defoe
really wanted was a secure Government office—like
that of Commissioner for the Glass Duty which he had
held for a time in the previous reign—in place of the
secret 'supplies' which Harley sent him so very ir-
regularly. In a voice that speaks to us of the rising middle
classes he had told Harley of his hopes of such a place and
of training his sons to succeed him. Men have received
much higher honours than that for doing considerably
less. Defoe had 'faithfully served,' as he pointed out
after six months had gone by with nothing more from
Harley than a hint that he should apply to Godolphin
at the Treasury if he thought any payment was due to
him. 'I baulked no cases,' went on Defoe, 'I appeared
in print when others dared not open their mouths,
and without boasting I ran as much risk of my life as
a grenadier storming a counter-scarp.' He repeated the
phrase when he came to make his *Appeal to Honour and
Justice.*

It was not till November, when the first combined
Parliament with its forty-five Scottish members was
meeting at Westminster, that a letter arrived for Defoe
in Edinburgh with a remittance of £100. In the winter
mud and darkness he rode slowly to London and the
family from whom he had been absent for more than a
year. Harley's personal preoccupations, though they
scarcely excuse the hardship and anxiety caused to the
Ministry's confidential servant, had certainly been
severe. With his underground intrigues towards a new

Government the conflict between the developing Party system and Queen Anne's inborn appetite for personal authority was coming to a head. The first victim of the crisis, despite all that the Queen could do to save him, was Harley himself. The full and fascinating story of his fall must be read elsewhere, but its immediate cause was something that Defoe had warned him about—carelessness with State papers. The Minister so prone to clandestine activity allowed a negligence in the despatching-room of which an underpaid clerk took treasonable advantage. The culprit was executed at Tyburn, fully exonerating his master, who struggled for some weeks but at length had to resign. Godolphin and Marlborough, against whom Harley had been intriguing, survived for the time on the great Duke's immense prestige. The Ministry was not upset, and it was Harley himself who urged Defoe to continue in the Queen's business by applying to Godolphin. It should be said to Defoe's credit that he first offered himself to the fallen Minister 'to be the servant of your worst days.'

*   *   *

In February 1709, the transfer having been effected, Defoe again kissed the Queen's hand as one for whom Godolphin had State employment. The famous *Appeal to Honour and Justice* came out in 1715 after the death of Queen Anne. In those six years moderation had dropped out of the political vocabulary. The self-assertion of Parliament against the royal (and Stuart) principle of supra-political control nourished extremism in party politics, and the middle-way men had to choose sides or go under. It was more than a coincidence that those six years should also produce the opprobrium of hireling and turncoat against which Defoe published his defence (though he begins his apologia with the earliest years of his public life). Defoe served both Tories and Whigs in succession. It would have been far better for his final reputation if he had avoided the temptation to refute the hostile personal charges in detail, and had confided himself to his very best observation that 'in such turns of tempers and times, a man must be tenfold a vicar of Bray, or it is impossible but he must one time or other be out with everybody;' or, as he wrote in the *Review* in a mood of desperation in September 1712, 'all is a mere show, outside, and abominable hypocrisy, of every part, in every age, under every government, in every turn of government; when they are OUT to get IN, when IN, to prevent being OUT.'

Robert Harley was out, but not for long. The fall of the patient, cautious, greatly experienced Godolphin was the next story, and Defoe's old enemy Dr. Sacheverell had a notable part in it. The celebrated sermon for which the Highflier was impeached, the new raising of 'the bloody flag of defiance' against Whigs, Dissenters, moderates, the Godolphin Ministry, and the Revolution Settlement itself, was preached in 1709 on 5 November: a date sanctified for the Whigs as the anniversary both of the arrest of Guy Fawkes and the landing of William of Orange, to whose memory Defoe's *Review* for that day carried one more tribute. Godolphin accepted the preacher's intemperate challenge and the Whig majority in the House of Commons supported him. But the trial, in February 1710, caused tremendous excitement not only in London but throughout the provinces. Forty thousand copies of the offending sermon were sold; and Samuel Johnson's father, the Lichfield bookseller, declared that in all his experience only Dryden's *Absolom and Achitophel* had caused such a stir. Defoe began by making fun of Sacheverell and his thunders, both in the *Review* and by pamphlet,[1] but he made it clear that the principle of constitutional toleration had been attacked and that he supported Godolphin in bringing the matter to trial. The majority that finally voted Sacheverell guilty was a narrow one, the sentence comparatively trifling, and the victory hollow. The bloody flag had roused the Tories, alarmed the Whigs and would soon wave over the ruins of centre-party government. For Sacheverell, as it turned out, had two allies beyond his own faction. One was the fickle London mob, that had cheered Defoe in his own quite opposite defiance but now returned to its former recreation of burning Dissenters' meeting-houses. The other was Queen Anne herself. In the summer of 1710 she felt strong enough to dismiss Godolphin, break altogether with the Duchess of Marlborough, and bring Harley back into office as Chancellor of the Exchequer.

It is in no way surprising that Defoe should already have resumed contact with Harley, and that he should now be prepared to support him again. But Harley's return, as it awkwardly turned out, was to a Ministry almost entirely weeded of Whigs; and in the elections that followed in October the predominantly Whig House of Commons was transformed into a Tory majority decisive and therefore coloured by extremism. Defoe's old enemies the Highfliers were pushing Harley with them. It was the Whigs who were now to turn on Defoe, long suspected of double-dealing and at last caught in the wrong camp. The

---

[1] *Instructions from Rome in Favour of the Pretender : Inscribed to the most Elevated Don Sacheverillio and his Brother Don Higginsco. And which all Perkinites, Non-jurors, High-Flyers, Popish Desirers, Wooden-shoe Admirers, and Absolute-Non-Resistance Drivers, are obliged to pursue and maintain (Under Pain of his Unholinesses Damnation) in order to carry on their intended subversion of a Government fixed upon Revolution Principles.*

author of the *Review* made no secret of the difficulty he was in:

'If a man could be found that could sail north and south, that could speak truth and falsehood, that could turn to the right hand and the left, all at the same time, he would be the man, he would be the only proper person that could now speak.'

In these last years of the reign, with their confusion and bitterness, Defoe raised up those 'worst enemies' to whom he appealed a little too strongly for honour and justice after the Queen was dead. Both he and Harley, men of the middle way, had to seek means of survival in a situation in which (as Defoe wrote of the Succession issue) 'the strife is gotten into your kitchens, your parlours, your shops, your counting-houses, nay into your very beds.' Harley employed his characteristic resources—intrigue and delaying tactics—but with at last a failing touch. Escaping an attempted assassination, awarded an Earldom on his recovery, he was to lurch finally from office in the Queen's last week of life, irresolute and scarcely sober, and with an impeachment to face when the Whigs found their power with their Hanoverian King. Defoe, in these years when he might have been silent to his own advantage, touched afresh the heights of his gifts as a political writer—a point sometimes overlooked in the effort to decide whether his later defence was honest and justifiable.

The *Review*, after doing its best to sail north and south, came at length to its end in 1713, the year of the Peace of Utrecht. Defoe's attitude to the war with France was one of the bones of contention on which his opponents seized. Another, which shows how far the temper of the times and his own bent for manoeuvre could obscure his fixed beliefs, was his attitude to the Protestant Succession.

Fundamentally the war policy was a Whig policy—
only by spectacular achievements could Marlborough
appease the Tories. Defoe had always supported the war
against the 'exorbitant power' represented by Louis
XIV, even though it interrupted trade and inflicted
grievous losses on merchants and shipowners. The Grand
Alliance, after all, was the heir to William's policy of
collective security, of which Defoe was an open-eyed
partisan. He showed an optimism rare in these days
about the future of his country in rivalry with continental
absolutism; and there is a passage in the *Review* which
anticipates some kind of international system for the
preservation of peace and the redressing of injustice.
This was written in 1709, before Godolphin's removal,
when the military situation seemed to favour an advantageous peace and Defoe was prepared to support it if
it could be made by large minds:

'It is now in the power of the present Confederacy
for ever to prevent any more war in Europe. It is in
their power to make themselves arbiters of all the
differences and disputes that ever can happen in Europe,
whether between kingdom and kingdom, or between
sovereign and subjects. A congress of this alliance may
be made a Court of Appeals for all the injured and
oppressed, whether they are Princes or People that are
or ever shall be in Europe to the end of the world. Here
the petty States and Princes shall be protected against
the terror of their powerful neighbours, the great shall
no more oppress the small, or the mighty devour the
weak; this very Confederacy have at this time, and, if
they please, may preserve to themselves, the power of
banishing war out of Europe.'

Peace was made in 1713 by the Tory Ministry of Harley and Bolingbroke. The Whigs were bitter at what they saw as a betrayal of England's Dutch allies, though the Treaty of Utrecht did secure many of the things for which we had gone to war, and the Dutch had given Marlborough no end of trouble. Defoe, still struggling to keep the *Review* on a middle course, found something good and something bad in the terms of the negotiation, and concluded rather weakly that we must now see what could be got out of peaceful commerce with France. In support of the Ministry he had written in 1710 his *Essay Upon Publick Credit* and his *Essay upon Loans* (both attributed to Harley); and he almost certainly helped Harley in his plan for the organization of the South Sea Company, which he supported in a pamphlet of the following year.[1] In these and other ways he served the new Ministry with zeal and skill, and sometimes even with conviction; but the task of placating the Whigs so as to save Harley from the extreme Tories—which is what it amounted to—was beyond him or any man. The final passing into law of the notorious measure against Occasional Conformity, as a result of a cynical bargain in the Lords, showed the sort of climate to which Defoe was now adjusting himself.

Having ceased to take a belligerent interest in the Spanish Succession, Englishmen had awoken to the realization that Queen Anne was by no means immortal and that the British Succession was a vital matter. Harley cautiously, and Bolingbroke more dangerously, were flirting with the cause of the Pretender whose acknowledgment by the French monarch had long ago

---

[1] *An Essay on the South Sea Trade . . . By the Author of the Review.* Defoe, the scourge of stockjobbers, was always interested in new trading projects, and considered this one sound enough for an investment on his own account. He sold his shares at a profit before the bubble burst.

stung England into war. Rumours were flying, and Defoe
found himself tarred with the brush of Jacobitism—
Defoe who claimed to have been out with Monmouth,
who had kept green the memory of William of Orange,
who had lived and breathed the Protestant Succession
throughout his political life, and who, in his brief
service under Godolphin, had been sent on a second
mission to Scotland precisely to report on the alleged
dangers of Jacobite disturbance. One might as justly
have accused Dr. Sacheverell of hatching a Presbyterian
plot. But Defoe's enemies were by now ready to use
any pretext; and this one was presented to them by
Defoe himself, who returned imprudently to the ironical
vein which had got him into trouble ten years before
with *The Shortest Way with the Dissenters*.

Two pamphlets published towards the end of 1712
exhibited Defoe quite unequivocally (as did his writings
in the *Review*) as a friend of the House of Hanover and an
enemy of the Stuart Pretender. One was *A Seasonable
Warning and Caution against the Insinuations of Papists and
Jacobites in favour of the Pretender*, which was given out as
'a letter from an Englishman at the Court of Hanover'
(it has been suggested that Defoe did go to Hanover on
a mission from Harley, who was trying to prepare for
either possibility in the succession; but this is more
probably one of Defoe's many literary disguises). The
other was *Hannibal at the Gates: or the Progress of Jacobitism
and the Danger of the Pretender*. So far so good. But early
in the following year came three more pamphlets with
these titles:

*Reasons against the Succession of the House of Hanover, with
an Enquiry how far the Abdication of King James, supposing
it to be legal, ought to affect the Person of the Pretender.*

And what if the Pretender should come? or some Considerations of the Advantages and Real Consequences of the Pretender's possessing the Crown of Great Britain.

An Answer to a Question that nobody thinks of, viz. What if the Queen should die?

It would be quite impossible in normal times to misunderstand this sudden volley of pamphlets, each of more than forty octavo pages. And though Defoe's name did not appear with them, his hand was plainly recognizable. Who else could so adroitly have turned argument inside out, persuading the reader that after all liberty didn't matter so much, for the French got on very well without it; that a dose of arbitrary rule from a Popish prince sent over from France might have the healthy effect of an emetic upon our diseased body politic; that in any case George of Hanover would hardly be in a hurry to come to a country so torn by dissension and so eager to sacrifice all that it had fought for; that the City should welcome, on the other hand, a monarch who would put a strong guard upon the Bank (the whole kingdom being a garrison), and suffer none to plunder but himself; and that 'pamphleteers shall then not be whipped or pilloried, but hanged'? It is the first two of these tracts that sustain the irony in Defoe's most spirited manner: the third simply demands serious attention to the question which concludes every paragraph: 'But what if the Queen should die?' Had the Pretender followed her upon the throne it was reasonable prophecy that the pamphleteer *would* have been hanged. Yet it was the Whigs, the ardent Hanoverians, who now swooped on Defoe, raided the printing-house, secured proof of authorship, tricked him out of his house in Stoke Newington, got him arrested and brought to trial under the astounding charge of uttering 'treasonable libels against the *House of Hanover.*'

M

Basing the charge largely on the titles, and observing that if that were irony it was of a kind for which hanging, drawing and quartering were prescribed, the judges committed Defoe (who had unwisely commented on the case in the *Review*) to the Queen's Bench prison. He was released after a week, and eventually pardoned by the Queen.

The irony was to go deeper yet. Under a Tory Government Defoe had been falsely accused, on the instigation of influential Whigs, of a Jacobite libel. Two years later under a Whig Government he had to answer in the King's Bench Court, a charge of libellously imputing Jacobitism to a Tory peer (the Earl of Anglesey). Queen Anne was dead, George I was on the throne, the Jacobite Rebellon had just been defeated, the long reign of the Whigs had begun. Godolphin was in his grave, Bolingbroke and Harley (now the Earl of Oxford) had been impeached for high treason. Defoe had not a friend to turn to. What he did at this juncture has been variously interpreted since William Lee discovered and published the remarkable bundle of letters written by Defoe to Secretary of State Lord Stanhope in 1718. But it shows, on any reckoning, incredible, undefeatable strategy. Lord Anglesey's charge against him petered out. Somehow Defoe had got round Lord Chief Justice Parker and no sentence was ever passed. But how? Apparently by entering yet another secret compact, this time with the Whig Ministry, a compact more tortuous than anything which his association with Robert Harley had produced. This is how Defoe described it in a celebrated passage from the correspondence with Stanhope:

'I am, Sir, for this purpose posted among Papists, Jacobites and enrag'd High Tories—a generation who, I profess, my very soul abhors; I am obliged to hear traitorous expressions and outrageous words against His Majesty's person and government and his most faithful servants, and smile at it all as if I approved it; I am obliged to take all the scandalous and, indeed, villainous papers that come, and keep them by me as if I would gather materials from them to put them into the news; nay, I often venture to let things pass which are a little shocking, that I may not render myself suspected.

'Thus I bow in the House of Rimmon, and I must humbly recommend myself to his Lordship's protection, or I may be undone the sooner, by how much the more faithfully I execute the commands I am under.'

His task was to insinuate himself among the Tories and Jacobites and to edit and manipulate certain papers of that colour—Mist's *Weekly Journal*, Dormer's *Newsletter*, and the *Mercurius Politicus*—in such a way as to take the sting out of them. They would thus, as he put it, 'be always kept (mistakes excepted) to pass as Tory papers, and yet be so disabled and enervated, so as to do no mischief, or give any offence to the Government.'

To impersonate a High Tory, though more repugnant to Defoe than the other disguises he had adopted, was not at this point in politics beyond him. He was known or suspected to be helping in the defence of Harley and his colleagues even after they had been discredited and impeached by the revengeful Whigs. Harley at this time was finished, and Defoe must have known it. Yet he wrote, among the publications designed to exonerate the late Ministry for its conduct over the Peace and the Succession, the *Secret History of the White Staff* (his denial is hard to believe), a sympathetic account of Harley's final dismissal which the accused cautiously repudiated.

He was also believed to be (though he never acknowledged it) the fabricator of the *Minutes of the Negotiations of Mons. Mesnager at the Court of England, Towards the Close of the last Reign*, which purported to reveal the peace preliminaries in a manner favourable to Harley—they were in fact closely followed by the acquittal which enabled the ex-Minister to end his days in quiet retirement. There is a mystery about these activities. Defoe, since he was now serving the Whig Ministry, was in no position to be candid about them. One thing, however, is certain. None but Defoe had the abilities and experience required for the remarkable assignment of toning down the Tory Press by stealth: and only at this stage of his career would he have accepted it. Once he had entered upon it he kept up the game for nearly ten years, even when he was making a success with the narrative works of his last great period.

In some of this later journalism we can find the sort of reporting, the elaboration of real-life stories and criminal confessions, which furnished material for his books. But only a specialized study could deal at all adequately with Defoe's newspaper-work after the death of the *Review*; beginning with the *Mercator* which followed immediately on the *Review* to publicize Bolingbroke's mercantile policy; passing through the dim and twisting corridors of the pseudo-Tory campaign; and so on to Defoe's own *Whitehall Evening Post* and the miscellaneous contributions to *Mist's Journal*, *Applebee's Journal*, the *Daily Post*, the *Universal Spectator*, and other papers.[1] It was William Lee who first explored this side of his work, and the pieces he identified in his *Life and Newly Discovered*

[1] Earlier, in 1710, Defoe had acquired control for a time of two Edinburgh papers, the *Edinburgh Courant* and the *Scots Postman*, besides the northern edition of the *Review*.

Writings of Daniel Defoe in 1869 are still accepted. Their title to our continued interest is that they came from the same hand that wrote *Robinson Crusoe*, *Moll Flanders*, *Roxana*, *Captain Singleton*, *Colonel Jack*, the *Memoirs of a Cavalier*, the *Journal of the Plague Year*, the *New Voyage Round the World*, the *Tour through Great Britian*, and so much else that gave him at last the reputation (to put it no higher) of 'the most extraordinarily prolific old man in the history of English literature.[1]

[1] *Cambridge History of English Literature*, Vol. IX, 1913 (W. P. Trent).

Chapter Five

MATERIALS OF A MASTERPIECE

IN the first year of the reign of George I Defoe was fifty-five; and if we are to judge by the *Appeal to Honour and Justice* of that year 1715, he had no great hopes of being an old man at all. His sense at that time of being 'near to the great ocean of eternity' was endorsed by 'the publisher's' concluding note:

'While this was at the press, and the copy thus far finished, the author was seized with a violent fit of an apoplexy, whereby he was disabled finishing what he designed in his further defence; and continuing now for above six weeks in a weak and languishing condition, neither able to go on nor likely to recover, at least in any short time, his friends thought it not fit to delay the publication of this any longer.'

The evidence of journalistic activity has thrown a doubt upon this fit of apoplexy—and hence upon the veracity of the *Appeal*. The dates, as far as they have been traced, are puzzling, but *some* interruption of work is credible. His highly tried physique had warned him. In February 1707 he had advised Harley, in one of his letters from Scotland, not to work himself into illness, adding:

'I speak my own immediate experiences, who having despised sleep, hours, and rules, have broken in upon a perfectly established . health, which no distressse, disasters, jails or melancholy could ever hurt before.'

Again in 1712, in the months before his series of pamphlets on the Succession issue, he had obtained leave from
Harley to go and recover his health at Buxton. As a rest-
cure this trip seems energetic, for he travelled first by
way of Lincoln, York, and Newcastle to the Border,
carrying out some commercial business for himself and
some political business for the Minister. Then he
returned south to Halifax and stayed there a few weeks
with friends, and only then repaired to Buxton to try
the waters and to view the sights of the Peak District.
Perhaps the visit did him good, for when he wrote his
Tour Buxton came off better than Bath:

'If . . . the nobility and gentry were suitably enter-
tained I doubt not but Buxton would be frequented, and
with more effect as to health, as well as much more
satisfaction to the company; where there is an open and
healthy country, a great variety of view to satisfy the
curious, and a fine down or moor for the ladies to take
a ring upon in their coaches, all much more convenient
than in a close city, as the Bath is, which, more like a
prison than a place of diversion, scarce gives the company
room to converse out of the smell of their own excre-
ments, and where the very city itself may be said to
stink like a general common-shore.'

It is easy to believe that in his forties the pace and
volume of Defoe's activities, and the troubles he had been
through, began to tell upon a robust constitution: the
only marvel is that the final lethargy was held at bay
until he was over seventy. If his health fluctuated from
time to time, his changes of material fortune may well
have been equally distressing to his dependents. Taking
farewell of his readers in the last number of the *Review*
he wrote:

'I sometime ago summed up the scenes of my life in this distich:

> No man has tasted differing fortunes more
> And thirteen times I have been rich and poor.'

There must have been a number of years when his literary earnings alone were reasonably good, not to speak of his political or commercial income. But in none of his means of support was there any security, and if we accept his own complaints the persecutions of his enemies must have made a regular drain upon his resources. He started his fresh career after the Newgate imprisonment with the ruins of his pantile business about him, and it is obvious that his need of Harley's patronage had a good deal to do with his debts. Perhaps he never caught up with them, and he even had to spend money in the prosecution of false claimants. Here are some of the harassments of which he complained in the *Review* in July 1705:

'Sham actions, arrests, sleeping debates in trade of 17 years' standing revived; debts put in suit after contracts and agreements under hand and seal; and which is worse, writs taken out for debts without the knowledge of the creditor, and some after the creditor has been paid; diligent solicitations of persons not inclined to sue, pressing them to give him trouble . . .'

From this we should conclude that Defoe did have a variety of undischarged debts at that time, but that he would have hoped to meet his obligations reasonably had he not been maliciously pursued. He had ways of making money, but probably none of raising credit—save in Scotland where he could penetrate unknown—and whatever capital he needed had doubtless to be brought into being by some successful venture at a high profit. When he came to write *The Compleat English Tradesman* at the age of sixty-six, he was not looking back only upon his experiences as a young merchant before the French wars but upon an almost continuous, though subsidiary, business activity throughout his professional life. Now it might be a deal in wool at the great Stourbridge Fair, another time a shipment of wine bought and sold, a linen-factory in Scotland, a share in a trading voyage to the West Indies, a venture in real estate. In his later years, after he had already been 'thirteen times rich and poor' it seems that he sometimes speculated unwisely; and the will of his brother-in-law Samuel Tuffley has been dug out to show that by 1714 those close to him were not too ready to trust him with money—for Tuffley left most of his estate to Mrs. Defoe for her own disposal 'absolutely and independently of her said husband Daniel Defoe,' who received one guinea for himself and one for each of his children.

This said husband, however, was a responsible one. We know next to nothing directly of his domestic relationships, but it was certainly not himself alone that he sought to raise to comfort and security. When he wrote of the crimes or misfortunes of men he seldom omitted to reflect upon the results for their families. And for himself the misery of bankruptcy or imprisonment was always seen in this light. The present sent to Mrs. Defoe by Queen Anne at the release from Newgate was in answer to the husband's pleas; and when Harley was dilatory, as he commonly was, in meeting his secret commitments with Defoe he was frequently reminded that his agent had dependents. It was not simply the problem of their daily provison that caused anxiety. What is very characteristic of Defoe—and it is a new

attitude in his time—is the emphasis he places on the
education of his children: a respectable education and
one for which (he proudly declared in his *Appeal*) he
refused to be 'indebted one shilling in the world.' To
Harley he had written when leaving alone on his mission
to Scotland: 'Thus, sir, you have a widow and seven
children on your hands.' Nine years later one is touched
to read in the *Appeal*: 'I have six children; I have educated
them as well as my circumstances will permit, and so as I
hope shall recommend them to better usage than their
father meets with in this world.' The second bereave-
ment (a young daughter) must by then have occurred,
leaving the Defoes with Daniel and Benjamin (who
seem to have proved, for some years at any rate, good and
useful sons), and with four girls whose marriage-settlements were to weigh heavily upon the writer's old age.

The standard of living which Defoe struggled to maintain for himself and his family was a 'very genteel' one.
So said Henry Baker, the naturalist, who subsequently
married one of the daughters. The house at Stoke
Newington where we find the Defoes installed in 1709
was not as handsome as the prospective son-in-law made
out (to judge by a print, for it has disappeared); but it
attracted attention on account of its size. Defoe probably
added to it later, which would explain Baker's remark in
1724 that it was 'newly built.' It had, of course, its
stables, also outhouses, orchards and 'a great garden'—
the designing of gardens was one of Defoe's interests.
There is a tradition that the building was 'gloomy and
irregular', with 'thick walls, curious cupboards, and
heavy locks;' and another that Defoe's apprehension in
April 1713 on account of the pamphlets on the Succession
was accomplished only by force and a strong posse of
bailiffs and constables, Defoe having barricaded himself

within. This latter story comes from his bitter enemy
Ridpath, the Whig journalist, who was in the plot to
lay him by the heels and as sensationally as possible. It
has survived, without real evidence, largely because it
gave later writers a chance to compare Defoe's domestic
stronghold with Crusoe's 'castle.'

This was the house in which *Robinson Crusoe* was
written, at just the time when its hard-pressed author
needed a new reputation if he were to have any at all.
Historians of literature see the accession of the first
Hanoverian as the end of a comparatively fortunate phase
for English writers and the beginning of the real miseries
of Grub-Street. Defoe's daily and weekly journalism,
continued till 1726, kept him in what seems today the
anonymous underworld. But it was not Grub-Street,
and though he had to take pains to keep out of trouble
and throw dust in the eyes of a variety of enemies, his
hand was more often visible to his contemporaries than
some later writers have realized. Nathaniel Mist, for
instance, the proprietor of the rabidly Tory *Journal*
which Defoe was supposed to be secretly emasculating,
was certainly not the innocent dupe of a master-plan;
and if, as Lee deduced, he once drew his sword upon
his fellow-journalist it can hardly have been in righteous
resentment at deception. It may indeed be doubted
whether Defoe's political services in this busy period
were worth very much to the Whig Government. But
if he were bowing in the House of Rimmon to no great
purpose, he was doing a great deal to enliven the pages and
increase the circulations of a whole sheaf of periodicals.
He may even have enjoyed doing it. But the days of walk-
ing with royalty in the gardens of Kensington Palace or
Hampton Court must sometimes have seemed very far away.

In 1715, however, when he was appealing for honour

and justice, Defoe also produced a book which found its way into the royal household, whither *Robinson Crusoe* was to follow it. This was his *Family Instructor*, a manual for the use of God-fearing parents in bringing up their children. It has been called sentimental, even crudely so. But this class of literature, once so popular, is now so completely out of fashion that it is difficult to find the right standpoint from which to judge it. Though it cannot move us as Bunyan will always move us, nor yet as Defoe can move us with the humanity of *Moll Flanders*, it has not, on the other hand, become an object of horrified ridicule like the early Victorian *Fairchild Family*. It is a document of English domestic puritanism produced by a writer who knew his business for a public which, in the result, received it very warmly. By 1720 there had been eight editions, and they were followed by many more on both sides of the Atlantic. Had it been written, as first the author intended, as a long didactic poem, it would hardly have had this success. The form of a series of dialogues consorted better with his own gifts and with the tastes of a wide circle of readers. In a preface composed later he declared that the stories he had woven together to teach godly living in the home were strictly based upon fact. We have no means of knowing how far that was true, but it is interesting that he thought the claim worth making.

The first edition of the *Family Instructor*, in three parts, ran to 444 duodecimo pages, and it appeared only five weeks after the *Appeal*. If it were inspired, as a religious work, by a near contemplation of eternity, it must be said that this and a score of other publications of 1715 point to a most satisfactory recovery from the apoplectic stroke. Among them we may single out another sizeable work, the *History of the Wars of his present Majesty Charles*

XII King of Sweden—the portentous conqueror who threw the statesmen of Western Europe (except Marlborough) into alarm and confusion until his course of victories, diverted towards the devouring plains of Russia, ended at Pultava. Defoe is not regarded as wholly responsible for this work, but he appears to have had a large hand in it—it was reissued in 1720 with a continuation to the King's death. The point for us, in our hurrying survey, is that it was given out as a work of 'a Scots Gentleman in the Swedish Service.' It is a convincing and characteristic disguise, but a more significant one was assumed by Defoe for the short piece that he wrote in 1717 (and followed up next year) called *The Conduct of Christians made the Sport of Infidels*. In his impersonation of 'a Turkish Merchant of Amsterdam' writing to the Grand Mufti at Constantinople of the curious goings-on in Christian countries Defoe hit upon a literary device which later, with Montesquieu and Voltaire and a host of lesser social critics, had an enormous vogue in Europe.

*   *   *

The costumes are various and worn with an air. Within the solid walls of the big house at Stoke Newington the ageing but unquenchably energetic writer who assumes them remains always himself, and superbly so in the goatskin cap and habit of Crusoe that we are coming back to at last. In his library there, and in a mind that must have been preternaturally retentive, was stored the raw material of the astonishing series of works that flowed from his hand during these last years of his life. After his death the *Daily Advertiser* invited attention to the sale of the library of:

'. . . the late ingenious Daniel De Foe, Gent., lately

deceased. Containing a curious collection of Books relating to the History and Antiquities of divers Nations, particularly England, Scotland and Ireland. . . . N.B. Manuscripts. Also several hundred curious, scarce tracts on Parliamentary Affairs, Politicks, Husbandry, Trade, Voyages, Natural History, Mines, Minerals, etc.'[1] Half of Defoe's *werkstoff*, as the Germans would aptly call it, came out of his own avid experience of life, the other half from a real love of books. It is easy to imagine his study as a heaped lumber-room, his mind stuffed with ill-digested miscellanea. But it was not so. He left his books, according to the notice of sale, 'in very good condition, mostly well bound, gilt and lettered.' And he read them, as he read life, with an exact attention. That his rapid composition and handling of proofs allowed of mistakes and inconsistencies is another matter.

He wasted nothing. Into all his writing he poured what he collected, and because *Robinson Crusoe* is a masterpiece men have studied to discover and analyse its ingredients. Defoe remains uncommemorated, but a statue of Alexander Selkirk, the unlettered Scottish sailor, looks out across the sea from a hill at Largo. There is no evidence that Defoe ever met Selkirk; but he could easily have done so, either in London when Captain Woodes Rogers brought back the castaway from Juan Fernandez in 1711 to become the talk of town and country, or afterwards when the tired and somewhat bewildered celebrity was living in Bristol. Defoe visited Bristol in 1713. It would have been very natural for him to seek out Selkirk and converse with him, as his own Colonel Jack loved to talk with 'old soldiers and tars'—

[1] The notice was quoted by a correspondent in *Notes and Queries*, February 17th, 1866.

natural but quite unnecessary. The account of Selkirk's four and a half years of solitude was available in the popular description by his rescuer, Woodes Rogers, of *A Cruising Voyage Round the World*, and in the *Voyage to the South Sea* by another member of the expedition, Edward Cooke. Both these books were published in 1712, and in December 1713 Steele wrote in the *Englishman* his essay on Selkirk's adventures. Defoe was just then engrossed in the politics of the last years of Queen Anne, but the story stayed in his mind. In 1718 Woodes Rogers' narrative earned a second edition; and on 25 April, 1719, with the colophon of the ship in full sail and the famous engraved frontispiece, William Taylor published *The Life and Strange Surprizing Adventures of Robinson Crusoe*.

Whatever else it has since turned out to be, *Robinson Crusoe* was a travel-book, written for those who enjoyed travel-books by one who enjoyed them himself. What was an episode in Woodes Rogers' voyage, and an episode that caught the public imagination, was here developed by Defoe into the chief (though not the only) element. But if we seek the significant background of Defoe's reading it will be found not in the dozen or more accounts of castaways, real or fictitious, with which he might have been acquainted. It will be found in the general literature of voyages and discovery, from Hakluyt and Purchas onwards, which he knew so well: the literature of winds and tides and climate, of strange peoples, their manners and the prospects of trading with them, of ports and islands and uncharted passages, of pirates and slavers and colonizers, of unfamiliar herbs and fruits, of beasts and birds wild and tamed, and of the many and marvellous hazards of the men who struggled back with the tale of them.

Captain Robert Knox's *Historical Relation of Ceylon*, though the island is so far from either Juan Fernandez or from Crusoe's Island at the mouth of the Orinoco, is reasonably included among the more important source-books.[1] John Ogilby's *Description of Africa*, Louis Le Comte's *Journeys through China*, and the *Three Years Travels from Moscow Overland to China* by E. Ysbrant Ides had all been known for twenty years or more: Crusoe, of course, begins his adventures in Africa, and the second and more purely travelling volume carries him across the world to China and back by Siberia. But the names that meant most to Defoe, it might be guessed, were Raleigh from the first great wave of voyaging and Dampier from the second. Raleigh he respected sufficiently to throw out a claim to a family connection. Dampier, nearly eighty years after Raleigh's execution, published the first of the four volumes of voyages that made him pre-eminent in the new age of travel-literature, and his book was in its sixth edition when Defoe was writing *Robinson Crusoe*. Swift bewailed the proliferation of travel-books and the public appetite for accounts of the South Seas; but he learned what he needed of seamanship from Dampier, and it was in the unknown regions of *Terra Australis* that Gulliver found his Lilliputians. Defoe may have meant Dampier when he wrote that 'a very good sailor may make but a very indifferent author', but he absorbed his abundant information on sea-routes and land-routes, winds, and currents, and tropical phenomena. Dampier's narrative style has some of the same attractions as Defoe's, and on at least one occasion

[1] It was undoubtedly at Defoe's elbow when he was writing *Captain Singleton*, which appeared after the First and Second Parts of *Robinson Crusoe* but before the Third. The best account of the possible and probable source-books for *Crusoe* is A. W. Secord's *Studies in the Narrative Method of Defoe* (University of Illinois, 1924).

the great explorer and sometime buccaneer displayed a resourcefulness wholly worthy of Crusoe:

'Foreseeing a necessity of wading through rivers frequently in our land-march, I took care before I left the ship to provide myelf a large joint of bamboo, which I stopt at both ends, closing it with wax, so as to keep out any water. In this I preserved my journal and other writings from being wet, tho' I was often forced to swim.'

The real Dampier with his bamboo cylinder and the allegedly real Crusoe with his notched date-stick, his salvage and his improvizations are in the same tradition. These were the things of which Defoe's contemporaries loved to read, and Defoe gave them good measure: twenty-eight years on the Island for Selkirk's four and a half, and in those twenty-eight years, as the book grew under his hand, so much of his own thought and feeling and reflected experience, his alternations of hope and despair, his religion of perseverance, even perhaps the night-fears of childhood and the memory of a boyish interest in the basket-weavers of Cripplegate.

The details that he took from the Selkirk story—the goats and the goatskins, the tribe of cats, some of the topographical features, and so forth—are really of less importance than the main points of deliberate divergence. Why, for example, did Defoe move the Island from the South Pacific to the North Atlantic (north of the Line, that is, by ten degrees), from Juan Fernandez (or Mas-a-Fuera in the same group) to the region of what is now Venezuela? Part of the answer, obviously, is that he had to make some radical changes for a new story. But this particular change is very personal. The current fascination was the exploration of the South

N

Seas by way of Cape Horn, and the search for the land-mass which was logically supposed to exist somewhere in that huge expanse of ocean. Such expeditions often ended in a circumnavigation of the globe: Dampier had three to his credit, and was present both when Selkirk was marooned and when his signal-fires at last attracted his rescuers. Defoe was certainly prepared to share and nourish the public appetite for geography. We have seen the part that he played in the establishment of the South Sea Company. But nine years before that he had put before William of Orange his detailed scheme for supplanting Spain in South and Central America and the West Indies in the then approaching war of the Spanish Succession. William died before this dazzling plan had been fully considered: and of it all the attack on Chile, the cutting of the treasure-route by seizing Havana, the conquest and development of Guiana—of it all there was only the treaty clause giving England the retention of any West Indian islands taken during the war. Yet Defoe's imagination never forsook these regions, and Raleigh's maps of Guiana remained in his library. He interested Harley in a project for establishing English colonies in South America, but Harley first procrastinated and then abandoned it. In 1719, the year of *Robinson Crusoe*, Defoe also wrote a short treatise (published January 1720), of which the title is eloquent enough:

An Historical Account of the Voyages and Adventures of Sir Walter Raleigh. With the Discoveries and Conquests he made for the Crown of England. Also a particular Account of his Several Attempts for the Discovery of the Gold Mines in Guiana, and the Reason of the Miscarriage, shewing, That it was not from any Defect in the Scheme he had laid, or in the Reality of the Thing itself, but in a Treacherous Discovery

of the Design and of the Strength he had with him to the
Spaniards. To which is added An Account how that Rich
Country might be now with Ease, Possess'd, Planted and
Secur'd to the British Nation, and What immense Wealth and
Increase of Commerce might be raised from thence. Humbly
proposed to the South-Sea Company.

Through the early summer of 1720 the South Sea Bubble
expanded with the speculation encouraged by the success
of Walpole's Sinking Fund. In August it burst. But
Defoe had sold his shares in the South Sea Company.
He had taken his castaway off the South Sea route and
given him, first a likely-looking tobacco plantation in
Brazil and then an island kingdom in an archipelago
vaguely indicated by Raleigh and other cartographers at
the mouth of the Orinoco, with Caribs for his nearest
neighbours, a local type of fever to lay him low and other
details (largely though not consistently accurate) which
have mysteriously failed to prevent the growth of a notion
that Juan Fernandez was 'Robinson Crusoe's Island.'

The immense success of *Robinson Crusoe* did not give
substance to the dream of a British colonial enterprise in
South America. The Purple Land was still, when W. H.
Hudson came to write of it, 'the purple land that England
lost.' But Defoe's great book played a part that can be
recognized, even if it cannot be measured, in keeping
the eyes of Englishmen fixed on the distant horizons that
have drawn their race to its destinies. Between Dampier
and Cook the fictitious Crusoe remained in popular
esteem the supreme adventurer of travel. Even Anson's
circumnavigation of 1740–44, the account of which was
internationally famous, still ranked only second to
Robinson Crusoe as a fertilizer of pioneering imaginations.
The rise of new nations where once was *Tetra Incognita*

has turned old maps and old ships into curiosities. But the story of a lonely man's mastery of circumstance is not yet out of fashion.

*　　　*　　　*

In another of Defoe's travel-books, the *New Voyage Round the World*, published six years after *Robinson Crusoe*, the supposed author introduces his work with a significant criticism. Most of the accounts of voyages, he complains, have too many technical data and too little, for the general and untravelled reader, in the way of diverting or exciting incident. They have, in a word, 'little or nothing of *story* in them.' The man who set out to remedy this defect, for a public that he knew, found thereby his place in the history of English fiction.

The word 'fiction,' of course, was openly rejected by Defoe. 'The Editor,' he tells the world in the preface to *Robinson Crusoe*, 'believes the thing to be a just history of fact; neither is there any appearance of fiction in it.' An *appearance* of fiction would have caused his readers to lose interest. It would have classed him, moreover, with the purveyors of romances, idle reading for idle minds and only less corrupting than the stage. When Gildon rushed in to challenge his veracity with *The Life and Strange Surprizing Adventures of Mr. Daniel De Foe*, it seemed imperative to produce a reply—the allegorical, but not fictional interpretation put forward in the preface to the *Third Part*. But though Defoe continued to write 'histories' rather than 'novels,' one detects in the preface to *Moll Flanders* a hint that if the disclaimer is not accepted it doesn't really matter—so long as people go on reading:

'The world is so taken up of late with novels and romances, that it will be hard for a private history to be

taken for genuine, where the names and other circumstances of the person are concealed, and on this account
we must be content to leave the reader to pass his own
opinion upon the ensuing sheets, and take it just as he
pleases.'

Professor Saintsbury once pointed out that the world
managed to get on without novels for more than two
thousand reading years. And the eventual introduction
into English literature of the form which later became
so dominating seems in some ways curiously accidental.
Defoe, mixing fiction with fact, disguising one as the
other (and perhaps not always sure himself of the
boundary between the two), became the first master
of the craft which he repudiated. From Richardson's
practice as an instructor in letter-writing to the new
middle classes came *Pamela* (nine years after Defoe's
death); and in humorous reaction to *Pamela* came
Fielding's *Joseph Andrews*. The growing reading public,
men and women from a widening range of society,
demanding in various degrees a story, a plot, characters,
moral examples, sentiment and fun, saw to the rest.
The history of literature is not merely a chronicle of outstanding writers. There are also the anonymous readers,
the audiences, the customers. The decline of Court
patronage and of the theatre which had flourished in its
rays diverted the creative energy of writers into new
channels; and the public—in many ways a prejudiced
public—helped to determine their course. The appetite
for facts which Defoe worked hard to satisfy was in itself
a criticism of the abundant prose-romances of his day,
forgotten by all now but the researcher seeking a gene-
alogy for Defoe, Richardson, Fielding, Sterne, and
Smollett.

Forgotten, also, are the *Serious Reflections* which form the final volume of *Robinson Crusoe*, though Defoe's attempt with this *Third Part* to prolong the interest and recover from the charge of writing fiction is highly curious. There is, first of all, the suggestion of allegory, which may or may not be a pure after-thought:

'The adventures of Robinson Crusoe are a whole scheme of a life of twenty-eight years spent in the most wandering, desolate, and afflicting circumstances that ever man went through, and in which I have lived so long in a life of wonders, in continued storms, fought with the worst kind of savages and man-eaters, by unaccountable surprising incidents; fed by miracles greater than that of the ravens, suffered all manner of violences and oppressions, injurious reproaches, contempt of men, attacks by devils, corrections from Heaven, and oppositions on earth; and had innumerable ups and downs in matters of fortune, been in slavery worse than Turkish, escaped by an exquisite management, as that in the story of Xury and the boat of Sallee, been taken up at sea in distress, raised again and depressed again, and that oftener perhaps in one man's life than ever was known before; shipwrecked often, though more by land than by sea; in a word, there's not a circumstance in the imaginary story but has its just allusion to a real story, and chimes part for part, and step for step, with the inimitable life of Robinson Crusoe.'

The explanation, which has sometimes been extended much too literally, was not given in his own name, but it is clear that Defoe's authorship was known or guessed almost immediately *Robinson Crusoe* appeared; and therefore he may have been taking the opportunity to confess and excuse and explain, in his characteristic manner, the

shady journalism in which he was still engaged in association with Nathaniel Mist. Crusoe himself, in the *First
Part*, has a natural and unforced piety of character. But
the Dissenting conscience is altogether too special a
phenomenon for us to be sure how much Defoe means
when he tells us in the *Third Part*:

'This supplying a story by invention is certainly a most
scandalous crime, and yet very little regarded in that
part. It is a sort of lying that makes a great hole in the
heart, in which by degrees a habit of lying enters in.'

Whether that hole in the heart were real or imaginary,
deep or shallow, the literary results of Defoe's art of
invention are important. It established a tradition of
realism so influential that we find Henry James laying
it down that 'the novel is history'—and so insisting for
almost the same reasons that actuated Defoe. For James
(in his essay on *The Art of Fiction*) found a lingering spirit,
in the English-speaking world, of 'the old evangelical
hostility to the novel . . . which regarded it as little
less favourable to our immortal part than a stage-play.'
The only effectual way to lay this hostility to rest, he still
felt, was to conceal and deny the element of make-believe,
to pursue truth as busily as the historian, and never to
fall into such shocking 'want of discretion' as did
Trollope by frivolously showing his hand. And one of
the most distinguished of writers in these latter days of
the novel, Mr. Somerset Maugham, has taken extraordinary pains to carry out this principle, with first-
person narration, circumstantial detail and even (in *The
Moon and Sixpence*) the adoption of a basic narrative from
actuality.[1]

[1] A comparison of Maugham with Defoe is made by Professor Pelham Edgar
of Toronto in *The Art of the Novel* (New York, 1933).

Technically, the first requirements of such an approach are an easy and flowing prose style, an ear for speech, and a *selective* eye for the concrete features of any given environment. Defoe had, or developed, all of these. His style had a miscellaneous ancestry in which the English Bible, as we should expect, is an element, but only one. His own practice of journalism shaped his writing into the instrument that he needed, and we can guess at influences from his favourite reading—travels, topography, histories, treatises on commerce, and the 'curious and scarce tracts' which no doubt included many of the narrative-pamphlets of the Civil Wars. What he may have derived from other literatures can only be a matter of speculation. He translated an *Art of Painting* from the French and he had a Dutch dictionary in his library. It is a pity that we cannot know whether his schoolboy studies of modern languages were kept up sufficiently for him to have read Cervantes in the original, for the Spanish characters in his books are as favourably drawn as one could look for from so staunch an Englishman. Though Defoe likes to remind us from time to time of his civilized acquaintance with the classics, the development of his prose is away from the classical, polite, and exclusive tradition. Only in his addiction to verse (at length abandoned) did he cherish memories of an ambition to scale the Augustan Parnassus, to be remembered, perhaps, as the Juvenal of his time.

The idea of a 'natural' style was not startling in itself. Montaigne (translated by John Florio in 1603) had declared:

'It is a natural, simple and unaffected speech that I love, so written as it is spoken, and such upon paper, as it is in the mouth.'

Such a way of writing might well gain ground in the age of Locke's philosophical influence, and Defoe was in every way fitted to adopt it. In those pleasant phrases he had recognized his 'natural infirmity of homely plain writing.' In prose as in religious politics he had no bent for high-flying, and in his design for an Academy in the early *Essay Upon Projects* he had set himself against jargon and pedantry. Yet simplicity is not the whole of the matter, for the exchange of speech varies in different societies, and speech is not always simple. Coleridge, and Lamb following him, drew attention to the fact that Defoe's eponymous heroes and heroines, coming from 'low life,' would be expected to tell their stories repetitiously and with an apparently trivial exactitude, elements which thus entered Defoe's style of writing. In fact there is more social variety among the narrators than that would suggest—from the son of a well-to-do gentleman supposed to have written the *Memoirs of a Cavalier*, through the confessedly middle-class Crusoe and the saddler of the *Plague Year* to outcasts like Moll Flanders and Colonel Jack. And the difficulty about someone like Moll Flanders was that her vocabulary would be unprintable, so that Defoe had to pretend that 'she is made to tell her own tale in modester words than she told it at first.'

That, however, was the least among the technical problems which Defoe set himself by maintaining the convention that he was providing authentic histories. He was limited to a single fully considered character, since the others cannot reveal themselves save in speech or action within the narrator's experience. The story, where the principal figure is absent, must be carried on by second-hand contrivances. Whatever perils may be encountered, whatever crimes may seem to call for the

direst punishment, we know that the hero or heroine
has lived to tell the tale before us, and usually to tell it
in a period of elderly, leisurely, and not always complete
repentance which carries all the dangers of anti-climax.
Again, since the author has to be prepared to provide a
sequel if the book creates a demand, there is the temptation to leave loose threads of narrative lying about.
Defoe's strongest gift was not for situation, plot, or character, but simply for *story*, the craft of carrying the reader
irresistibly from incident to incident and making him ask
for more. Of *Robinson Crusoe* Dr. Johnson demanded:
'Was there ever anything else written by mere man that
was wished longer by its readers, except *Don Quixote* and
Pilgrim's Progress?' Our usual response is to abridge all
three. Indeed *Robinson Crusoe* began to earn pirated abridgments almost immediately on its appearance, and we are
not to know in which edition Johnson had enjoyed it.

Certainly Defoe offers temptations to the publisher's
pruning-hook. He may be cut, but not compressed.
His narrative works are little concerned with form. In-
asmuch as they are episodic the part has the virtue of
the whole. The true addict of his story-telling style
will happily read that part of *Robinson Crusoe* which gives
the castaway's journal of a year, although (as the author
admits) the same ground is covered in the remainder of
the text; but the impatient may question such artless
construction. Was it, perhaps, that Defoe had contracted
with William Taylor at the Ship for a book of three
hundred and sixty octavo pages and needed to fill out
his subject?[1] Or was this his notion of the rambling sort

[1] The story that Defoe hawked his manuscript from one bookseller (or
publisher) to another without success rests on no discovered evidence. 'If
the facts were known,' says Henry Clinton Hutchins in his study of *Robinson
Crusoe and its Printing* (Columbia, 1925) 'I have no doubt that Taylor was the
first and last publisher to handle the manuscript of *Robinson Crusoe*.'

of tale, telling the same particulars in two ways, that the
real seafarer would produce? Or was it rather his own
spontaneous, uncalculating way of getting his story on
paper? There is an unplanned look about all these
personal histories of his, though the first part of *Crusoe*,
like the *Journal of the Plague Year*, imposes a certain
unity in its subject. But however unpremeditated may
be the shape and the framework (which is not easy to
determine) the skill with which it is filled is undeniable.
There is a lifetime's practice behind it, and when a theme
as rich as that of the island-citizen presents itself, the
man has only to sit down and write. Defoe wrote rapidly,
as will be well understood, and the expertise is set off
by the sort of mistake which only his magical vividness
can redeem. One might be tempted to think that even
the mistakes were part of the machinery of illusion, as
are the natural hesitations, the self-corrections, the
repetitions, the cautious processes of recollection:

'When they were on shore, I was fully satisfied that
they were English men; at least, most of them; one or
two I thought were Dutch; but it did not prove so:
There were in all eleven men, whereof three of them I
found were unarmed, and as I thought, bound; and when
the first four or five of them were jumped on shore, they
took those three out of the boat as prisoners. One of the
three I could perceive using the most passionate gestures
of entreaty, affliction and despair, even to a kind of
extravagance; the other two I could perceive lifted up
their hands sometimes, and appeared concerned indeed,
but not to such a degree as the first.'

But the man who could give his evidence thus, for page
after page, could also dress Crusoe in goatskins in the
warm weather of a tropical latitude. He could transport

Selkirk's seals and penguins from the South Pacific to an unnatural habitat near the equator. He could cause the eyes of the old goat in the cave to shine where there was no light. He could stuff biscuits into Crusoe's pockets after he had taken off his clothes to swim. Some of his mistakes Defoe corrected after Charles Gildon had impugned his veracity; for to risk disbelief was certainly no part of the plan of 'natural' writing. By the time that he came to add *Roxana* to his successes the hallooing of the sceptics had died away. But it can only be hasty composition which allowed Defoe, with his precise and superstitious interest in dates, to represent Roxana as about ten years old in 1683 and eventually, after a variety of fortunes as a grown woman, attracting the attention of King Charles II (who died in 1685).

In *Robinson Crusoe* Defoe is almost bewilderingly quotable. At random one can pick passages that show the run of his prose, the easily understood metaphors with never a glance at classical antiquity, the hints that carry the reader forward and the asides that remind him of what has gone before, the use of detail not to bludgeon but to beguile, not to stupefy but to illumine. Swift evolved a prose of brilliant clarity. Richardson can suddenly transform the mawkish into something truly and touchingly observed. Fielding knew 'low life' as well as Defoe and could incorporate it in a human comedy beyond Defoe's conception. Sterne's egregious style *talks* like none other. But Defoe alone could stoop from heaven to earth in a sentence:

'I walked about on the shore, lifting up my hands, and my whole being, as I may say, wrapt up in the contemplation of my deliverance, making a thousand gestures and motions which I cannot describe, reflecting upon all my comrades that were drowned, and that there should not be one soul saved but my self; for, as for them, I never saw them afterwards, nor any sign of them, except three of their hats, one cap, and two shoes that were not fellows.'

Here is the well-known picture of Crusoe at dinner—before his little kingdom was troubled by visitors—with the explanation about the cats into which he is characteristically led:

'Then to see how like a king I dined too all alone, attended by my servants. Poll, as if he had been my favourite, was the only person permitted to talk to me. My dog, who was now grown very old and crazy, and had found no species to multiply his kind upon, sat always at my right hand; and two cats, one on one side the table, and one on the other, expecting now and then a bit from my hand, as a mark of special favour.

'But these were not the two cats I brought on shore at first, for they were both of them dead, and had been interred near my habitation by my own hand; but one of them having multiplied by I know not what kind of creature, these were two which I had preserved tame, whereas the rest run wild in the woods, and became indeed troublesome to me at last; for they would often come into my house, and plunder me too, till at last I was obliged to shoot them, and did kill a great many; at length they left me with this attendance, and in this plentiful manner I lived; neither could I be said to want any thing but society, and of that in some time after this, I was like to have too much.'

In his fifty-ninth year Defoe had fashioned a best-seller. He may or may not have been surprised. He must certainly have been elated, for one thinks of

Robinson Crusoe as written with a peculiar gusto, a special concentration of himself and his powers on a task that challenged his craftsmanship. Even so was his hero challenged by the need of a good, sound pot, 'a great employment upon my hands' which took two months and more of thought and search and experiment, until finally:

'No joy at a thing of so mean a nature was ever equal to mine, when I found I had made an earthen pot that would bear the fire; and I had hardly patience to stay till they were cold, before I set one upon the fire again, with some water in it, to boil me some meat, which it did admirably well; and with a piece of a kid I made some very good broth, though I wanted oatmeal, and several other ingredients requisite to make it so good as I would have had it been.'

Daniel Defoe had made a piece of earthenware that would last for centuries.

Chapter Six

AUTUMN HARVEST

O F the last twelve years in Defoe's career the
patient research of biographers has yielded little.
The record—and it is an extraordinary record even if we
select only the more interesting titles—is in the bookseller's lists.

The catalogue of William Taylor indicates that he
valued *Robinson Crusoe* sufficiently to retain a whole share
in all three parts of it, though the commoner practice
was to distribute shares among several booksellers. It
seems that he cleared the considerable profit of £1000
on Part I. When Taylor died a few years later, of a fever,
he was said to be worth between forty and fifty thousand
pounds; which is comparable (for he was not an old man)
with the eighty thousand accumulated by the more
celebrated Jacob Tonson, publisher of the last works of
Dryden and the first of Pope. What Defoe himself may
have made out of *Robinson Crusoe*, starting with a royalty
of £10 on every thousand copies printed of Part I,
cannot be assessed; but he was at all events quick to
exploit the vein that he had struck.

When the *Farther Adventures of Robinson Crusoe* appeared
on 20 August, 1719, the *Life and Strange Surprizing
Adventures* had already reached its fourth edition in as
many months, finding readers in all classes of society. By
that time, also, Taylor had publicly protested against the
first, but not the last, pirated edition, the 'Amsterdam

Coffee-house' abridgment, which was selling at two shillings as against the comparatively high price of five shillings charged for the genuine article. By October of the same year *Robinson Crusoe* was declaring its popularity (and making publishing history) by a serial reprinting in a tri-weekly paper, *Heathcote's Intelligence*. In October also Defoe, who had meanwhile published a number of economic tracts, had a small book ready which might be considered in an indirect sense a sequel to the story of the lonely castaway. This was *The Dumb Philosopher*, an account of one Dickory Cronke, a poor Cornishman whose solitude was that of being born dumb and so continuing for fifty-eight years, until he 'came to his speech' with prophetic effect a few days before his death. And then in December the public for roving adventure was offered some shavings from the workshop of *Robinson Crusoe* in a pamphlet called *The King of Pirates*. Captain Ben Avery of Bideford, whose exploits were thus re-dressed, had for twenty years been a by-word for successful piracy. The theme had everything that could excite the public and pack Drury Lane (as it had done in 1713 for Charles Johnson's play about him)—brisk encounters at sea, feuds over booty, execution at Wapping Dock for some of the pirates, and for Avery himself a marriage to a Mogul princess, a piratical kingdom in Madagascar, and a bag of jewels too valuable ever to be disposed of in safety.

The library-exploration of Madagascar, and of Avery too, were behind *The Life, Adventures and Piracies of the Famous Captain Singleton*, one of three full-length books which all came from Defoe in the summer months of 1720: the other two were the *Memoirs of a Cavalier* and Robinson Crusoe's *Serious Reflections*. Captain Singleton is a kind of fictional counterpart of the successful buccaneering of Captain Avery (who enters the narrative at one point), though as usual given out as history. But it is a good deal more than that. It follows Defoe's prescription of the travel-book with a story, and it has enough incident to fill a dozen novels, besides the half-told stories, with a beginning and no end, with which he enticingly sprinkles his pages. Two things have chiefly caused *Captain Singleton* to be reprinted in our own day: the character of William the Quaker, to which we shall come in a moment, and the geographical riches of the whole work, from the Persian Gulf by Ceylon and the East Indies to Formosa and Japan, from Madagascar to Central Africa and across that then mysterious continent from coast to coast. With twenty-seven men Singleton:

'. . . took one of the rashest, and wildest, and most desperate resolutions that ever was taken by man, or any number of men, in the world; this was, to travel over-land through the heart of the country, from the coast of Mozambique, on the east ocean, to the coast of Angola or Guinea, on the western or Atlantic ocean, a continent of land of at least 1800 miles, in which journey we had excessive heats to support, unpassable deserts to go over, no carriages, camels, or beasts of any kind to carry our baggage, innumerable numbers of wild and ravenous beasts to encounter with, such as lions, leopards, tigers, lizards, and elephants; we had the equinoctial line to pass under, and, consequently, were in the very centre of the torrid zone; we had nations of savages to encounter with, barbarous and brutish to the last degree; hunger and thirst to struggle with, and, in one word, terrors enough to have daunted the stoutest hearts that ever were placed in cases of flesh and blood.'

o

The narrative well fulfils this exciting summary. More than that, it has encouraged the belief that Defoe knew, or guessed, certain things about Central Africa which nobody else knew until the days of Speke, Grant, Livingstone and Stanley. He knew of great lakes, and that the Congo runs north of the Line, with incidental details which modern scholars have checked and collated. The result is to establish, not that Defoe had the gift of second-sight, but that he studied with care, intelligence, and imagination the sources available in his time. For it seems that information assembled from Portuguese and Arab travellers, sometimes tentative but often near the truth, was in circulation in Defoe's lifetime, although afterwards discredited and removed from the maps until the nineteenth-century explorers restored and extended it.[1]

As for William Walters the Quaker, captured in one of Singleton's piratical fights, 'he was a comic fellow indeed, a man of very good solid sense, and an excellent surgeon; but what was worth all, very good-humoured and pleasant in his conversation, and a bold, stout fellow too, as any we had amongst us.' William gives a flavour to the story which a mere succession of adventures, however interesting in themselves, would have lacked. And if Defoe's own character intrigues us, the preacher and the keen tradesman together, the constitutionalist and the adventurer, he offers here for our curiosity a Quaker and a pirate in the same skin. This is in no sense a satire on the Friends, who were often the butt of contemporary writers. Quakers had visited and helped Defoe in his first imprisonment, when the other sects would do nothing but revile him, and he more than once

[1] See A. W. Secord, *op. cit.* Also G. A. Aitken's introduction to *Captain Singleton* in the Aldine edition.

had a good word to say for their Society. William's faith is as real as his worldly wisdom, he has a certain dry humour and a zest for action that would have done credit to Rabelais' Friar John. 'It pleased God to make William the Quaker everything to me,' says Singleton at the end of the book, after this lively keeper of his conscience had produced satisfactory arguments to show that repentance of piracy need not be accompanied by any vain attempts to restore the spoils of crime to their rightful owners.

By what accident did this rounded and various and in many ways delightful character find himself among what Saintsbury called Defoe's 'unreal beings who are yet so profoundly real, though they live and move and have their being only in their own and their author's fantasy?' Part of the answer, as in the case of Friday, is doubtless functional. The relation of unlawful adventure must have its useful purpose, its occasion for moral and practical reflection. But Singleton is to be a *successful* pirate, telling his own tale not at Execution Dock with a rope round his neck but in the ease of retirement. His wickedness can be explained by the entire absence of a Christian upbringing (he was stolen by a gypsy as a child). What there is of good in him can only be brought out slowly (and without spoiling the story) by one of his own kidney, yet a Christian—the first of such with whom he had had any close relationship. It is a relationship, in Defoe's showing, not without pathos.

The third considerable work of 1720, the *Memoirs of a Cavalier*, has more affinity with the *Journal of the Plague Year* than with the fabricated adventures, since the Cavalier's function is that of a witness. The interest lies in the presentation of historical events, in the second phase of the Thirty Years' War, and then in the Civil

War in England; not in the character or exploits of the narrator. For example, the Cavalier's decision (after witnessing the horrors of the sack of Magdeburg) to transfer from the Imperialist to the Protestant cause, is significant only as a means of having his observations of both camps and the personages therein, Tilly and Wallenstein on the one side, Gustavus Adolphus and his colonels on the other. The style is in the main brisk and close-knit. The device of circumstantial detail is sparingly used (the events being matters of common knowledge), and there are few of the conversational asides, the hesitations, and recapitulations. An extract from the description of the battle of Naseby will show of what economy Defoe was capable when it suited his theme:

'Ireton seeing one division of his horse left, repaired to them, and keeping his ground, fell foul of a brigade of our foot, who coming up to the head of the line, he like a madman charges them with his horse. But they with their pikes tore him to pieces; so that this division was entirely ruined. Ireton himself, thrust through the thigh with a pike, wounded in the face with a halberd, was unhorsed and taken prisoner.

'Cromwell, who commanded the Parliament's right wing, charged Sir Marmaduke Langdale with extraordinary fury, but he, an old, tried soldier, stood firm, and received the charge with equal gallantry, exchanging all their shot, carabines and pistols, and then fell on sword in hand. Rossiter and Whalley had the better on the point of the wing, and routed two divisions of horse, pushed them behind the reserves, where they rallied and charged again, but were at last defeated; the rest of the horse, now charged in the flank, retreated fighting, and were pushed behind the reserves on foot.'

And here, from the German part of the narrative, is a thumb-nail sketch of Tilly's Imperialists:

'. . . but I that had seen Tilly's army and his old weather-beaten soldiers, whose discipline and exercises were so exact, and their courage so often tried, could not look on the Saxon army without some concern for them when I considered who they had to deal with. Tilly's men were rugged surly fellows, their faces had an air of hardy courage, mangled with wounds and scars, their armour showed the bruises of musket bullets, and the rust of the winter storms. I observed of them their clothes were always dirty, but their arms were clean and bright; they were used to camp in the open fields, and sleep in the frosts and rain; their horses were strong and hardy like themselves, and well taught their exercises; the soldiers knew their business so exactly that general orders were enough; every private man was fit to command, and their wheelings, counter-marchings and exercise were done with such order and readiness, that the distinct words of command were hardly of any use among them; they were flushed with victory, and hardly knew what it was to fly.'

But did Defoe write the *Memoirs of a Cavalier*? He himself, characteristically, assumed the office of a mere editor or publisher of a manuscript 'written threescore years ago by an English gentleman.' Some have been inclined not only to take him at his word but to identify a known Cavalier as the author, a practice begun by the editor of the second (Leeds) edition of the *Memoirs* after Defoe's death. The evidence, says the preface to this second edition, points to a certain Andrew Newport as the genuine compiler of the military journal. But many of the circumstances of Andrew Newport's career make it improbable, and the date of his birth in 1623 makes it impossible, for him to have been the man concerned in the account as it stands. No other name has been seriously put forward: yet surely a man who had stood high in the counsels of King Gustavus Adolphus of Sweden and then of King Charles I of England would have left some other trace on history if he had existed. Defoe had manuscripts and 'curious scarce tracts' in his library. He often spoke of his interest in such things, and it is by no means unlikely that he had read, besides the printed sources that we can assume, some unpublished and now lost accounts. The *Memoirs* contain some inaccuracies, balanced elsewhere by admirable and accurate descriptions. They contain writing which is not entirely characteristic of Defoe's usual style, but they also contain much that points to his now direct authorship. It is not the way in which we write history nowadays, yet historians have praised it. And Defoe, placed by his literary device in a position to praise it himself, concludes his preface on a note with which we can agree:

'The relation, we are persuaded, will recommend itself, and nothing more can be needful, because nothing more can invite than the story itself, which, when the reader enters into, he will find it very hard to get out of till he has gone through it.'

In 1721, as though content to rest upon the variegated laurels of the previous year, Defoe put out very little beyond the contributions he was still making to *Mist's* and *Applebee's* and the *Daily Post*—work which more than once put him on the track of material for something bigger. But he must have been writing *Moll Flanders*, which appeared in Janurary 1722 to usher in an astonishing year: *Moll Flanders* in January, *Due Preparations for the*

Plague and *Religious Courtship* in February, *A Journal of the Plague Year* in March, *Colonel Jack* in December. Looked at merely as quantity, that was well over seventeen hundred pages of reading-matter; and in addition the four hundred and twenty pages of *The Life and Actions of Peter Alexowitz, the present Czar of Muscovy*, published either at the end of that year or the beginning of the next, are usually accepted as by Defoe, though now quite unread.

Quantity, however, is a commonplace with Defoe. It is the quality of 1722 that is arresting. We have already noticed the two plague-books, and the connection between them, in the first chapter. *Religious Courtship*, like *The Family Instructor* (of which a second part had been issued in 1718), is a series of imaginary dialogues, in this case largely concerned with the advantage of religious harmony between husband and wife and master and servants. It is the work of Defoe the Puritan, remembering in old age, no doubt, the pieties of his childhood's home; but it is dead, where *Moll Flanders* is alive, the great book which Defoe presented to his public not so much with a title as with a *menu*:

'The Fortunes and Misfortunes of the Famous Moll Flanders who was born in Newgate, and during a life of continued Variety for Threescore years, besides her Childhood, was Twelve year a Whore, Five Times a Wife (whereof once to her own Brother), Twelve year a Thief, Eight year a Transported Felon in Virginia, at last grew Rich, liv'd Honest, and died a Penitent. Written from her own Memorandums.'

The exhibitor of that bill of contents has been identified by Lee as the author of an anonymous denunciation in the *Weekly Journal* of the famous, or infamous, Edmund

Curll, whose catalogue he attacked as 'lewd abominable pieces of bawdry, such as none can read even in miniature, for such an advertisement is to a book.'[1] There has been much argument as to whether Defoe was being hypocritical in avowing a moral purpose for his narratives of delinquency. Was he pandering, with his tongue in his cheek, to the popularity of vice? He was certainly writing for a market—there were three editions of *Moll Flanders* within the year and an abundance of them ever since. Yet it is reasonable to conclude that his moral intent was an honest one.

The matter has been confused by the shyness of Victorian admirers of *Robinson Crusoe* and the *Plague Year* and the *Shortest Way*; and yet more so by the persistent life of *Moll Flanders* and *Roxana* in the company of near-pornography. The fact is that among the writers whose works stand incongruously assembled with sex-manuals and restorers of vigour, Defoe, with the exception perhaps of Aristotle, is the least salacious. 'All possible care,' the preface to *Moll Flanders* tells us, 'has been taken to give no lewd ideas, no immodest turns in the new dressing up this story.' But one has the feeling that Defoe needed small effort to eliminate an element which seems to have interested him as little as the insipid extravagancies of contemporary romances. The amours of Moll and Roxana are conducted without appetite or fantasy. They are, for the most part, transactions, but under Defoe's contrivance they are no less interesting for that. That these transactions are wicked the author does not allow us to doubt, nor that wickedness must be followed by repentance. But he does not promote sexual irregularity to a special place in the calendar of

---

[1] However, if *Duncan Campbell* is regarded as even partly by Defoe it means, that he was not above accepting a commission from Curll, who published it.

offences. Roxana relates of the French prince who kept her that 'whoring . . . was the worst excursion that he made, for he was otherwise one of the most excellent persons in the world.' Moll Flanders graduates in the school of viciousness from harlot to thief, not *vice versa*. It is our own, not Defoe's, preoccupation with sex that has distinguished between *Robinson Crusoe* and *Moll Flanders* as different *kinds* of reading-matter, the one recommended to the young and the other, if possible, concealed from them. They were written by the same hand, and for the same public, and they are not essentially different in kind. We think of Crusoe as virtuous, the others as offenders, but Defoe knew that all men, and women, are sinners. Crusoe's conscience, after all, gives him plenty of trouble. His particular sins are to have forgotten God and the Bible until he found he needed both, and to have rebelled against domestic restraint. An uninhabited island offered few opportunities for more active wickedness, and the theme was rich enough without introducing crime.

Crime, it may next be noticed, shared with exploration and military memoirs the attractions of eventfulness. For a feminine character the road to such necessary adventure begins with sex. That, in Defoe's day at any rate, was part of the social contract. Had he been concerned with sexual relations for their own sake, his heroes would have been gallants, which they are not: they are too busy for that, and even Colonel Jack's experience of being 'five times married to four whores' has not placed his exploits in the company of *erotica*. When Defoe turned for material to his knowledge of Newgate and its inmates, his characters, so similar in their attitude to life, simply went the way of their sex. They were 'cat and dog, and rogue and whore.'

What Defoe was justifying by the moralizing that is a feature of his personal histories was not immodesty, for there is really none. It was not only wickedness in general. It was the storyteller's trade itself. He would have dissented profoundly from the dictum of Oscar Wilde (who hailed him with Herodotus and others in *The Art of Lying*) that 'all art is utterly useless.' In a prospectus written for the *Universal Spectator* (started by his son-in-law Henry Baker), Defoe proclaimed:

'The character of a good writer, wherever he is to be found, is this, *viz.*, that he writes so as to please and serve at the same time.'

The improving intention of his tales arises from this characteristically utilitarian outlook; but there are practical as well as moral lessons to be learned by the reader, who is advised (for example) in the preface to *Moll Flanders*, to protect his possessions against the tricks employed by Moll the thief. The moral lessens themselves have very often a materialistic flavour. Just as Captain Singleton and his Quaker counsellor lived as reformed characters on the proceeds of piracy, so it will have been noticed that Moll at last grew rich, lived honest and died a penitent. Her mercantile instincts of course, were always sound, if less obvious than Roxana's, and transportation to Virginia gave her opportunity to prove herself a colonizer of the Crusoe breed (Minto suggested long ago that Defoe, in writing *Robinson Crusoe*, may himself have been haunted by the fear of transportation). She and her husband purchased for £35 as much land 'as would make a sufficient plantation to employ between fifty and sixty servants,' and after eight years of work it was yielding £300 a year in produce. Again there is a Quaker to help, and again there is luck—

the sort of luck that Crusoe had with the honest woman who looked after his property while he was away, the sort of luck of which Defoe was often dreaming for himself. But we are made to undersand that sober and industrious management was chiefly responsible for success—'a story fruitful of instruction to all the unfortunate creatures who are obliged to seek their reestablishment abroad, whether by the misery of transportation or other disaster.'

There is a converse to the picture of virtue and repentance in the comfortably off. It is the prayer 'Give me not poverty, lest I steal,' which Moll remembers in temptation. Moll was born in Newgate Gaol, the offspring of a woman condemned to death who 'pleaded her belly' and was transported instead. The child then wandered with the gypsies, as did Captain Singleton as a boy. Roxana was deserted by her husband and left without means to support her children. Colonel Jack was 'a dirty glass-bottle-house boy,' who never knew his parents. So consistently does Defoe show us poverty, misfortune, and bad social conditions as the parents of wrongdoing that he has been hailed as a prophet of economic determinism. Fabians have taken him up, and even Marxists have tried on occasion to overlook his belief in God and the Devil and his insistence on the bourgeois virtues.

It is enough to recognize in him the reforming spirit of Protestantism. He was compassionate, sensitive to injustice, and an early critic of specific social ills: electoral corruption, the treatment of the insane and of debtors, the neglect of orphans and the exploitation of unwanted children by baby-farmers, and at least the worst excesses of the slave-trade. He was too solid a realist to ignore, as the authors of gallantries customarily do, the living issue of unlicensed love. The resort of Moll Flanders to the old woman who managed such matters is as important as anything in her story—we are even given three specimen tariffs at different rates for clandestine deliveries. It is the final fate of Roxana to be pursued—whether recognized or not remains uncertain —by the daughter of her first marriage who had been deposited by a trick with a distant relative; and the expectation of a child by her princely protector provokes reflections on the fate of bastards, even though high-born. In this liaison, unlike Roxana's previous activities, human affections are allowed their discreet but telling part. Roxana lets the Prince feel the child moving in her body, and at the lying-in 'I sent word I would make as few cries as possible, to prevent disturbing him.' The father's delight in his illegitimate child is noticed:

'He would sit and look at it, and with an air of seriousness sometimes, a great while together, and particularly, as I observed, he loved to look at it when it was asleep.'

It is a family man who is writing the memoirs of the Fortunate Mistress.

The Fortunate Mistress, usually referred to as *Roxana*, dates from 1724 and is the last of Defoe's well-known fictions. In the mastery of clear and natural narrative, in the even but never tedious pace of the prose, in concentration upon the essential theme which is the story of one woman's life, *Moll Flanders* is the greater book. Its fascination is incommunicable except by quotation, and at the same time the style is remarkable (as Brimley Johnson has observed) for the absence of purple passages. One piece of writing, it is true, is commonly picked out as an example of Defoe's special gifts. This is the vivid account of Moll's theft of a bundle from a woman about to board the Barnet coach, which Herbert Read reproduces at length in his *English Prose Style*. But any page could exhibit much the same skill in the use of the simplest means, so that a scene or an event is put sharply before the reader with the *right* detail: avoiding unnecessary description of buildings, clothes, weather, and any other extraneous factor, let alone the analysis of sensation and emotion which the later romantic novel took on board as essential cargo. Here is Moll the Whore declining into Moll the Thief:

'Wandering thus about, I knew not whither, I passed by an apothecary's shop in Leadenhall Street, where I saw lie on a stool just before the counter a little bundle wrapped in a white cloth; beyond it stood a maid-servant with her back to it, looking up towards the top of the shop, where the apothecary's apprentice, as I suppose, was standing upon the counter, with his back also to the door, and a candle in his hand, looking and reaching up to the upper shelf for something he wanted, so that both were engaged mighty earnestly, and nobody else in the shop.

'This was the bait; and the Devil, who I said laid the snare, as readily prompted me as if he had spoke, for I remember, and shall never forget it, 'twas like a voice spoken to me over my shoulder, "Take the bundle; be quick; do it this moment." It was no sooner said but I stepped into the shop, and with my back to the wench, as if I had stood up for a cart that was going by, I put my hand behind me and took he bundle, and went off with it, the maid or the fellow not perceiving me, or anyone else.

'It is impossible to express the horror of my soul all the while I did it. When I went away I had no heart to run, or scarce to mend my pace. I crossed the street indeed, and went down the first turning I came to, and I think it was a street that went through into Fenchurch Street. From thence I crossed and turned through so many ways and turnings, that I could never tell which way it was, nor where I went; for I felt not the ground I stepped on, and the farther I was out of danger, the faster I went, till, tired out and out of breath, I was forced to sit down on a little bench at a door, and then I began to recover, and found I was got into Thames Street, near Billingsgate.'

Can we doubt that that happened?

There are three episodes in *Roxana* which are almost as clearly seen—for example the chance discovery of the heroine's first husband among the troops parading at Versailles, an incident without the expected sequel. Both women engage our interest from the beginning, Moll learning to sew for gentlewomen in a charitable house in Colchester, Roxana living eight years as the wife of a wealthy brewer ('never, ladies, marry a fool') and then facing disaster with the resourceful companionship of her maid Amy. The difference in the two books is perhaps the difference in the two heroines. Saintsbury found Roxana 'disgusting' because of the absence of passion, and could not quite account for the different effect of a similar deficiency in Moll Flanders. May not the explanation be, quite simply, that the one was a whore and the other a mistress? The shorter word is frequently on Roxana's lips, and Moll, on the other hand, has her taste of the life of a gentlewoman. Yet the social difference does seem decisive. Even Defoe's forthright and human approach does not entirely strip Roxana of artificiality, but Moll is real and solid from first to last. We can believe that Defoe had seen and talked to her, or her prototype, in Newgate Gaol. With Roxana, we feel, he had a more formal, though a sympathetic acquaintance. Her very name, adopted from antiquity to suit her appearance in eastern costume at a royal rout, smacks of the romances from which Defoe was in fact turning the reading public. A liaison with a French prince was for such a writer more dangerous ground than Moll's honeymoon at the coaching-inn at Brickhill. He avoids the danger, but he skirts it. 'It would look a little too much like a romance,' says Roxana, 'here to repeat all the kind things he said to me on that occasion, but I can't omit one passage.' And on the next page, on receipt of a necklace:

'If I had an ounce of blood in me that did not fly up into my face, neck and breasts, it must be from some interruption in the vessels. I was all on fire with the sight, and began to wonder what it was that was coming to me.'

Moll has her excitements and her shames and her fears, but her circulation is on the whole in better condition.

There is at least one chapter of Roxana's life in which one feels the author to be thoroughly involved, and that is when she consults Sir Robert Clayton, an experienced man in the City, about the best way of maintaining and enhancing her financial capital. When at length he brings her an advantageous offer of marriage from a merchant, she finds that:

'Sir Robert and I agreed exactly in our notions of a merchant. Sir Robert said, and I found it to be true, that a true-bred merchant is the best gentleman in the nation; that in knowledge, in manners, in judgment of things, the merchant outdid many of the nobility; that having once mastered the world and being above the demand of business, though no real estate, they were then superior to most gentlemen even in estate. . . . That an estate is a pond, but that a trade is a spring; that if the first is once mortgaged it seldom gets clear, but embarrasses the person for ever; but the merchant had his estate continually flowing; and upon this he named me merchants who lived in more real splendour and spent more money than most of the noblemen in England could singly expend, and that they still grew immensely rich.'

By contrast with this satisfactory picture, poor Moll Flanders got herself tied up with an 'amphibious creature, this land-water thing called a gentleman-tradesman.' The one may have been Defoe's dream of success in his early days, the other his fear of failure.

That different dream, the reward of honest labour in a colony where the wicked cease from troubling, re-visits us in *Colonel Jack*; and it is here, in the middle phase in Virginia, that Man Friday's understudy appears, the negro slave Mouchat, and gives the author the opportunity for those remarks on the treatment of slaves to which attention has often been drawn. But *Colonel Jack*, despite the rapid gusto of its writing, is somewhat uneven and ill-constructed in comparison with Defoe's best narratives. There is first the superb account, a book in itself, of the foundling's boyhood and apprentice-ship to crime, praised by Lamb and not surpassed by the heavier artillery of Dickens. It is one more example of the view 'that to be reduced to necessity is to be wicked,' but Defoe does not let it go at that. The boy joining in the escapades of his ragged companions, the childish terrors and excitements, the element of hero-worship for the senior expert, the discovery that thieving brings the new problem of where to keep the goods or how to dispose of them, the nagging of a human feeling of wrong-doing to others in the mind of a lad without any kind of moral instruction—all these are woven with a touching simplicity into a pattern of adventure about the city streets and open places. When Jack and his companion leave London and head for the north on a criminal version of one of Defoe's own tours we begin to miss something—it is hard to say what, since the pace of incident is still brisk. And when they are enticed aboard ship and carried off to the colonial labour-market it is the beginning of another story. Thereafter Defoe adds fresh ingredients to the dish—adventures in the wars of Europe, and in Colonel Jack's lightly told matrimonial affairs a spice of fun that foreshadows Fielding and Smollett. Even the repentance has a dry touch to it:

'Here I wrote these Memoirs, having, to add to the pleasure of looking back with due reflections, the benefit of a violent fit of the gout, which, as it is allowed by most people, clears the head, restores the memory, and qualifies us to make the most just and useful remarks upon our own actions.'

There was a second edition of *Colonel Jack* in 1723 and a third in 1724. John Masefield has called it 'the best work of fiction ever done by Defoe,' and his opinion has been sufficiently influential to give it, along with *Moll Flanders*, a reissue in a contemporary collection of the world's classic novels.

If the old man did not again touch the heights of inventiveness and narrative charm, it was neither from

P

lack of material nor of industry in using it. The *New Voyage Round the World* does not really succeed, as it sets out to do, in improving upon the actual journals of voyages. But it is prodigally packed with incident and information, and even in the Andes Defoe remembers things familiar to his stay-at-home self and his readers— a waterfall 'twenty times as high as our own Monument,' a view into the valley that 'looked as the lowlands of England do below Box Hill in Surrey.' The *New Voyage* appeared in 1724, the year of *Roxana*, and the first volume of the *Tour thro' the whole Island of Great Britain*, and a book about servants called *The Great Law of Subordination Consider'd.* If we add to these, at the suggestion of Professor J. R. Moore of Indiana, the celebrated *General History of the Robberies and Murders of the Most Notorious Pyrates* which has been hitherto attributed to Captain Charles Johnson, we get a productivity comparable to that of 1722. But the grounds for this attribution have not yet been made public. What Professor Moore has done, however, is to put in a strong case for Defoe in the matter of *Robert Drury's Journal*, a story of shipwreck, fifteen years' captivity in Madagascar, and eventual rescue, which came out in 1729 and has always been recognized as owing something to the author of *Robinson Crusoe* and *Captain Singleton*.[1] Without analysing the internal evidence we can perhaps say that if anyone but Defoe wrote *Robert Drury's Journal*, it might well have aroused his professional jealousy. Similarly with *The Four Years' Voyages of Captain Roberts* (1726) and the better known *Military Memoirs of Captain George Carleton* (1728): the first including an account of

[1] *Defoe's Sources for Robert Drury's Journal* (Indiana University, 1943). In W. Minet's notes on *Daniel Defoe and Kent* (1914), the Captain Young who figures in the Journal is shown to have married into the family of Mrs. Veal, whose 'apparition' Defoe had reported in 1706.

two years' solitude on one of the Cape Verde Islands, the second a narrative of the Earl of Peterborough's romantic campaign in Spain, and both embellished with the customary descriptions of towns and cities, manners, religion, and natural products. All these are the sort of books with which Defoe had already found popularity. But that popularity was leading now to imitations in style and content, and the 'traces of Defoe's hand' are less easy to assess.

*　　*　　*

With the shower of miscellaneous works of the last years, several of which are highly interesting, we return from the far places of the earth to Defoe himself; sitting in his library at Stoke Newington, brooding upon the insolence of servants, the ill-treatment of the aged, the increase in crime in the city; or completing his knowledge of his own country by a last tour; in business again, and in trouble again, struggling to preserve his estate for his children and worried about their marriage-settlements; looking back upon his long experience to write *The Compleat English Tradesman* and *A Plan of the English Commerce*; looking forward, with something of that buoyancy of spirit that gave us the early *Essay Upon Projects*, to write the short and exhilarating *Augusta Triumphans*; and writing too, of the supernatural that he had felt so often at his elbow, the voice of conscience and the voice of temptation, the last companions of the lonely.

The personal references in the *Tour thro' the Whole Island of Great Britain* take us back sometimes to Defoe's early manhood—as when he watched the ill-fated Duke of Monmouth racing at Aylesbury. But the first volume dates from 1724, when the author was sixty-five, the second from 1725 and the third (most probably) from 1726. His own witness on so many journeys served him well, and the comparatively blank appearance of the year 1723 in the bibliography of his publications probably means that he had been taking pains to bring his observations up to date and to study other sources. England was changing every day. Defoe was proud of the national energy and more hopeful than his cotemporaries of its future fruits. Antiquities and matters of historic interest were worth a passing mention, but 'the situation of things is given not as they have been, but as they are.' In the preface to the third volume the note of urgency is repeated:

'Every new view of Great Britain would require a new description; the improvements that encrease, the new buildings erected, the old buildings taken down; new discoveries in metals, mines, minerals, new undertakings in trade; inventions, engines, manufactures, in a nation, pushing and improving as we are. These things open new scenes every day, and make England especially shew a new and differing face in many places on every occasion of surveying it.'

That was written in 1726, not in 1826. One result of the close study of Defoe's delightful and informative book can be seen in the recent tendency to look some decades earlier than had previously been the custom for the beginnings of that long development which we call the Industrial Revolution. In Defoe's pages we can find the domestic system and the factory system side by side, and his description of the manufacture and marketing of woollens and textiles in the West Riding of Yorkshire and other areas is accepted as important evidence on the eighteenth century's chief industry, especially on account of his abiding interest in 'the common people, how they live, and what their employment.' A guide-book of Defoe's time might rather be expected to tell us of the gentry and their parks and houses and possessions. We do indeed catch sight of these in the *Tour*, but it is significant that Defoe has less to say (for instance) of the Duke of Devonshire's famous seat at Chatsworth than of the extravagant glories of Edgware, north of London, where the newly created Duke of Chandos was busy outshining the ancient chivalry. The gentry that interest him most are the successful merchants and City men who have been encircling London with their new country houses in Surrey and Kent and Essex and Buckinghamshire. Moreover he tells us more about those who are on their way up than those who are established and retired; and much more about the business of fairs and market-places and harbours than about the cultivation of leisure in watering-places and rural retreats.

The centre of Defoe's picture of his times, though he takes us to Land's End and the wilds of Scotland, is London: rebuilt since the Fire, expanding in all directions, prosperous and vigorous, its port and river alive with traffic. But it is the Londoner Defoe who widens our view of his times—and not only in the *Tour*—more than any other writer of that metropolitan age. His curiosity is as eager in his late sixties as when he first contemplated the 'projecting temper' in the England of William and Mary. Though his notes on industry have aroused such interest, it is trade that concerns him most, and trade means movement, locomotion, transport. On matters of communication he is as exact as possible, critical of the state of the roads, observant about horses and inns, adventurous on cross-country routes, interested in coastal shipping and in inland water-transport in pre-canal days. Of agriculture he tells us something, but comparatively little—for that we have to await Arthur Young. Nor can we expect, in the seventeen-twenties, romantic descriptions of the English countryside or the grandeur of Wales or Scotland: fifty years later, after all, Boswell could only wring from Johnson the admission that he had noted in the Highlands 'some considerable protuberances.' Defoe is by no means insensitive to a pleasing view, but it pleases him best when he can assess it in terms of human activity and benefit; as when, looking from the terrace at Windsor Castle, 'over part of the finest and richest vale in the world,' he contemplates 'the river, with a winding and beautiful stream, gliding gently through the middle of it, and enriching by its navigation, both the land and the people on every side.' There remain, when we have tried to distinguish Defoe's special attitudes, the ample digressions, rewarding the reader in themselves. Despite his intention to avoid the antiquarian descriptions to be found in other books, he does in fact provide more than a little about ancient buildings, inscriptions, and remains. Ely he may pass over, but Lichfield Cathedral and York Minster he describes with a warmth which has given him the reputation of a precursor of the Gothic Revival. One reader will leave a bookmark at Defoe's account of the jockeys at Newmarket or his version (probably the first) of the story of Dick Turpin; another at his passing reflections as a good democrat upon 'rotten boroughs' like Old Sarum (which gave Pitt his seat) or Aldborough (Sir Richard Steele's constituency); a third at such wonders as the seasonal appearance of the birds in East Anglia or the dearth of women in the Essex marshes (in which matter one of his witnesses, he confesses, must have 'fibbed a little.') A fourth may pause where Defoe pauses at a battlefield of the Civil Wars, to hear the tale of Marston Moor or to study fresh material on the siege of Colchester. There are riches enough: and let us not forget the ageing writer's vision as the last corrections go to the printer in the effort to keep pace with the changing face of England:

'Every age will find an encrease of glory. And may it do so, till Great Britain as much exceeds the finest country in Europe, as that country now fancies they exceed her.'

The age that followed Defoe certainly provided an increase of editions of the *Tour*, but Samuel Richardson and others revised it out of all recognition. It is significant that in our own day it fell to a popular writer on economic and sociological topics, Professor G. D. H. Cole, to rescue the original work from these encrustations.[1] Some of Defoe's forecasts went wrong, but his vision of 'the situation of affairs in this great British Empire' (his word for the United Kingdom) is still stimulating; and we can be grateful that he resisted the temptation, hinted at in the preface to his first volume, to make the *Tour* a satire—'to have complain'd how much the conduct of the people diminishes the reputation of the island, on many modern occasions.' In his last years Defoe alternated between the still vigorous exposition of his life-long beliefs and an old man's sometimes querulous disapproval of the decadence of his time. His *Compleat English Tradesman*, published in two parts in 1725 and 1727, supplemented the *Tour* in its illumination of the movements of internal trade. It offers the counsel of sad experience against over-trading and other mistakes of the young merchant, and it explains business principles

[1] In 1927, and partly reprinted in the Everyman Edition. Professor Cole was in error, however, in supposing that *The Storm* had been written and published while Defoe was in Newgate Gaol.

with the frankness that revolted Charles˙Lamb. After this came, in 1728, *A Plan of the English Commerce*, which has been reprinted in the ten-volume Oxford edition of Defoe's chief works. Its ideas are those which he had so often expressed in his *Review* and elsewhere, and it was 'humbly offered to the consideration of the King and Parliament' as a tonic for the pessimists of the day. In face of 'loud complaints' Defoe argues that the English commerce is *not* declining, and he is ready with proposals for fresh enterprise such as the opening up of new markets in West Africa. In the same year appeared that remarkable little bundle of reforming projects which he called *Augusta Triumphans*:

'. . . or, the Way to make London the most Flourishing City in the Universe. I. By Establishing a University where Gentlemen may have Academical Education under the Eyes of their Friends. II. By an Hospital for Foundlings. III. By forming an Academy of Sciences at Christ's Hospital. IV. By Suppressing Pretended Mad-Houses, where many of the Fair Sex are unjustly confined, while their Husbands keep Mistresses etc., and many Widows are locked up for the Sake of their Jointure. V. To Save our Youth from Destruction, by clearing the Streets of impudent Strumpets, suppressing Gaming Tables, and Sunday Debauches. VI. To Save our lower class of People from utter Ruin, and render them useful, by preventing the immoderate use of Geneva. With a frank Exposition of many other common Abuses, and incontestable Rules for Amendment. Concluding with an Effectual Method to prevent Street Robberies, and a Letter to Col. Robinson, on Account of the Orphan's Tax.'

The title-page speaks for itself. London had to wait another century and a half for its University, with 'many colleges quartered at convenient distances.' But the Hospital for Foundlings, to be supported by Hogarth and by Handel as well as by Defoe, was on the way to realization: 'to my great joy I find my project already anticipated, and a noble subscription carrying on for this purpose.' In their own way Roxana and Moll Flanders had campaigned for this reform, and the plea in *Augusta Triumphans* is the same as Defoe put into their mouths. 'The fault is in the parents, not the child.' If Defoe were really the father of the illegitimate Benjamin Norton Defoe, his conscience told him that he shared the general guilt, and he would not have it said that humane treatment of unwanted children was an encouragement to vice. 'I am as much against bastards being begot, as I am for their being murdered.' The reference to Richard Savage (whose claim to aristocratic bastardy may have been an imposture) has been remarked in an earlier chapter. 'What a figure might this man have made in life,' writes Defoe, 'had due care been taken.' As it was, Savage turned on him.

As for the cleansing of the London streets of their bad characters, their Molls· and their Jacks and so on, this became a preoccupation of Defoe's old age—a design, one might say, of literary infanticide. Besides the works that have survived, he had given an eager public a type of crime-reporting which is no less popular today, though in England the law now provides fewer opportunities for securing interviews and gallows confessions. Jonathan Wild and Jack Sheppard were two of the notable criminals whose exploits he treated, and it is said that Sheppard, on the day of his execution, was persuaded to hand over publicly to Defoe a manuscript 'autobiography' which the latter had himself prepared. At the price of sixpence it sold eight editions in little more than a month. This sort of enterprise was a by-product of the anonymous weekly journalism which he continued up to March of 1726, to the manifest increase in circulation of such papers as *Applebee's Journal*. The serious attack on the social problem of street-robbers whose every trick and form of violence he knew so well came in 1728, his sixty-ninth year, with the proposals in *Augusta Triumphans* and two or three further pamphlets urging schemes for a kind of police-protection and for better lighting of the streets. These and some further works had come out under a new pseudonym, that of 'Andrew Moreton,' but the disguise must have been penetrated when 'Andrew Moreton' had the honour of presenting his plan for a safer city to King George II and Queen Caroline, the last little mark of royal notice in the life of him who had known 'the dungeon of Newgate and the closet of a king.'

Defoe was an old man, and often ill. He could no longer protect himself against thieves and bullies as he went about his sometimes mysterious business on his trips to London from Stoke Newington. Even servants, it would seem, gave him trouble. This was a not unusual complaint of the age, and Swift's *Directions to Servants* made famous fun of it. But Defoe plunged solemnly into the matter. Immediately after *Roxana* (whose maid Amy was 'as faithful to me as the skin of my back') he had published, in 1724, quite a thick volume called *The Great Law of Subordination Consider'd: or, the Insolence and Unsufferable Behaviour of Servants in England duly enquired into*. And in the next year there came (from 'Andrew Moreton') the successful pamphlet *Everybody's Business is Nobody's Business*, on the same theme. To the reforming zeal of the last years must be attributed also the *New Family Instructor* of 1727 and, in the same year the title

that exploded like a jumping cracker on the bookstalls:
Conjugal Lewdness, or Matrimonial Whoredom. It was later
slightly modified to *Use and Abuse of the Marriage-Bed*,
but it should be added that its language approaches the
topic (including the matter of birth-control) with
deliberate delicacy.

The master of fact, who lent a strange immortality to
ordinary people and everyday objects, has left us also a
group of studies in the occult; indeed it would have been
strange if the journalist in Defoe had neglected so fruitful
a field. But the series is not all ephemeral. It may be said
to begin with that fascinating rehearsal for his narratives,
the *Apparition of Mrs. Veal*, in 1706. A few years later he
was dabbling, like others, in almanacs, prognostications,
and second-sight, sharing with both Swift and Steele the
celebrated pseudonym of Isaac Bickerstaff. There was
Dickery Cronke, the dumb Cornishman who spoke
miraculously on his death-bed. There was Duncan
Campbell, a Scottish wonder-worker who was also deaf
and dumb. Defoe probably wrote a pamphlet of 1726
about Duncan Campbell called *The Friendly Daemon*; but
the lengthy *Life and Adventures of Duncan Campbell* which
has often been published in collections of his work seems,
for the most part, utterly unlike his writing, though he
may have edited and added to it for the publisher Curll.
The Political History of the Devil and *A System of Magick*, both
published in 1726, are a different matter. From these
we can judge what Defoe did and did not believe in. He
believed in a polarity of good and evil as candidly as he
read the two columns of his account-books; he had come
across evidence of apparitions which convinced him that
they were a possibility, if a rare one; and he had
experience of his own 'voices.' 'There is a converse of
spirits,' he had concluded (writing in the *Review*), 'I

mean those unembodied, and those that are encased in flesh.' Crusoe knew of the warning voices. Moll Flanders heard the actual words of temptation: 'Take the bundle; be quick; do it this moment.' Defoe himself, when in danger of a new imprisonment and ruin, received the bodiless advice 'Write to the Judge,' obeyed it, and thus entered upon the contract to write secretly for the Tory Press that kept him free and active.

'I have had, perhaps, a greater variety of changes, accidents and disasters in my short life, than any man, at least more than most men alive; yet I had never any considerable mischief or disaster attending me, but sleeping or waking I have had notice of it beforehand, and had I listened to these notices, I believe I might have shunned the evil.'

The converse of spirits, if rightly understood, was a practical and useful phenomenon, far removed from necromancy and hocus pocus. In his three serious books on the subject Defoe had a Protestant concern for the elimination of superstition. His *Political History of the Devil*, which Henry Kingsley found brilliant and John Masefield, for some reason, nauseating, strips the invisible antagonist of his vulgar attributes, traces his work in the world's history while mocking at the fables and even criticising Defoe's admired Milton for his portrayal of Satan. It was a provocative book in its own day, widely read in England and abroad, placed upon the Papal Index and eventually quoted by George Eliot in *The Mill on the Floss*. It is readable today partly because its theme called forth, at the end of the writer's life, the irony and wit of his earlier pamphlets as well as the contemplation of things beyond the veil. The *System of Magick* exposes popular credulity in the black arts, and shows that Defoe had studied the literature of the pseudo-sciences that he rejects. The *History and Reality of Apparitions* examines carefully what he saw as the sense and nonsense of the subject. He makes fun of the ghost-stories of the idle or the interested, but:

'There is such a drumming in the soul, that can beat an alarm when he pleases, and so loud as no other noise can drown it, no power silence it, no mirth allay it, no bribe corrupt it.'

*　　*　　*

In the last sentence of *The Farther Adventures of Robinson Crusoe* we seem to hear once again the authentic voice of its author:

'And here, resolving to harrass myself no more, I am preparing for a longer journey than all these, having liv'd 72 years, a life of infinite variety, and learn'd sufficiently to know the value of retirement, and the blessing of ending our days in peace.'

Defoe nearly achieved the age which he had set for Crusoe, but retirement was a thing beyond him. He did not stop writing—two unpublished manuscripts, *Of Royall Educacioun* and *The Compleat English Gentleman*, were left behind him at his death. He could not keep out of business—there was an abortive beginning to a new tile-making enterprise in 1724, and the papers that after-wards found their way into the Courts mention deals in cheese, oysters, honey, and bacon. And he spent his last year of life in hiding, a fugitive, as it now appears, from one more creditor.

In *Robinson Crusoe* Defoe had created the Protestant hermit. In 1726 he published (as Andrew Moreton) a little book called *The Protestant Monastery*, the title-page of which explains its interest for his biographers:

'*The Protestant Monastery*, or, a Complaint against the Brutality of the Present Age, Particularly the Pertness and Insolence of our Youth to Aged Persons. With a Caution to People in Years how they give the Staff out of their own Hands, and leave themselves to the Mercy of others. Concluding with a Proposal for Erecting a Protestant Monastery, where Persons of small Fortune may end their Days in Plenty, Ease and Credit, without Burthening their Relations, or accepting Publick Charities.'

But he was not to find his Island or his Monastery. Worse still, after a lifetime of writing, he could not find a publisher for *The Protestant Monastery* and had to bring it out at his own risk. He was 'almost worn out with age and sickness,' he said in his preface, and added: 'The Old Man cannot trouble you long.' A year later his favourite daughter Sophia was writing in a letter of 'a violent sudden pain' which afflicted her father. 'I fear it is a messenger from that grand tyrant which will at last destroy the (to me) so-much-valued structure.'

She was writing to her suitor, Henry Baker, whose personal papers are almost the only evidence we have of Defoe's private life at Stoke Newington. The protracted negotiations for Sophia's marriage-settlement consequently bulk largely, and perhaps too largely, in the story of these last years as it has come down to us. Nevertheless the four years of haggling over the dowry cannot be written off, even allowing for Baker's own acquisitiveness. They reveal the tradesman in Defoe as often as the affectionate father, anxious for his children's security, which he undoubtedly was. A man of Defoe's nervous energy might well become more difficult to deal with as he felt his strength slipping from him. To 'give the staff out of his own hands' would go hard with such a man, and 'the mercy of others' was something in which experience had given him little confidence. His procrastination, his 'hiding in mists,' of which Baker warmly complained, is easier to understand now that we know how doggedly he must have been striving to preserve from other claimants what he hoped to bequeath to his family. It would be amusing to fancy, at the same time, that the language of Henry Baker's addresses to his daughter was sometimes an irritant to the creator of 'homely plain English.' Here is a brief specimen:

'My Sophy, ah, how I languish for thee! What soft sensations seize me! What fondness inexpressible possesses me when'er I think of thee! This very moment my soul is stretching after thee with ardent longings. Methinks I fold thee in my eager arms, and bask and pant and wanton in thy smiles; and now I hold thee off and gaze upon thy charms with infinite delight, and now all ecstasy I snatch thee to me, and devour thy lips, strain thee with breathless rapture to my bosom, till feeble mortal faints, unable to endure bliss so excessive, and sinks with joys celestial.'

The story, however, ends in a happy marriage, though only after Henry Baker had proposed a poetic suicide and Sophia Defoe had fallen ill with the strain. The financial bickering was not yet over, but a compromise was effected, an agreement made, and Sophia provided with a bond for £500 payable on her father's death, the house at Stoke Newington being engaged as security.

There were three other daughters living. Maria was married and on Hannah her father had settled some

property at Colchester. Henrietta was still unprovided.
To safeguard the arrangements he had made and to leave
something after his death Defoe went on working,
writing, speculating, venturing. At the time that Henry
Baker was pining with unfulfilled passion and trying to
raise the old man from four per cent to five per cent,
Defoe was already once more in the grip of the inveterate enemy, pursuit for debt: a grand tyrant less
merciful than the one that Sophia feared. It dated back
to the real disaster of his life, the second bankruptcy of
1704, brought on by his arrest and imprisonment. Did
his voices, the drumming in his soul, never warn him of
where *The Shortest Way with the Dissenters* was to lead him?.

The debts of his first bankruptcy he had settled. For
the second he compounded with his creditors through a
trustee, James Stancliffe, Nevertheless actions on the
same account pursued him at various points of his subsequent career. Stancliffe was long dead, Defoe claimed
that everything had been discharged; but the affair, with
a remorselessness that would today be legally impossible,
had now got as far as the widow of the administrator of
Stancliffe's estate. Her name was Mary Brooke. Had he
been younger Defoe might have fought this case more
openly. Feeling his strength ebbing and the security of
his dependents once more endangered, it looks as though
he first safeguarded what he could by making it over to
his eldest son Daniel, and then, in his seventieth year,
went on the run.

On 12 August, 1730, Defoe wrote to Henry Baker
from a place 'about two miles from Greenwich'—an
area which he had praised in his *Tour* as enjoying 'the best
air, best prospect, and the best conversation in England.'
Now it was his hiding-place, 'nor have I a lodging in
London, nor have I been at that place in the Old Bailey,

since I wrote you I was removed from it.' He wrote 'under the load of insupportable sorrows' and 'under a weight of very heavy illness, which I think will be a fever.' The letter—it is a celebrated one in the chronicles of Defoe—is not without that self-dramatization which a reader of the *Appeal to Honour and Justice* will understand; and the 'poor dying mother' of his children in fact survived him by two years. The chief cause of his distress, the 'inhuman' failure of his son to provide for the family with which Defoe had entrusted him, is probably exaggerated. But not deliberately: the old man, though his spirit had carried him 'thro' greater disasters than these,' was in an agony of distress which caused him to lean upon the son-in-law who had once called him his evil genius.

'I only ask one thing of you as a dying request. Stand by them when I am gone, and let them not be wrong'd, while he is able to do them right. Stand by them as a brother; and if you have anything within you owing to my memory, who have bestowed on you the best gift I had to give, let them not be injured and trampled on by false pretences, and unnatural reflections. . . .

'I would say, (I hope) with comfort, that 'tis yet well. I am so near my journey's end, and am hastening to the place where the weary are at rest and the wicked cease to trouble; be it that the passage is rough, and the day stormy, by what way soever He pleases to bring me to the end of it, I desire to finish life with this temper of soul in all cases: *Te Deum Laudamus* . . .

'It adds to my grief that I must never see the pledge of your mutual love, my little grandson. Give him my blessing, and may he be to you both your joy in youth, and your comfort in age, and never add a sigh to your

Q

sorrow. But, alas! that is not to be expected. Kiss my dear Sophy once more for me; and if I must see her no more, tell her this is from a father that loved her above all his comforts to his last breath.'

That last breath was drawn on 26 April, 1731, in an obscure lodging in Ropemaker's Alley, close to the house where a son had been born to James Foe, butcher and tallow-chandler, in the first year of the reign of King Charles II, when the maypole was raised in the Strand again and even Dissenters could hope that better days were coming. Daniel Defoe died alone, and he had fought that last secret fight alone, but there is now good reason to think that he had won it. Mrs. Mary Brooke was granted letters of administration on his goods, but rightly or wrongly her persistence probably brought her little. He had put his dependents' livelihood beyond her reach. The most reliable of his biographers, Professor Sutherland, has observed that she was still arguing about a clock some years afterwards.

And with that clock, that little object of contention, that item of an inventory, we may take our last look at the writer who stored our literary experience with so vivid a profusion of the world's various goods, and with men and women who share the solid existence of their chattels. Defoe's clock joins the barometer that he tapped in the great storm of 1703; and Crusoe's pot, and his ingenious umbrella, and the treasure-trove of the wreck; the 'joynted baby' that the urchin-gang stole at the fair in *Colonel Jack*, the dish of stewed oysters that Colonel Jack and the widow left for the servant, Mrs. Veal's elbow-chair and her gown of scoured silk, the little bundle in a white cloth that Moll Flanders snatched up while the apprentice peered into the upper shelf with a candle in his hand. Confronted with the merchandise of Defoe's unflagging industry, even admiring critics are sparing in their use of the language of aesthetic appreciation. But if 'facts become art through love,' as Sir Kenneth Clark has written of Giovanni Bellini, then Defoe, who loved facts, had the art not merely to preserve but to fashion them.

Yet it is possible that an unassailed reputation for realism has obscured the creative element in a career of self-renewing vigour. In his life and in his work Defoe was anything but dull. He may not exhibit the sustained and disciplined and, as it were, privileged power of Swift or Pope or Addison, but he has left one book which can still enchant readers who have scarcely heard his rivals' names (or indeed his own); and beyond that an abundance of fresh and stimulating reading which, if it were now presented as it deserves, would seem more the gift of a generation than of an individual. He may be thought of as excluded, an outsider, a 'plebeian genius'; but without the products of his activity and his curiosity, how much less we should know and understand of his England, his united Britain, its daily business, its movement, its conflicts and its calms, the legacy of its people to ourselves. Daniel Defoe is not the fine flower of the great century. He is its root.

READING NOTE

THE bibliography of Defoe, established in the *Cambridge History of English Literature*, Vol. IX (1913), has been revised and extended in the *Cambridge Bibliography of English Literature*, Vol II (1940. Fresh suggestions and attributions continue to be made, especially from America. For the ordinary reader there is no difficulty of approach to *Robinson Crusoe* (the First Part), *Moll Flanders*, *Captain Singleton*, the *Memoirs of a Cavalier*, the *Journal of the Plague Year*, the *Tour* (except Scotland), *Colonel Jack* and *Roxana*, which are all to be had in modern editions (the first six in *Everyman*). None of the various 'collected editions,' including Defoe's own, is adequate or complete, and some contain works that are not his; but odd volumes, particularly of the *Romances and Narratives* edited by Aitken, are worth the search among the second-hand bookshops. The same editor's *Later Stuart Tracts* (*An English Garner*, Vols. II. and III, 1903) provides one means of access to some of Defoe's political writings, and Morley's *De Foe's Earlier Life and Chief Earlier Works* (1899) includes complete texts. Though Defoe's first biographer (Chalmers, 1790) has of course been superseded, one occasionally finds the 1841 editon containing texts of important tracts and the *True-Born Englishman*; and a later biographer (Lee, 1869) filled two volumes with his own discoveries of the periodical contributions between 1716 and 1729. There are well selected extracts in Masefield's volume on Defoe in the *Masters of Literature* series (1909) and in W. P. Trent's *Daniel De Foe and How to Know Him* (1916), an American publication; and Mr. Roger Manvell has in preparation a new Defoe anthology. The facsimile *Review* and its separate index are only to be found in the largest libraries.

CHRONOLOGY

(mentioning a selection only of Defoe's publications)

CHARLES II: 1660–1685

1660. Defoe (presumed) born in London a few months after the Restoration.

1665–6. The Plague and Fire of London.

1680. (about). Defoe, educated as a Dissenter's son at Morton's Academy, Stoke Newington, embarks on a commercial career in the City.

1684. Marriage to Mary Tuffley.

JAMES II: 1685–1688

1685. Defoe takes some part in the unsuccessful Monmouth Rebellion in the West, but escapes the Bloody Assize.

WILLIAM AND MARY: 1688–1694

1689. The Act of Settlement. Defoe, now a City Liveryman, rides with a ceremonial escort of London citizens when the King and Queen go to Guildhall.

1691. First definitely ascertained publication (verse satire), though there are hints of earlier writing by Defoe.

1692. Business failure and bankruptcy.

1694. Defoe, having compounded with his creditors, attracts influential interest and is seen at Court.

WILLIAM III: 1694–1702

1697. Defoe's brick and tile works at Tilbury in a flourishing condition.

1698. Defoe's first considerable book, *An Essay Upon Projects*, and pamphlets on Occasional Conformity, a standing army, and the reformation of manners (*A Poor Man's Plea*).

1700–01. Pamphlets supporting King William's continental policy and denouncing electoral corruption. Emboldened by the great success of his poem, *A True-Born Englishman*, satirizing the King's detractors, Defoe involves himself in the affair of the Kentish Petition.

ANNE: 1702–1714

1702 (March). Death of Defoe's great hero, King William, shortly after Marlborough's signature of the Grand Alliance, implemented in the new reign by the opening of the War of the Spanish Succession. Alarmed by Queen Anne's partiality to the High Church Party Defoe, though a critic in principle of Occasional Conformity, resists the Bill seeking to penalize it and publishes anonymously his brilliantly ironic pamphlet, *The Shortest Way With The Dissenters*.

1703. Defoe arrested, fined, imprisoned, and pilloried for *The Shortest Way*. His *Hymn to the Pillory* and first collected volume of his writings prepared in prison, whence he is released on the intervention of Robert Harley. Collapse of the brick-making business.

1704. The year of the Battle of Blenheim. First numbers appear of Defoe's one-man paper the *Review*, to be carried on for nine years, supporting moderate policies of Harley and Godolphin at home and the war against France. Narrative of *The Storm* (of 1703), pamphlet *Giving Alms No Charity*, and a dozen other topical pieces. Beginning of Defoe's journeys through Britain as Harley's confidential agent.

1705. Much controversial pamphleteering, some verse, and the long, allegorical prose satire *The Consolidator*. Defoe on the road again, mainly in the West.

1706. Two important works, the brief *True Relation of the Apparition of Mrs. Veal* and the immense political poem *Jure Divino*; also writings advocating the Union of the English and Scottish Parliaments under negotiation in Edinburgh, for which Defoe goes to Scotland (September) on Harley's instructions.

1707. Defoe's work for the Union (which includes his poem *Caledonia*) completed by the royal assent of 6 March, he returns to London at the end of the year. His *Review* (4th annual volume) becomes *A Review of the State of the BRITISH Nation*.

1708–09. On Harley's dismissal (February, 1708) Defoe re-enlists in the Queen's service under Godolphin and is sent again to Scotland (August, 1709) to investigate reported Jacobite stirrings. His 700-page *History of the Union* published. Sensational trial of High Churchman Dr. Sacheverell weakens Godolphin's Government.

1710. Replacing her Ministers by Tories, Queen Anne dismisses Godolphin but restores Harley. Defoe, once more serving Harley, finds growing Tory power a challenge to his agility as a political writer. Two financial essays for the Government, on *Loans* and on *Publick Credit*.

1711. Arrival of the ex-castaway Alexander Selkirk in London with a story which Defoe is too busy to deal with. He settles his family in a substantial house at Stoke Newington and pours out pamphlets defending Harley, explaining the policy of now seeking peace with France and popularizing the South Sea scheme.

1712–14. More pamphleteering, much of it of a high order, on the issues of peace with France (Treaty of Utrecht, 31 March, 1713) and the Protestant (Hanoverian) Succession to the throne. Three ironical titles on the latter are used by Whig enemies to secure Defoe's arrest and prosecution, from which Harley retrieves him. The *Review* comes to an end (May, 1713), but Defoe writes anonymously for a new paper, the *Mercator*, supporting Bolingbroke's trade policy. Harley's final removal from office and the Queen's death (July, 1714).

GEORGE I: 1714–1727

1715. Harley (now Earl of Oxford), impeached with the absent Bolingbroke by the Whig Government of the new reign, still has Defoe's anonymous support. Defoe's own peace with the new régime and his rescue from the consequences of a libel charge are secured by a secret compact to 'take the edge off' the extreme Tory Press. His defence against enemies on all sides in the *Appeal to Honour and Justice* stands out, with the popular *Family Instructor* and the first part of the *History of the Wars of Charles XII of Sweden*, among more than 30 publications.

1716–18. Contributions and collaborations in several weekly and monthly journals; also many controversial writings, political and ecclesiastical, and the interesting *Turkish Spy* letters. Woodes Rogers' *Cruising Voyage Round The World*, containing the Selkirk story, appears in a second edition (1718).

1719. The years of journalism and polemics suddenly illuminated with *Robinson Crusoe* (Parts I and II), beginning the great narrative series of Defoe's sixties.

1720. *Memoirs of a Cavalier; Captain Singleton; Serious Reflections of Robinson Crusoe.* Periodical contributions continue through these years (to 1726).

1722. *Moll Flanders; Due Preparations for the Plague* and *A Journal of the Plague Year; Religious Courtship; Colonel Jack.*

1724. *The Fortunate Mistress* (Roxana); *The Great Law of Subordination Consider'd; A Tour thro' the Whole Island of Great Britain,* Vol. I; *A New Voyage Round the World; Robberies and Escapes of John Sheppard.* Defoe takes up some new business activities.

1725. *Everybody's Business is Nobody's Business; Jonathan Wild; The Compleat English Tradesman,* Vol. I; the *Tour,* Vol. II.

1726. *Political History of the Devil; Four Years, Voyages of Captain Roberts* (?); *The Protestant Monastery; A System of Magick;* the *Tour,* Vol. III.

GEORGE II: 1727–1760

1727. *Conjugal Lewdness; History and Reality of Apparitions; A New Family Instructor; The Compleat English Tradesman,* Vol. II; also a few pamphlets, chiefly on trade.

1728. *Augusta Triumphans; A Plan of the English Commerce; Memoirs of Captain Carleton* (?); and pamphlets on prevention of street-robberies. Defoe's daughter Sophia married to Henry Baker.

1729. Trade pamphlets and (uncertainly) *Madagascar, or Robert Drury's Journal.* Defoe complains of illness.

1730. *A Brief State of the Inland or Home Trade of England* and a further *Scheme for the Immediate Preventing of Street Robberies.* Defoe leaves home in the summer, pursued for an alleged debt.

1731. Defoe dies in lodgings in London (April), leaving *The Compleat English Gentleman* and *Of Royall Education* in manuscript.

INDEX

Addison, Joseph, 78, 122, 125, 142, 227

Africa, 143, 193–4, 216

Anne, Queen, 4, 19, 73, 101, 117, 124, 133, 135, 148, 152–3, 175; interest in Defoe, 18, 107, 110–11, 114–15, 149, 154, 162, 169; foreign policy, 102; support of Established Church, 102, 103; relations with her Government, 118, 121, 154, 156

Annesley, Dr. Samuel, 44, 50–2

Anson, George, Admiral Baron, 179

Applebee's Journal, 31, 53, 164, 198, 218

Arbuthnot, John, *John Bull*, 24

Arne, Thomas, *Rule Britannia*, 24

Athenian Gazette (later *Mercury*), 66, 141

Athenian Society, 65–6

Avery, Capt. Ben, 192–3

Baker, Henry, 170, 202, 222–3, 224–225

Battersby, Defoe's schoolfellow, 52

Baxter, Richard, 41, 42, 57, 64

Behn, Aphra, 17, 28; *Oroonoko*, 17

Bethlem Hospital, 76

Bible, 23, 27, 44, 51, 53, 184, 201

Bickerstaff, Isaac, *pseud.*, 219

Bloody Assize, 52, 58, 137

Bolingbroke, Henry St. John, Viscount, 133, 159, 162, 164; *Idea of a Patriot King*, 133

Brooke, Mrs. Mary, 224, 226

Bunyan, John, 1, 54, 86, 172, 186; *Pilgrim's Progress*, 5, 54, 186

Caroline, Queen, 218

Cervantes, 184; *Don Quixote*, 186

Ceylon, 176

Charles I, 45, 198

Charles II, 27–8, 30, 44, 45, 56, 57, 73, 124, 137, 188, 226; Defoe's opinion of, 43, 98

Cobbett, William, 91, 108 n.

Coffee-houses, 20, 60, 66, 122, 136, 147

Colepeper, William, 108–9, 110

Collier, Jeremy, 82

Conventicle Act, 45

Cooke, Edward, *Voyage to the South Sea*, 175

Cromwell, Oliver, 1, 41, 90, 196

Cromwell, Richard, 44

Croome, George, printer, 106

Crusoe, Timothy, 38, 52, 54

Curll, Edmund, 199–200, 200 n., 219

Daily Advertiser, 173

Daily Courant, 137

Daily Post, 164, 198

Dampier, William, 2, 11, 176–7, 178, 179

Davis, Robert, 147

Defoe, Benjamin, 170

Defoe, Benjamin Norton, 86–7, 217

Defoe, Daniel, works by or attributed to: *Advice to the Electors of Great Britain*, 26; *Appeal to Honour and Justice*, 33, 137–8, 143, 152, 154–5, 166, 170, 172, 225; *Argument for a Standing Army*, 26, 90, 91; *Art of Painting* (tr.), 184; *Augusta Triumphans*, 85, 87, 211, 216–7, 218; *Brief Reply to the History of Standing Armies*, 90; *Caledonia*, 151; *Captain Singleton*, 13, 19, 34, 130, 139, 150n., 165, 176–1, 192–5, 203, 210; *Colonel Jack*, 2, 14, 19, 23, 34, 47, 60–2, 80, 150 n., 165, 174, 185, 199, 203, 208–9, 226; *Compleat English*

235

Gentleman, 41, 221; *Compleat English Tradesman*, 20, 21, 35, 41, 43, 64, 65, 67, 69, 145, 146, 169, 211; *Conduct of Christians the Sport of Infidels*, 173; *Conjugal Lewdness*, 85, 219; *Consolidator*, 33, 131–3; *Danger of the Protestant Religion Consider'd*, 26, 92; *Due Preparations for the Plague*, 47, 198–9; *Dumb Philosopher*, 192, 219; *Duncan Campbell* (?), 200, 219; *Elegy on the Author of the True-born Englishman*, 134; *Enquiry into Occasional Conformity*, 101; *Essay at Removing National Prejudiceo*, 150–1; *Essay on the South Sea Trade*, 26, 159 n., *Essay upon Loans*, 159; *Essay upon Projects*, 10, 65, 74–80, 83, 90, 185, 211; *Essay upon Publick Credit*, 159; *Everybody's Business is Nobody's Business*, 218; *Family Instructor*, 24, 85, 172, 199; *Four Years' Voyages of Captain Roberts* (?), 210–11; *Friendly Daemon*, 219; *Giving Alms No Charity*, 145; *Great Law of Subordination Consider'd*, 210, 218; *Hannibal at the Gates*, 26, 160; *History and Reality of Apparitions*, 221; *History of the Devil*, 35, 219, 220; *History of the Kentish Petition*, 94; *History of the Pirates* (?), 210; *History of the Union*, 116, 152; *History of the Wars of Charles XII*, 173; *Hymn to the Pillory*, 111–13; *Instructions from Rome in Favour of the Pretender*, 156; *Journal of the Plague Year*, 4, 6, 19, 28, 29, 31, 34, 46–9, 165, 185, 187, 195, 199, 200; *Jure Divino*, 116, 133–4; *King of Pirates*, 192; *King William's Affection to the Church of England*, 111; *Legion's Memorial*, 93–4, 107, 119; *Life and Actions of Czar Peter Alexowitz*, 199; *Life and Actions of Jonathan Wild*, 217; *Memoirs of a Cavalier*, 28, 34, 165, 185, 192, 195–8; *Military Memoirs of Captain Carleton* (?), 210–11; *Minutes of the Negotiations of M. Mesnager* (?), 30, 164; *Mock Mourners*, 100; *Moll Flanders*, 19, 20, 28, 34, 47, 80, 113, 130, 150 n., 165, 172, 180, 185, 198, 199–206, 207, 208, 209, 217, 220, 226; *More Reformation*, 100; *New Discovery of an Old Intreague*, 65; *New Family Instructor*, 85, 218; *New Voyage Round the World*, 165, 180, 210; *Ode to the Athenian Society*, 65; *Original Power of the Collective Body of the People of England*, 119; *Pacificator*, 90; *Plan of the English Commerce*, 35, 143, 211, 216; *Poor Man's Plea*, 80, 84, 90, 110, 113; *Present State of Jacobitism Consider'd*, 95; *Present State of Parties*, 52; *Protestant Monastery*, 222; *Reasons Against the Succession of the House of Hanover*, 160–2; *Reasons Against a War with France*, 95; *Reformation of Manners*, 17, 22, 85, 110; *Religious Courtship*, 85, 199; *Review*, 6, 31, 54, 69, 82, 88, 89, 100, 113, 116, 117, 118, 122, 125, 134, 135–45, 147, 148, 150, 152, 155, 156, 157, 158, 159, 160, 162, 164, 164 n., 167, 168, 219, 220; *Robberies and Escapes of John Sheppard*, 217–18; *Robert Drury's Journal* (?), 210; *Robinson Crusoe*, 1, 2, 3, 4–18, 19, 28, 34, 37, 38, 44, 51, 54, 55–6, 70, 72, 80, 106, 116, 127, 130, 139, 143, 150 n., 165, 171, 172, 173–92, 200, 210, 202, 210, 220, 221, 226; *Roxana* (The Fortunate Mistress), 19, 20, 30 n., 34, 70, 80, 139, 165, 188, 200, 204, 206–8, 210, 217, 218; *Royal Education*, 221; *Seasonable Warning Against Insinuations in Favour of the Pretender*, 160; *Secret History of the White Staff* (?), 163; *Shortest Way to Peace and Union*, 111; *Shortest Way with the Dissenters*, 26, 27, 29, 35, 41, 71, 102–7, 109, 110, 111, 136 n., 160, 200, 224; *Six Distinguishing Characters of a Parliament Man*, 93; *Storm, The*, 125–7, 215 n.; *System of Magick*, 219, 220; *Tour Through the Whole Island of Great Britain*, 6, 13–14,

19, 20, 35, 42, 43, 50, 58, 59, 62,
87, 127, 146, 147, 152, 165,
167, 210, 211–15, 224; *True-Born
Englishman*, 24, 35, 81, 96–9, 107,
110, 122, 134; *True Relation of the
Apparition of Mrs. Veal*, 29, 35, 116,
127–31, 210 n., 219, 226; *Two
Great Questions Consider'd*, 91;
*Voyages and Adventures of Sir Walter
Raleigh*, 178–9; *What if the Pretender
Should Come?* 26, 161–2; *What if
the Queen Should Die?* 26, 161–2

Defoe, Daniel (junior), 170, 225
Defoe, Hannah, 87, 170, 223–4
Defoe, Henrietta, 87, 170, 224
Defoe, Maria, 87, 170, 223
Defoe, Martha, 87
Defoe, Mary, 87
Defoe, Mrs. Mary (*née* Tuffley), 62
87, 107, 169, 225
Defoe, Sophia, 87, 170, 222–3, 226
Dissenters, 1, 22, 27, 38–41, 43,
44–5, 50, 51, 52, 56, 57, 82, 100–
105, 120, 131–2, 147, 148–9,
155, 156, 226
Dormer's Newsletter, 163
Dottin, Paul, 6, 50, 56
Dover, Treaty of, 57
Drelincourt, Charles, 128
Dryden, John, 22, 33, 96, 191;
Absalom and Achitophel, 155; *Hind
and the Panther*, 40
Dunton, John, 19, 32, 38–9, 50, 52,
74, 99, 141; *Life and Errors*, 109–
110, 117; *Secret History of the
Weekly Writers*, 32; *Whipping-Post*,
141
Dutch, 20, 21, 26, 93, 97–8

Edinburgh, 123, 140, 149–53, 164 n.
Edinburgh Courant, 164 n.
Eliot, George, *The Mill on the Floss*,
220
Elton (Hunts), 42 n.
Englishman, 175
Etton (Northants), 42

Fielding, Henry, 24, 36, 82, 142,
181, 188, 209; *Joseph Andrews*, 181
Flying Post, 137
Foe, Alice (Defoe's mother), 44

Foe, James (Defoe's father), 1–2, 38,
41–2, 44, 226
Foe, Daniel (grandfather), 6
Foe, Henry (uncle), 46, 48
Foxe, John, *Book of Martyrs*, 23
Foundling Hospital, 87, 217
France, 63, 76, 81, 90, 103, 139,
143, 159, 161; Revolution, 18,
23, 24; at war with Britain and
Allies, 68, 74, 89, 92–3, 102, 140,
157–8

George I, 4, 19, 31, 33, 121, 162,
166
George II, 4, 218
Gildon, Charles, 54, 64, 180, 188;
*Life and Adventures of Mr. Daniel
De Foe*, 180
Godolphin, Sidney Godolphin, Earl
of, 18, 110, 114, 124, 125, 139,
153, 154, 155, 156, 158, 160, 162
Guiana, 178–9

Hakluyt, Richard, 175
Halifax, Charles Montagu, Earl of, 74
Halifax, George Savile, Marquis of
('The Trimmer'), 120
Hampton Court Palace, 80, 100
Handel, George Frederick, 217
Harley, Robert (Earl of Oxford and
Earl Mortimer), 93–4, 124, 133,
166, 167; Defoe's political patron,
9, 18, 19, 73, 119, 120, 122,
124–5, 138, 139, 147, 148, 156;
delivers Defoe from prison, 107,
110, 113–14, 121; sends him to
Scotland, 123, 149, 150–3, 170;
first fall from power, 125, 153–5,
168, 169, 170, 178; second fall
and impeachment, 30, 162, 163,
164
Hart, Christopher, 147
Heathcote's Intelligence, 12, 192
Hewling, Defoe's schoolfellow, 52
High Tories (High Church party,
Highfliers), 19, 27, 32, 102, 105,
109, 112, 117, 123, 124, 134,
137, 147, 148, 155, 156, 159,
162
Hogarth, William, 24, 217
Holland, 63. *See* Dutch

Ides, E. Ysbrant, *Travels from Moscow Overland to China*, 176
Ireland, 26, 140, 174
Italy, 63

Jacobites, 26, 92, 95, 96, 133, 160, 162, 163
James I, 44
James II, 4, 57, 58, 73, 95
James, Henry, 183
Jeffreys, George, Baron, Lord Chief Justice 57, 137
Jenkyns, Defoe's schoolfellow, 52
Johnson, Captain Charles, 210
Johnson, Charles (dramatist), 192
Johnson, Dr. Samuel, 21, 41, 58, 86, 123, 155, 186, 214
Juan Fernandez Island, 174, 176, 177, 179

Kensington Palace, 73, 80, 171
Kentish Petition, 93–4, 108
Kingsley, Henry, 120
Kit-Cat Club, 20, 74
Kitt, Defoe's schoolfellow, 52
Kneller, Sir Godfrey, 67
Knox, Captain Robert, *Historical Relation of Ceylon*, 11, 176
Krinke Kesmes, 17

Lamb, Charles, 13, 21, 64, 85–6, 185, 208, 216
Law, John, 143
Le Comte, Louis, *Journeys Through China*, 176
Lee, William, 33, 88, 162, 164, 171, 199
Le Motteux, Peter, 99
L'Estrange, Sir Roger, 136–7, 136 n.
Leslie, Charles, 117, 137
Locke, John, 24, 66, 74, 91, 133, 185
London, 1, 2, 3, 21, 30, 38, 39, 42, 57, 59–62, 66, 67, 68, 88, 94–5, 98–9, 100, 101, 125, 126, 127, 136, 153, 155, 156, 174, 207, 209, 210, 213, 216–17, 218, 224, 226; Great Fire, 1, 2, 26, 44, 45–6, 49, 50, 56, 213; Plague, 1, 26, 44, 45–9
London Gazette, 67, 106, 137, 141

Louis XIV of France, 21, 26, 40, 66, 81, 91–3, 95–6, 99, 140, 143, 158

Macaulay, Thomas Babington, Baron, 4, 29
Madagascar, 192–3
Marlborough, John Churchill, Duke of, 4, 58, 95, 149, 154, 158, 159, 173
Marlborough, Sarah, Duchess of, 124, 156
Marston Moor, battle, 215
Marvell, Andrew, 45
Mary II, Queen, 4, 23, 26, 59, 60, 73, 80–1, 213
Masefield, Dr. John, 35, 209, 220
Masham, Mrs. (Abigail Hill), 124
Maugham, Somerset, 183, 183 n.
Mercator, 143, 164
Mercurius Politicus, 163·
Mexico, 92
Milton, John, 1, 22, 35, 45, 46, 220; *Areopagitica*, 121
Minto, William, 27, 91, 116, 125, 202
Mist, Nathaniel, 171, 183
Mist's Weekly Journal, 31, 163, 164, 171, 198
Monmouth, James, Duke of, 57, 58, 59, 211
Monmouth Rebellion, 52, 58, 59, 137, 160
Montaigne, Michel, 184
Montesquieu, 24, 120, 173
Monthly Oracle, 141
Moreton, Andrew, *Pseud.* for Defoe, 4, 218, 221–2
Morley, Professor Henry, 35, 42
Morton, Dr. Charles, 39, 52, 57–8

Naseby, battle, 196
Netherlands (Spanish), 93, 107
Newgate Gaol, 18, 68, 82, 106, 108 n., 109–14, 116, 121, 125, 133, 139, 147, 149, 168, 169, 201, 203, 207, 218
Newport, Andrew, 197–8
Newton, Sir Isaac, 24, 66, 74
North American Colonies, 18, 63, 92, 144–5, 202

Nottingham, Daniel Finch, Earl of, 106, 107, 110, 113, 114

Oates, Titus, 30, 57, 108
Oblivion, Act of, 45
Observator (L'Estrange), 137
Observator (Tutchin), 70, 122, 137
Occasional Conformity, 55, 100–5
Occasional Conformity Bill, 102, 148
Ogilby, John, *Description of Africa*, 176
Oldmixon, John, 59
Orinoco, River, 4, 6, 10, 176, 179
Oxford, Earl of, *see* Harley

Parker, Thomas, Earl of Macclesfield, Lord Chief Justice, 162
Partridge, John (almanac-maker), 30
Paterson, William, 107, 108, 110
Penn, William, 107, 108, 110
Pepys, Samuel, 44, 50
Phipps, Sir William, 75
Poland, 140
Pope, Alexander, 22, 30, 32, 37, 86, 96, 108, 191, 227; *The Dunciad*, 37
Popish Plot, 30, 57
Portland MSS., 107, 108, 113, 151
Portugal, 13, 63
Post-Boy, 89, 137
Post-Man, 137
Presbyterians, 39, 40, 150, 151
Pretender (James Stuart), 95, 96, 160, 161
Prior, Matthew, 30, 74, 96
Purchas, Samuel, 175

Quakers, 17, 40, 64, 194

Raleigh, Sir Walter, 43, 176, 178–9
Ramillies, battle, 136
Read, Herbert, *English Prose Style*, 205
Rehearsal, 137
Richardson, Jonathan, 45
Richardson, Samuel, 181, 188, 215; *Pamela*, 181
Ridpath, George, 171
Rogers, Captain Woodes, 174, 175; *Cruising Voyage Round the World*, 175
Roman Catholics, 39, 50

Rousseau, Jean-Jacques, 14, 15, 17, 18; *Emile*, 14
Royal Exchange, 60, 67
Royal Society, 28
Russia, 12
Ryswick, Peace of, 81, 89

Sacheverell, Dr. Henry, 102, 105, 109, 112, 155–6, 160
Saintsbury, Professor George, 133, 181, 195, 206
Savage, Richard, 86–7, 217
Schomberg, Frederick, Duke of, 98
Scotland, 26, 123, 135, 140, 149–52, 160
Scotland, Parliamentary Union with England, 19, 120, 125, 140, 149–53
Scots Post-Man, 164 n.
Scott, Sir Walter, 29, 128
Sedgmoor, battle, 58
Selkirk, Alexander, 11, 17, 28, 124, 174, 175, 177, 188, 217
Sheppard, Jack, 214
Sheridan, Richard Brinsley, 5
Smith, Adam, 143
Smollett, Tobias, 181, 209
South America, 9, 177, 178–9, 210
South Sea Company, 159, 178–9
South Seas, 176, 177–8
Spain, 12, 13, 63, 91, 92, 93, 159, 178, 211
Spanish America, 92, 95–6, 143, 178
Spectator, 78, 83, 135
Stancliffe, James, 224
Stanhope, James, Earl of, 33, 162
Steele, Richard (divine), 41, 64
Steele, Sir Richard, 74, 78, 88, 141, 142, 175, 214, 219, 226
Sterne, Laurence, 181, 188
Stevenson, Robert Louis, 5
Stoke Newington, 6, 18, 38, 52, 54, 63, 69, 161, 170, 211, 218, 222, 223
Stothard, Thomas, 1
St. Vincent, Island, 31
Sutherland, Professor James, 22, 40 n., 74, 112, 133, 226
Sweden, 140, 173, 198
Swift, Jonathan, 3–4, 7, 10, 27, 30, 53, 66, 74, 99, 119, 124, 131,

152, 176, 188, 219, 227; *Directions to Servants*, 218; *Gulliver*, 4, 7, 131, 176; *Tale of a Tub*, 131
Swiss Family Robinson, 17

Tate, Nahum, 74, 96, 99
Tatler, 78, 83, 135, 141
Taylor, William, 175, 186, 186 *n.* 191
Tilbury, 13, 88, 126
Toleration, Act of, 100–1, 102, 103, 107, 120
Tories, 22, 25, 26, 31, 82, 92, 93, 95, 96, 99, 102, 112, 119, 121, 155, 156, 157, 158, 159, 162, 163, 164
Trent, Professor W. P., 3, 35, 106, 165 *n.*
Trevelyan, G. M., 24, 118 *n.*, 123–4, 133
Tuffley, Samuel, 169
Turks, 56, 57, 173
Tutchin, John, 53–4, 70, 97, 106, 122, 137

Uniformity, Act of, 39, 44

Universal Spectator, 164, 202
Utrecht, Peace of, 30, 157, 159

Voltaire, 24, 120, 173

Weekly Journal, 199
Wesley, Charles, 1, 38, 52
Wesley, John, 52
Wesley, Samuel, 38, 39, 52, 54, 66
Whigs, 19, 22, 25, 26, 32, 41, 57, 74, 81, 82, 94, 99–100, 102, 109, 110, 112, 117, 119, 120, 121, 124, 143, 149, 155, 156, 157, 158, 159, 161, 162, 163, 164
Whitehall Evening Post, 164
William III, 4, 21, 23, 26, 58, 60, 73, 84, 90, 99, 103, 118, 155, 213; supported by Defoe, 18, 35, 38, 59, 80–2, 84, 89, 96–100, 103, 107, 109, 111, 119–20, 133, 155, 160, 178; war coalition policy, 66, 68, 72, 92–3, 95–6, 158; death, 81, 100, 178
Windsor Castle, 110, 124, 214
Wren, Sir Christopher, 66, 73